في ذكرى

مارك لينز

Abd al-Aziz al-Babtain, mid 1960s. Courtesy of the al-Babtain Foundation.

POET AND BUSINESSMAN

POET AND BUSINESSMAN

Abd al-Aziz al-Babtain and the Formation of Modern Kuwait

Leif Stenberg

GINGKO

THE AGA KHAN UNIVERSITY
(International) in the United Kingdom
Institute for the Study of Muslim Civilisations

First published in 2022 by Gingko in agreement with the
Aga Khan University – Institute for the Study of Muslim Civilisations

Gingko, 4 Molasses Row, Plantation Wharf, London SW3 3UX
AKU-ISMC, 10 Handyside Street, London N1C 4DN

A CIP catalogue record for this book is available from the British Library.

ISBN: 978-1-914983-00-9

Typeset in Garamond by MacGuru Ltd
Printed and bound in the United Kingdom by TJ Books

www.gingko.org.uk
www.aku.edu/ismc

CONTENTS

ACKNOWLEDGEMENTS   xi

1 THE STATE OF KUWAIT AND ABD AL-AZIZ SAʿUD AL-BABTAIN   1
   Abd al-Aziz al-Babtain: businessman and poet   5
   Introducing Kuwait, the life of al-Babtain and
       the al-Babtain Foundation   6
   The Iraqi invasion of Kuwait and identity insecurity   15
   The National Assembly and the politics of citizenship:
       gender, statelessness and tribal traditions   19
   A second war in the Gulf   24
   Studying Kuwait and Abd al-Aziz al-Babtain   26

2 ARABS, TRIBES, THE DESERT AND OIL:
   BACKGROUND AND KEY THEMES   33
   The notion of being Arab   33
   Tribal history and the founding of Kuwait   38
   Escape from the Najd   44
   Desert, depression and downturn   47
   The game-changing discovery of oil: the opportunity
       for entrepreneurship   54

3 SETTING THE SCENE: THE FOUNDING OF MODERN KUWAIT   59
   Early years of the oil industry: political and economic changes   59
   Property, the State, Islam and Arabism   69
   The emergence of the State of Kuwait: from Sheikh
       Mubarak to Sheikh Abd Allah   74
   Transformed by wealth: changes for government
       and citizens alike   79

4 KUWAIT ON THE WAY UP: THE WORLD OF AL-BABTAIN   83
   A fertile business environment   83
   The financial services rush   88
   A society in flux: citizenship laws, limitations, difference
      and identity   91
   A loss of heritage? Kuwaiti culture and the *diwaniyya*   101
   Crafting Kuwaiti citizens: the rise of a welfare state for nationals 106
   Developing healthcare   108
   From local to global media   110
   Education: schooling modern Kuwaitis   117

5 KUWAIT EXPERIENCING CHALLENGES:
   THE SUCCESS OF AL-BABTAIN   131
   1960s boom and 1970s chaos: the desire to diversify
      and industrialize   131
   Speculation and Kuwait's *nouveau riche*   138
   Crash and aftermath   140
   War in the Gulf   144
   A state on its knees, and an exodus   149
   The international community and an end to the war   151

6 CONTEMPORARY KUWAIT AND THE
   AL-BABTAIN FOUNDATION   159
   Developments after the liberation of Kuwait   159
   Economic recovery after the Gulf wars   163
   Striving to become a major financial centre   170
   The al-Babtain Foundation: aid programmes and foreign policy 177
   Kuwaiti politics and uprisings in the Middle East   189
   Politics, Islamists and the quest for democratization 198
   Demography and Kuwait's migrant workers   208
   Women in Kuwaiti society: political participation   213

7 ABD AL-AZIZ AL-BABTAIN: THINKING ABOUT
   A LIFE OF CONTINUITY AND CHANGE   223
   Abd al-Aziz, Kuwait and the first scholarships   223
   Expanding the al-Babtain Foundation   227

The library, changing ambitions and the "dialogue
    among civilizations"   229
The al-Babtain Foundation and the media   234
Promoting a culture of peace and influencing new generations   236
Poetry, Arab culture, Islam, identity politics and nationalism   241

8   FINAL REFLECTIONS   249

KUWAIT TIMELINE   257
BIBLIOGRAPHY   263
INDEX   285

ACKNOWLEDGEMENTS

I consider myself a fortunate person. I have a loving, supportive family, been reasonably healthy and I have always found my work stimulating and engaging. In many ways, I am truly blessed. The rationale informing this deeply held conviction could be analysed academically, but I prefer a simpler explanation, which is that I have never planned too much for my future, and I basically grabbed any opportunities that appeared along the way. Put even more simply, I rarely say no to something I find interesting. Hence, when I was offered the chance to participate in a meeting with the businessman, poet and philanthropist Abd al-Aziz Saʿud al-Babtain and his Foundation in Kuwait City, I couldn't resist the temptation to go to a country I had never visited previously.

The outcome of those visits to Kuwait over the years is this book. Even if the intention had been to write a straightforward chronological overview of the modern history of Kuwait amalgamated with the life of Abd al-Aziz, especially that part of his life where he spearheaded the al-Babtain Foundation, it would not have been possible without the support of several friends and colleagues. However, I would like to start by thanking the al-Babtain Foundation and Abd al-Aziz Saʿud al-Babtain for their generous support in providing information and all sorts of materials, as well as making time for interviews and giving me the opportunity to participate in several events organized by Abd al-Aziz and the Foundation. The kind encouragement and assistance of the General Director of the al-Babtain Foundation, Dr Touhami Abdouli, has been invaluable. Dr Farouk Abu Chakra and Dr Abderrahman Tenkoul have also been very helpful and sympathetic to the project. Their support and knowledge about the Foundation was instrumental in carrying out the research that led to this book.

Friends and colleagues have also supported me by helping to collect materials, making suggestions for improvement, assisting in translating interviews and editing the book. Many and warm thanks to the following:

Simon Fiedler, Carl Stenberg, Dr Anders Ackfeldt, Sara Williams, Omar Mokhles, Mohamad Meqdad, Nahel Yiziji, Dr Michael Degerald, Edward Grassby, Dr Charlotte Whiting, Joe Barnes, Dr Sarah Bowen Savant, Dr Gianluca Parolin, Dr Jonas Otterbeck, Dr Philip Wood, Donald Dinwiddie and all my colleagues at the Aga Khan University Institute for the Study of Muslim Civilisations (AKU-ISMC) in London. Let me also extend a warm thank you to Dr Spyros Sofos for his much-appreciated support and suggestions on how to improve the manuscript.

Finally, many thanks to the editorial team at Gingko, especially Barbara Schwepcke and Harry Hall.

Writing a combined history of a country and person has its risks. Mistakes can be made, but I do think that the reader who would like to know more about the history of Kuwait can make good use of the bibliography. All mistakes are my responsibility. Transliteration of Arabic names and terms have been simplified for the general reader.

Finally, my love and thanks are due to my supportive family members Agneta, Johan, Matilda, Tova and Tom, Carl and Chelsea and, last but not least, Rufus.

1

THE STATE OF KUWAIT AND ABD AL-AZIZ SA'UD AL-BABTAIN

One evening in November 1977, a hunting party led by Abd al-Aziz Sa'ud al- Babtain[1] pitched its tents between the cities of Ali al-Gharbi and al-Amarah in the south of Iraq. They were not far from the border between Iraq and Iran, alongside one of the roads that run north from the city of Basra towards Baghdad. The party was out hunting with falcons.

After a night's sleep, in the early morning just before sunrise, a black Mercedes approached the camp. Abd al-Aziz and some of his friends walked towards the car intending to welcome the driver as their guest, offer him breakfast and enquire who he was and why he was coming this way.

A man rolled down the window and requested their permission to address them. He then asked who they were and if they had a hunting licence. The men responded that they were Kuwaitis and had a licence to hunt in the name of Abu Sa'ud. The man in the car asked if Abd al-Aziz al-Babtain was among them.

"I am Abd al-Aziz", replied Abu Sa'ud.

The man then asked if they would accept a guest.

"We are Arabs like you", was the reply from Abd al-Aziz, signalling his assent.

The man in the car replied that the invitation for breakfast was not for him. He switched on the car's headlights, to reveal to all those watching that a white Mercedes was approaching the camp. The car came to a stop and a handsome man got out. He struck a casual note, declaring that he was

---

1 This is the full name of Abd al-Aziz al-Babtain. He is also called Abu Sa'ud in accordance with the tradition of being called the father (Abu) of his first son, who was named Sa'ud.

lucky – explaining that, when the leadership of the state of Iraq had summoned him back to Baghdad from Basra, it had been too early for the hotel he'd been staying in to prepare him breakfast. He said he was hungry and that he had noticed breakfast being prepared at the camp. "Those birds I see cooking look like a great meal", he added.

After they had eaten breakfast, Abd al-Aziz asked his guest, "Who are you?"

"I am Adnan Khayr Allah al-Talfah, Saddam Hussein's brother-in-law and cousin", came the reply. The Iraqi leader at the time, Saddam Hussein, (1937–2006) had recently married the guest's sister, Sajida al-Talfah.

With a poet's curiosity and respect, Abd al-Aziz asked the guest if his father was the former mayor of Baghdad, a man who was also the author of 50 books. Adnan replied that he was. The discussion continued and Abd al-Aziz asked his guest about his work. He answered that he had been made a minister of the State of Iraq (*Wazir al-dawla*) 20 days before, but also that he was trained to lead the parliament of Iraq (*Majlis al-Wuzara'*). Subsequently, following this meeting, he was also appointed as the minister of defence.

As their conversation drew to a close, Adnan invited his host to join him for dinner in Baghdad. Abd al-Aziz accepted the invitation and drove to the capital of the Republic of Iraq later that same day.

At dinner, the host and his guest were engaged in friendly chat when Adnan suddenly changed tone and made a formal announcement to the Kuwaiti businessman and poet.

"Since you are linked to the leadership of the state of Kuwait, I am giving you a message to convey to the Kuwaitis", he said.

"So, what is the message?" was Abd al-Aziz's courteous and cautious reply.

"We, the Iraqi leadership, strive to abolish borders between Arab countries", said Adnan Khayr Allah al-Talfah.

He continued in this vein, emphasizing that there was one Arab people and one Arab nation (*umma*) – ideas that reflected the rhetoric of the Iraqi Ba'ath Party.

"We don't need borders and barriers between us as Arabs", Adnan concluded, looking pointedly at Abd al-Aziz.

"But there is a border between your country Iraq and the Kingdom of Saudi Arabia", the Kuwaiti businessman and poet pointed out. "Moreover", he went on, "there's even a border between you and Syria, and you claim to be of the same political party, the Hizb al-Baʿath (the Baʿath Party).[2] Adnan, what you say reminds me of the chicken of Abu al-Ala al-Maʿarri: You make it weak, you kill it and then you eat it!"[3]

Adnan gave him a hard stare across the dinner table. "We don't make anyone weak, and we don't kill them! Look, there is an American, Iranian, and Israeli conspiracy to create a sectarian belt from Lebanon to Tehran." Adnan then told Abd al-Aziz that the minister of defence of Saudi Arabia had recently visited Baghdad and confirmed this conspiracy. "Do you trust Prince Sultan?"[4] he asked Abu Saʿud. He said that he considered the Shah of Iran a secular man with no interest in religion and sectarianism – a man who aspires to make Iran the sixth strongest country in the world and also the "policeman" of the Gulf. "If the Shah does not comply with the American-Israeli guidelines, they will replace him with religious leaders", declared Adnan darkly.

The above story was recounted by Abd al-Aziz Saʿud al-Babtain in a conversation that took place in the presence of Dr. Touhami Abdouli, former State Secretary of Arab, African and European Affairs, Ministry of Foreign Affairs, Tunisia, and now the General Director of the al-Babtain Cultural Foundation for Poetic Creativity in Kuwait City (hereafter the al-Babtain Foundation). Only at the end of his account did Abd al-Aziz reveal the timing: his encounter with Adnan Khayr Allah al-Talfah took place around 15 months before the Shah of Iran, Muhammad Reza Pahlavi, was deposed and left Iran.[5]

---

2 For an overview of the relation between Iraq and Syria and the two Baʿath parties, see Lawson 1996: 98–128 and Devlin 1991.

3 Abu al-Ala al-Maʿarri (d. 1057) is a celebrated Arab poet from Syria, who also spent some time in Baghdad during his lifetime. He is well known for his critical and sarcastic views on religions in general. He was also renowned for his contention that reason is the primary source in the search for truth. Many people see him as one of the first famous atheists in Muslim history. A statue of him in his hometown of Marrat al-Numan in Syria was decapitated by jihadists from the al-Nusra Front in early 2013. For a short introduction to his life, see Smoor 2006: 6f, and for the beheading of the statue, see http://www.bbc.co.uk/news/magazine-35745962. Accessed August 24, 2017.

4 Prince Sultan bin Abd al-Aziz Al Saʿud later became the second deputy prime minister in 1982 and in 2005 he was appointed as the crown prince. He died in 2011.

5 The timing of the encounter, November 1977, as given in the initial paragraph of the chapter was added by the author. Abd al-Aziz revealed the time the event took place after telling the story.

This was one of several instances recounted to me by Abd al-Aziz himself or his close associates that revealed the complex ways in which his life has been intertwined with the politics and history of Kuwait and the broader region. This particular narrative was shared with me in reply to a question I posed on how the businessman and poet Abd al-Aziz felt about the politics of his native Kuwait, his involvement in it and his potential role in a political context. I wondered if he perhaps saw a role for himself as a mediator in disputes between Sunni and Shi'a Muslim communities in which these identities are mobilized to justify, motivate and incite conflict between individuals or groups.

If I judged the intentions of the Kuwaiti leader of the al-Babtain Foundation correctly, his point in telling the story about his 1977 meeting in Iraq was to explain that discussion of identities like Sunni, Shi'a or Arab has been complicated for a long time in the Middle East. His recollection of his exchange with his Iraqi interlocutor revolved around the realization that these forms of belonging are sometimes conceptualized in mutually antagonistic terms – not only in the sense that they mark and signify a binary difference, but also that they incorporate an obligation to take certain actions or uphold principles (such as the notion put forward by Adnan al-Talfah that there should be no borders between Arabs).

To Abd al-Aziz, Sunni, Shi'a or Arab identities appear as problematic since they are, in his understanding, often placed in opposition to each other. Accordingly, to enter into the recounted conversation, "(...) no political culture is revered in Tehran as deeply as in the Kingdom of Saudi Arabia." One possible understanding of this statement is that Abd al-Aziz appears to regard the political culture of Saudi Arabia as easier to interpret and more stable over time. In this discussion, Abd al-Aziz provides glimpses of a topography of belonging that is informed by his status as a notable Kuwaiti national, something that I will discuss presently. Even if not expressly articulated, it is a conscious choice on his part to explore avenues other than politics to achieve his ambitions and influence the human condition more broadly, especially among Arabs and Muslims.

As a result of his personal analysis, Abd al-Aziz has, for the better part of his long life, favoured and actively worked to achieve what he describes as "cultural interventions" rather than those more familiar interventions of the political variety, although, to an onlooker, Abu Sa'ud's firm belief that the two can be separated might not look convincing. Nevertheless, in

Abd al-Aziz's view, the vital, urgent work of promoting a foundation for peaceful developments in societies is better accomplished by sponsoring the education of thousands of young people, or by supporting an annual poetry conference, than it is by fomenting social upheaval and conflict by engaging in politics.

Abd al-Aziz belongs to a particular group of social actors whose lives shaped, and were shaped by, the emirate of Kuwait, and whose position and lifestyle embeds them squarely within the politics of their country and region, notwithstanding his claim to be disinterested in politics.

Abd al-Aziz al-Babtain: businessman and poet

Abd al-Aziz al-Babtain is a Kuwaiti citizen. He was born in 1936, around the same time that oil was discovered in his homeland. Abu Saʿud and the modern state of Kuwait are not just of the same age, but also presumably products of similar forces, with hardships and histories in common.

The state and Abd al-Aziz Saʿud al-Babtain can be seen as intimately connected to each other, and one of the key ambitions of this book is to mirror each through the other and piece together the way they have traversed the turbulent past eight decades. In many respects, Abd al-Aziz and the state of Kuwait are in a symbiotic relationship. This interdependence is not only mutually beneficial, but also a relationship in which they are influenced by each other as statecraft, his public persona and personality have become intertwined along the way. The life of Abu Saʿud and the history of the state parallel each other. We can look upon the life of the successful Kuwaiti businessman and poet as a form of Weberian ideal type:[6] he can be understood as a representation of a class of people who have been subjects of the state, challenging as well as supporting it, and of a generation of individuals who, through their personal aptitudes, have been an intrinsic part of the development of the contemporary state through their entrepreneurship, financial success and initiatives in the broad field of culture.

Abd al-Aziz al-Babtain has lived through the period of the establishment of the new states of the Gulf and the advent of oil economies that

---

6 The term "ideal type" is in this context simply understood as a broader category, a mirror image of reality, abstracting a generation of socially and financially successful nationals who were part of the development of the current state of Kuwait.

utterly changed the lives of people in the region. His personal life story is linked to the dramatic developments of the country, shaped by a tsunami of new financial wealth created by the export of petrochemicals, and by a problematic relationship with its northern neighbour, Iraq. One purpose of this book is to illustrate the developments of the state of Kuwait and the life of Abu Sa'ud as expressions of a particular history, a particular time, culture and conditions, and to elucidate more recent developments in the 20th and 21st centuries informed by unique insights into episodes from the life story of Abd al-Aziz Abu Sa'ud al-Babtain. Together, these descriptions form the foundation for a discussion of how to comprehend the many achievements of an individual such as Abu Sa'ud. The focus is on his activity in fields that can be commonly designated as poetry, language, literature, and culture.

Another aim of the book is to explore Abd al-Aziz al-Babtain's theories on cultural phenomena such as language and Arab identity, how these conceptions are manifested in the institutions he built and how they relate to a broader discourse within Kuwaiti society.

Introducing Kuwait, the life of al-Babtain and the al-Babtain Foundation

The state of Kuwait is a small country along the Arabian or Persian Gulf. In the north and northeast it borders Iraq, and to the south and southwest, Saudi Arabia. It is a recently created nation-state centring on one principal urban area, Kuwait City, just like several other countries bordering the Gulf. This city is currently perhaps not as spectacular and famous as others – take, for example, the manifestations of financial extravagance evident in Doha in Qatar, or Dubai in the United Arab Emirates – but it does have a distinctive history of its own.

The geographical area that constitutes the current state of Kuwait is linked to the cultures of the Euphrates and Tigris as well as to early trade routes that passed through the area. In more recent history, Kuwait developed into an outpost thriving on commerce established during the 18th and the 19th centuries. In a sense, the port of Kuwait became a place of mercantile exchange, and a city that flourished due to its key position on intersecting trading routes, but also, like other societies along the Gulf, its economic prosperity was linked to the business of pearl-diving – an industry that was a principal source of livelihood for locals before the advent of oil.

In the 20th century, conditions changed more dramatically than ever before in Kuwaiti history. The two world wars and the discovery of oil, as well as the world's rapidly increasing hunger for oil and gas, brought waves of change to the social, cultural and economic structures of Kuwait. Living conditions, Kuwaiti society and the physical infrastructure of the country were all transformed. The predominately maritime city of Kuwait quickly evolved into a modern commercial city – a process that had begun in earlier times, but that rapidly accelerated after the end of the Second World War.

The life of Abd al-Aziz parallels and reflects these developments as well as the opportunities and challenges these changes brought to Kuwaiti society in general. Abd al-Aziz was not born wealthy, yet even at the age of 20 he embarked on his first business project. Like many others in the Kuwaiti society of the time, his idea was to open a small shop in a village outside Kuwait City.[7] However, the first steps he took as a businessman were not particularly successful. Abd al-Aziz persevered in his determination to pursue a business career, yet it took a certain period of time before he found his first prosperous niche in trading – a niche that I will discuss in greater depth in chapter 4 – and whose success is intimately bound up with the overall evolution and economic prosperity of the independent state of Kuwait. It suffices here to say that his initial idea of distributing goods to shop owners in a village outside Kuwait City developed into a business empire comprising a number of companies on the Arabian Peninsula. Abu Sa'ud's later financial accomplishments unquestionably form the basis for the creation of the al-Babtain Foundation, through which his various activities in the field of culture are channelled and organized.

As with many other countries in Africa and Asia, Kuwait became an independent state in the period following the Second World War.[8] The British protectorate came to an end and Kuwait attained sovereignty in 1961 with Abd Allah al-Salim al-Sabah as the first amir of the new state. The years from the end of the Second World War in 1945 until the early 1980s have often been described as Kuwait's Golden Era. This boom period was

---

7 Although not all Kuwaitis shared the same notions, the possibilities to enter into a business life were fairly limited and linked to particular economic and cultural resources, such as capital and kinship.
8 For an overview on politics and society in Kuwait between the 1920s and the early 1960s, see Alebrahim 2019.

fuelled by black gold: by the early 1950s, Kuwait was the largest exporter of oil in the Gulf region and soon numbered among the wealthiest countries in the world.[9] But this era was about more than just money. While Kuwait's prosperity and the popular notion of a Golden Era may have been primarily associated with the economic transformation of the country and the affluence it brought, it also brought with it the drafting of a new, liberal constitution, and elections to Kuwait's newly established parliament in 1963.[10] These developments heralded an era characterized by freedom of expression, the flourishing of cultural phenomena such as theatre, a modern art scene, a literary revival, the founding of institutions of higher education and successful participation in various international sporting events, especially football.

This so-called Golden Era coincided with Abd al-Aziz's first successful years as a businessman, influenced him and nourished his idea to cultivate what, in his view, constituted an essential aspect of Arab culture or even human life: language, literature and, especially, poetry. In this sense, the modern Kuwaiti state and Abd al-Aziz are intimately linked by a shared and roughly contemporaneous experience of self-realization through language, literature and poetry. For Abd al-Aziz, this parallel development would have a lasting, defining impact.[11]

These transformations experienced by Kuwaiti society are usually understood as factors that improved living conditions as a whole – both socially as well as financially. The period of prosperity continued until the country faced an economic crisis in the early 1980s after a speculation boom fuelled by oil wealth culminated in a stock market crash in 1977 and, following the imposition of stricter stock-market regulations by the government, a

9 AlShehabi (2015) identifies three distinct oil booms in Kuwait, the first from 1931 to 1973, the second from 1973 to 1985 and the third from 2000 to 2014. These three periods all have their individual characteristics. For example, AlShehabi characterizes the last period as an era of privatization.
10 In describing the National Assembly of Kuwait in this text, I use the term "parliament" as synonymous with the term "assembly". For an introduction to and analysis of the National Assembly of Kuwait, see Herb 2016.
11 To link language, literature and poetry to supra-national and national identities is not unique, neither in the case of Abd al-Aziz nor in Kuwait. For a comparative study on the production and reproduction of Arab identity and an everyday nationalism in Jordan and Syria, see Phillips 2016.

further and more devastating crash of the parallel, unregulated and unofficial stock market, the Suq al-Manakh, in 1982. Oil prices were slashed, sending the economy into a state of shock. Many economic sectors were affected, and private sector investments were either frozen or deferred. Beyond significant financial losses for individuals, property prices fell by 30 per cent in 1985 and banks experienced a severe liquidity crisis which would have rendered all banks apart from the National Bank of Kuwait insolvent, had the Kuwaiti Central Bank not intervened.[12] The stock-market crash left behind many casualties, as thousands of Kuwaitis faced bankruptcy. But, in the end, the government intervened and set up various schemes that either allowed Kuwaitis to pay off their debts or have liabilities written off. The financial turmoil contributed to the government's decision to impose restrictions on the free press and to dissolve the constituent assembly.[13] The near collapse of Kuwait's economy, combined with the intervention of the government, not only in the economy, but also in political life, brought Kuwait's Golden Era to an end.

The Golden Era is also associated with a series of physical and social demographic changes in Kuwait driven by the establishment of a revenue-generating oil and gas industry. After oil and gas became the foremost source of income for the State of Kuwait, the new extraction industry and the service economy attracted foreign workers whose number increased dramatically over the years. Foreign workers in Kuwait were, and still are, primarily from other Arab countries and Asia, especially from the Indian subcontinent and, to some extent, from Southeast Asia, with a smaller number arriving from the US and Europe. Today, the non-Kuwaiti labour force is estimated to compose close to 70 per cent of a total population of just over 4.4 million people, thus far outnumbering Kuwaiti nationals.[14] The largest group is broadly defined as South Asian and is estimated to constitute about 40 per cent of the population. Yet, due to strict citizenship laws, migrants residing in Kuwait for decades or the children of migrants

---

12 al-Nakib 2016: 115 and Crystal 1992: 108

13 Crystal 1992: 108

14 Labour migration will be discussed in more detail in the part that concerns contemporary Kuwait; see http://stat.paci.gov.kw/englishreports/#DataTabPlace:Pi eChartNat. Accessed October 1, 2017. See also Khalaf, AlShehabi and Hanieh (2015) for a more extensive discussion of various aspects of labour, migration and citizenship in the Gulf.

born in the country do not have the option of becoming naturalized as citizens. They do not have the right to "belong" and their presence and right to work in the country is conditional upon the possession of a residence and/or work permit. Indeed, the question of citizenship and migration is a central, and often controversial, one in Kuwaiti society and is inextricably linked with issues of identity and societal security, as will be further discussed in chapter 6. But it is worth pointing out at this juncture that these demographic patterns have, without doubt, shaped modern Kuwait and generated debates and controversies regarding Kuwaiti identity.

The demographic changes resulting from such a large foreign workforce have changed social dynamics and the composition of the population in several areas. The use of English in everyday life is one example. It has affected the daily language usage of all individuals living in Kuwait, irrespective of their origins and whether they are citizens or not. Largely as a result of its status as a global language dominating commerce and communications, and its use as lingua franca, English has made considerable inroads. It is spoken in media outlets, used in advertisements and is widely utilized in the shopping malls and *suqs*. In addition, one cannot help but notice the influence of languages from the Indian subcontinent, which are also visible and audible in parts of Kuwaiti society. However, in contrast to the use of English, which has permeated the social fabric of Kuwait, the use of Indian subcontinental languages is more overt and widespread in certain areas, particularly the neighbourhoods where South Asian migrants live and work.

English and languages from the Indian subcontinent also affect Arabic, and especially the so-called "Gulfi" spoken dialect, or *Khaliji*. The exposure of local Arabic speakers to sounds and words originating in these languages and of foreign workers to the local Arabic has contributed to a language development whereby local Arabic has acquired many new loanwords and expressions. In addition to the incorporation of foreign elements into *Khaliji*, it is not uncommon for Kuwaitis and other residents in the country to engage in a form of language mixing that is common in many multi-language societies. The economic, cultural and demographic changes that have shaped contemporary Kuwait and rendered identity and language-related boundaries fluid have had a profound effect on Kuwaiti society and are very likely to have had stimulated Abd al-Aziz's interest in issues revolving around the Arabic language, literature and poetry. His decision to engage in educational and cultural activities can be attributed to a desire to preserve the language and its heritage, and to secure its future.[15]

Another change in Kuwaiti society that is linked to demographic developments is the discernible increase of other religious affiliations besides the predominant one – Muslim. According to most reference sources, the number of people in the country professing various forms of Christianity today approaches 20 per cent of the population. Additionally, 7 per cent of the population is in the category of "Other/Not Stated" religious affiliation.[16] It is difficult to judge the accuracy of figures/statistics concerning religious allegiance due to uncertainties over how the Kuwaiti Public Authority for Civil Information collects the data, but numbers show a shift in religious affiliation over time, primarily due to the arrival and settlement of foreign workers. Having said that, the relative stability of a large non-Kuwaiti workforce in the country indicates that the number of non-Muslims is not likely to decrease. The only policy likely to change these numbers dramatically is if a decision is taken to decrease or even empty the country of foreign labour or non-Muslim foreign labour.[17]

Another issue that makes it hard to obtain an accurate snapshot of the population of the country in terms of religion relates to the difficulty of devising a reliable methodology for calculating the number of adherents to different branches of Islam in Kuwait, primarily the Sunnis and the Shiʿas. Several reports from the early 2000s have estimated the number of Shiʿa Muslims in Kuwait at somewhere between 25 per cent and 40 per

---

15 Through media and actions taken by states in the Gulf Cooperation Council (GCC) it is obvious that all the states recognize that Arabic is under threat as a spoken language. This can be seen in local papers like the United Arab Emirates-based newspaper, the English speaking *The National*. For example in https://www.thenational.ae/arts-culture/linguistic-twist-1.287316 and https://www.thenational.ae/uae/government/arabic-must-be-main-language-of-uae-urge-fnc-members-1.651886. Accessed July 18, 2017. See also the Qatari newspaper the *Gulf Times* for an example of how state supported organizations are founded to address the question of the status of Arabic: http://www.gulf- times.com/story/475962/Call-to-protect-and-preserve-the-Arabic-language/. Accessed April 24, 2017.

16 See http://stat.paci.gov.kw/englishreports/#DataTabPlace:ColumnChartEduAge. Accessed July 5, 2017.

17 I will outline current discussions in Kuwait concerning the composition of the labour force and citizenship presently, especially in the parts that concerns the contemporary developments in Kuwait.

cent of the population of Kuwaiti nationals.[18] It was with these numbers of Shi'as and Sunnis in the country in mind that I asked Abd al-Aziz the question which prompted him to narrate the story from Iraq. The intricacy of the relationship between different branches of Islam and the relationship between the complexity of religious affiliation and local and regional politics constitute a sensitive aspect of life in Kuwait and may have played a role in the more global emphasis of Abd al-Aziz's cultural and educational work. Perhaps organizing events and activities that bridge perceived political, cultural, social and religious gaps under the "Dialogue of or among Civilizations" umbrella is a better course of action than engaging with them as political or religio-political issues. The dialogue approach refers to a notion in which a mutual understanding and intercultural dialogue among civilizations are prerequisites for human development. At the same time, it is a notion about the human condition which implies that there are differences, borders that need to be crossed and gaps to be bridged. And although the Kuwaiti political system has been hailed at times as one of the more participatory in the Gulf region, and the Middle East more broadly, politics is still a complex terrain where one needs to tread carefully. It is less problematic within authoritarian settings to express criticism of global political matters rather than of local ones. Middle Eastern regimes tend to host dissidents of other countries while persecuting internal opposition. In the eyes of a regime, it is a significant difference if an opposition leader expresses criticism of a royal family or if he or she makes a critical statement about politics in a neighbouring country or about US foreign policy.[19]

In the case of the al-Babtain Foundation's global aspirations, there is also the matter of the ambition expressed within the institution. For example,

---

18 Louër (2008: 45) states that about 25 per cent of the nationals in Kuwait are Shi'a. However, in the *International Religious Freedom Report, 2001* published by the U.S. Department of State it is claimed that 36.5 per cent of Kuwait's citizen population are Shi'a. See https://www.state.gov/j/drl/rls/irf/2001/5593.htm. Accessed May 22, 2017. Azoulay (2020: 19) says that Shi'as constitute between 25 per cent and 35 per cent of Kuwaiti citizens.

19 For instance, while Algerian Islamists had no opportunity to engage in public debate within Algeria itself during the 1980s and most of the 1990s, Algerian Islamist texts were being freely printed and distributed in Cairo at a time when the Egyptian regime did not extend the same courtesy to its domestic Islamist opposition; see Stenberg 1996.

in 2012 the Foundation, in collaboration with the Altiero Spinelli Centre (Centro di Eccellenza Altiero Spinelli) in Rome, Italy, the Foundation of Mediterranean Studies in Tunisia and the Centre for Mediterranean Europe Studies (Meseuro Foundation) in Belgium, founded the Euro-Arab Institute for the Dialogue between Cultures. This Institute, located at Roma Tre University, is one of many recent international efforts by the Foundation and Abd al-Aziz to institutionally support dialogue between communities throughout the world.[20] Other examples are the schools, colleges, study programmes and academic chairs in Arabic that Abu Saʿud and the al-Babtain Foundation have supported and founded in Arab and Muslim countries, Central Asia, Europe and North America. One recently established relationship is with the Centre for Middle Eastern Studies at Oxford University, where the chair of Laudian Professor of Arabic was named after Abd al-Aziz in 2016.[21] This is only one of many efforts Abu Saʿud and the Foundation have been pursuing in order to establish or financially support chairs in Arabic at various universities in Europe with the aim of promoting teaching in Arabic and Arab culture in general.[22]

The outward orientation of the al-Babtain Foundation and the ambition to promote dialogue beyond the borders of Kuwait are also mirrored in the creation of the Cooperation Council for the Arab States of the Gulf, or, as it is more commonly known, the Gulf Cooperation Council (GCC). The idea behind the GCC, established in Abu Dhabi in the United Arab Emirates in the spring of 1981,[23] with the Kuwaiti diplomat Abd Allah Bishara as its first secretary general, has been to foster closer cooperation between its six member states. Security and trade concerns are often regarded as a significant aspect of the cooperation, but the GCC also aims to strengthen social, economic, educational and scientific ties between member countries. Many of the goals such as closer economic relations – for example

---

20 See *An Overview of Abdul Aziz Saud al-Babtain* 2015: 45; also stated in *Abdulaziz Saud al-Babtain: Biography & Cultural Achievements* 2017.

21 The new title of the chair is the Abd al-Aziz Saʿud al-Babtain Laudian Professor in Arabic. Also, in 2018 the al-Babtain Leiden University Centre for Arabic Culture was launched at Leiden University in the Netherlands.

22 See http://www.albabtainprize.org/default.aspx?pageId=40&nid=8212. Accessed June 10, 2017.

23 For a discussion on the GCC and origin and development of the Council, see Legrenzi 2015.

the establishment of a free market and a common currency – have yet to be fulfilled for the most part as cooperation within the GCC is characterized by inner tensions. Kuwait has sought to promote dialogue and has assumed the role of mediator in some of these disputes between member countries.[24] One aspect of the relationship between the GCC and Kuwait concerns the Peninsula Shield Force, a joint GCC military force stationed on Kuwait's border, which did not, however, intervene when Kuwait was invaded by Iraq in 1990. Thirteen years later, fellow GCC members dispatched reinforcements to shield Kuwait from potential fallout from the US-led invasion of Iraq in 2003. Another example of the internal divergences in the GCC comes from 2011, when Saudi Arabia and the United Arab Emirates sent troops to Bahrain as part of the Peninsula Shield Force following a request from the ruling family of the Gulf state for help to quell the Bahraini pro-democracy protest movement in which the country's Shi'a majority played a significant role. Kuwait did not send ground troops, but contributed by sending a naval unit which, according to the Kuwait News Agency (KUNA), contributed to the protection of the maritime border of Bahrain.[25] The Kuwaiti rulers and government have also kept a low profile and have acted as a mediator in the tensions between Saudi Arabia, the United Arab Emirates and Egypt on one hand and Qatar on the other when relations between the states worsened in June 2017, with the former countries breaking off diplomatic relations with the small Gulf state and enforcing a partial blockade of the country.[26]

In the broader region, Kuwait has been involved in mediation efforts between Saudi Arabia and Egypt, which had supported opposing sides in North Yemen in 1968. Kuwait sent a delegation headed by the then foreign minister and later amir, Sheikh Sabah al-Ahmad al-Jabir al-Sabah

---

24 This mediating role was established through Sheikh al-Sabah's decades-long effort to counter Kuwait's geographic vulnerability as the British forced the emirate to cede two-thirds of its territory to the al-Saud family in the 1920s while it also had to face a Saudi economic blockade and the threat of complete annexation by both Saudi Arabia and Iraq over the years. See https://www.washingtoninstitute.org/policy-analysis/kuwaits-precarious-mediation-role-may-be-imperiled-emirs-passing.

25 See http://www.kuna.net.kw/ArticlePrintPage.aspx?id=2154115&language=en,, also https://now.mmedia.me/lb/en/archive/kuwait_ends_bahrain_naval_mission_state_media_says. Accessed March 7, 2017.

26 Sailer and Roll 2017

(r. 2006–20), to Dhaka in 1974, to persuade Bangladesh to attend that year's Organization of Islamic States summit meeting with a view to normalizing the relationship between Bangladesh and Pakistan.[27] Moreover, in 1982 the Gulf Emirate was instrumental in healing a rift between Saudi Arabia and Libya resulting from a dispute over the former's high rate of production of Saudi crude oil,[28] and also played a role in reconciling Oman and South Yemen in the 1980s after the latter had lent its support to a guerrilla movement in the former's Dhofar region and openly sought to undermine the Omani dynasty.[29]

The Iraqi invasion of Kuwait and identity insecurity

The Iraqi invasion of Kuwait in early August 1990 resulted in the seven-month occupation and annexation of Kuwait, which the Iraqi president, Saddam Hussein, declared to be his country's 19th province. This was not the first time an Iraqi leader had laid claim to Kuwait. When the country achieved formal independence in 1961, Iraq summarily claimed it as part of its territory. Under international pressure, Iraq grudgingly watered down, though never renounced, its claim, thus creating a long-standing atmosphere of insecurity.[30] The reasons for the invasion in 1990 and the occupation are manifold. The most frequently cited grounds were financial, as Iraq's request to have debts it incurred through borrowing during the Iran-Iraq War (1980–88) written off was repeatedly turned down by Kuwait. Another related and oft-cited motive was that Kuwait, capitalizing on a lack of consensus on export quotas within the Organization of the Petroleum Exporting Countries (OPEC), refused to reduce oil extraction and exports, thus keeping oil prices low and depriving Iraq of much-needed revenue. Others have argued that the invasion was the product of Iraq's aspirations towards regional hegemony, whereas some commentators cite the problematic and unclear communication between US diplomats and

---

27 Shakoor 1989: 109–33
28 https://www.nytimes.com/1982/03/07/world/libya-and-saudis-renew-their-war-of-words.html. Accessed October 12, 2021.
29 See Halliday 1984: 355–362.
30 Herb 2016: 14

the regime of Saddam Hussein.[31] In addition, Michael Herb suggests that the Iraqi leadership saw an opportunity in persuading the Kuwaiti opposition to support the invasion because of their dissatisfaction with the amir's decree of 1986 abolishing the Assembly and instead setting up the National Council (*Majlis al-Watani*) with its sharply limited powers.[32]

Kuwait's amir, Jabir al-Ahmad al-Jabir al-Sabah (r. 1977–2006), was deposed and fled to Saudi Arabia, where he created a government in exile, and Iraq installed a puppet regime to lead the "Republic of Kuwait", as the state was renamed. Kuwaiti nationals and non-nationals alike mounted comprehensive resistance, and there are many accounts of how ordinary people in the country defied Iraqi forces[33] by engaging in civil disobedience such as boycotting or delaying work, collecting intelligence information for the allied troops and even launching direct military operations against the occupying army.[34] Most countries in the world protested, but the Iraqi leadership refused to return the country to its former ruler. In response, a US-led coalition comprising 34 countries sanctioned by the United Nations Security Council participated in a military operation to oust Iraqi forces from Kuwait. The First Gulf War ended the occupation, and in late February 1991 the pre-occupation government returned to power.

During my first visit to Kuwait, whilst visiting the al-Babtain Foundation and Abd al- Aziz, I was taken to a *diwaniyya*, a reception room of an individual and/or a family – a social space linking the public and the private spheres to participate in a social event that brought together various associates of Abu Sa'ud. The assembled party had come to eat and award prizes to young men who had excelled in a competition that involved reciting the Quran. While strolling around the large reception hall, I was introduced to a relative of Abd al-Aziz who pointed out to me portraits on the wall and described the meetings between those figures and Abu Sa'ud.

---

31 See https://www.nytimes.com/1990/09/23/world/confrontation-in-the-gulf-us-gave-iraq-little-reason-not-to-mount-kuwait-assault.html. Accessed April 10, 2018.

32 Herb 2016: 18

33 In "The Iraqi Occupation of Kuwait: An Eyewitness Account", Shafeeq Ghabra (1991a), at the time a political scientist at Kuwait University, Ghabra describes his personal experience of the looting, anarchy and resistance during the time of the occupation. Also, see Rajab 1993 for a personal account of the Iraqi occupation.

34 See Levins (1995) for a review of the activities and organization of the Kuwaiti resistance.

Reception room, al-Babtain *diwaniyya*. © the author.

After just a few steps, I found myself facing a picture of General Norman Schwarzkopf (1934–2012), the US commander of the First Gulf War coalition and a close confidante of the former and current leaders of the State of Kuwait. Pointing to an image of Jabir al-Ahmad al-Jabir al-Sabah, the exiled ruler of Kuwait during the Iraqi invasion, Abd al-Aziz's relative told me that when amir al-Sabah returned from his refuge in Saudi Arabia he used the *diwaniyya* of Abd al-Aziz as his residence. The story was presented without any commentary concerning political or other implications or any detail why the amir chose Abu Saʿud's *diwaniyya* as his first residence upon his return from exile. Perhaps it was considered unnecessary, since the story made it abundantly clear that the Kuwaiti amir desired a safe and trustworthy place of residence and host. More likely, the story simply served to underline that Abd al-Aziz al-Babtain is an important figure in Kuwaiti society, close to and trusted by the ruling family.

The Iraqi occupation and annexation of Kuwait is widely regarded as the

Framed photo in the al-Babtain *diwaniyya* showing an informal meeting
between US general Norman Schwarzkopf and the amir of Kuwait,
Jabir al-Ahmad al-Jabir al-Sabah (r. 1977–2006). © the author.

most traumatic moment in the country's recent history. Despite extensive post-war reconstruction, many houses in Kuwait City still bear the scars of this war in the form of bullet holes or in their deserted emptiness even as the city is undergoing profound changes in its physical infrastructure. The pace of change in Kuwait City may be considered slow compared to other capital cities in the Gulf, but the transformation does not stop as old and sometimes abandoned buildings are demolished, new streets added, old infrastructure improved and new buildings erected.[35]

The relationship between Iraq and Kuwait did not improve after the restoration of the pre-occupation government and the amir Jabir al-Ahmad al-Jabir al-Sabah in February 1991. After his return the amir imposed a period of martial law lasting three months. During this time, Kuwaiti leaders and particularly the amir were under pressure from domestic political opposition and from international forces to present plans for how to increase political participation for Kuwaiti nationals. Discussions had already taken place at the 1990 Jeddah conference between representatives of the international community, led by the US and the Kuwaiti ruling family, where it was made clear that international support for Kuwait and the goodwill of the domestic opposition would be contingent upon the restoration of democracy and the liberal constitution of 1962.

The National Assembly and the politics of citizenship: gender, statelessness and tribal traditions

As already noted, the former elected parliament (*Majlis al-Umma*) had been disbanded in 1986 and the political power of its successor *Majlis al-Watani* in the early 1990s was weak.[36] At the Jeddah conference in 1990, the rulers of Kuwait consented to the restoration of the *Majlis al-Umma* and to new elections, which were held in October 1992. However, the power of the restored elected Assembly is limited, in as much as the amir can present decrees and laws without consulting the *Majlis*. On the other

---

35 For a detailed depiction and analysis of the physical and social transformations of Kuwait City with a special focus on urban planning, see al-Nakib 2016.

36 Herb 2016: 17. However, even if parliaments in the Gulf share certain structures and contexts, they differ in the way they function. For an overview of parliaments in the Gulf, see Parolin 2016: 152ff.

hand, the Assembly has the power to challenge government ministers, and eventually remove them (following a vote of no confidence). In the 1992 elections, candidates opposed to the government took a majority of 31 out of 50 seats.[37]

There are no political parties in Kuwait and candidates run as independents, but after elections the members of the parliament usually form different blocs. In addition, there are 15 members appointed by the government.[38] They are government ministers and *ex officio* members of the Assembly. The National Assembly of Kuwait is considered one of the strongest and most independent parliaments in the Middle East, but has also been dissolved several times since parliamentary elections were introduced in the country in 1962 (when the constitution was ratified). As stated in a chronology of the parliament published in *Kuwait Times* (October 17, 2016), Kuwait's Assembly has been dissolved nine times in its existence and only six parliaments have been able to run their full terms since 1962.[39]

The practice of repeatedly dissolving the Assembly demonstrates the vulnerability of the political structures of Kuwait, reflected also in the work of scholars in the field.[40] In a sense, this tension between the weaknesses of Kuwaiti representative institutions and the authority of the amir has contributed to the scepticism that Abd al-Aziz al-Babtain and other figures like him maintain about politics – Abd al-Aziz has never been directly involved in domestic politics and has never been a candidate to the Assembly, yet has prospered as a businessman loyal to the ruling al-Sabah family. He has been instrumental in developing a Kuwaiti identity whose key cohesive elements comprise citizenship of the Kuwaiti nation and the Arabic language.

The history of the National Assembly can be seen as a reflection of the challenges inherent in creating and forming a viable political system as well as a national identity in Kuwait.[41] Questions concerning, for example, citizenship, the role of religion in society and gender have a major bearing

---

37 For two studies on the election to the Kuwait National Assembly of 1992, see Ghabra 1993 and Karam 1993.

38 No Gulf parliament is entirely elected by its constituencies. In Kuwait, 2/3 of the parliament is elected by voters and 1/3 appointed by the rulers; see Parolin 2016.

39 *Kuwait Times*, October 17, 2016.

40 See for example Herb 2016, Ulrichsen 2012 and 2014.

41 For a discussion on authoritarian patterns of governance in the Gulf and the role and function of constitutions, see Parolin 2016 and Schlumberger (ed.) 2007.

not only on the formation of a sustainable legal system, but also on how to shape society as a whole.

After a campaign lasting several decades, a decree was issued in 1999 by the amir granting women the right to vote and run for office, only for it to be annulled by the Assembly. Four years later, in the 2003 election, women activists held a mock ballot[42] in an attempt to highlight their disenfranchisement and, after sustained pressure from activists the Assembly voted to grant the right to Kuwait's female citizens to vote and run for office in 2005. Between 2009 and 2011, four women were elected to parliament, bringing with them different perspectives and issues not only in the general Assembly sessions, but also in the Women and Family Affairs Committee that became an additional forum for airing and discussing issues related to women. On the other hand, since winning the right to vote, only ten women have ever been elected to the Assembly, ande the 2020 ballot returned not a single female representative.[43]

Although women are underrepresented in the Assembly, Rania Maktabi (2017), reflecting on the experience of a decade of female presence in the Assembly, argues that this has influenced the way male members of the Assembly relate to issues concerning women's social and economic rights. Questions that concern women are more often on the agenda – even if those discussing them are men, and participation in the Assembly has fostered a greater understanding of women's roles within society. Having said that, it should be stressed that women still find it difficult to fundraise in order to campaign for votes and entry to the Assembly, and face structural inequalities and prejudice in their attempt to secure a presence and voice in politics.[44] It is these inequalities that have prompted women to establish a significant extra-parliamentary movement lobbying for women's issues and rights to be recognized.[45]

However, as Maktabi shows, the strengthening of women's civil rights has also enhanced authoritarian features within the government of Kuwait.

---

42 PeaceVoice (2016-05-11). "Blue Revolution – Kuwaiti Women Gain Suffrage". http://www.peacevoice.info/2016/05/11/blue-revolution-kuwaiti-women-gain-suffrage/. Accessed September 20, 2021.

43 Shalaby, 2015

44 https://blogs.lse.ac.uk/mec/2021/06/24/have-efforts-for-womens-political-participation-in-kuwait-failed/ Accessed September 20, 2021.

45 https://blogs.lse.ac.uk/mec/2021/06/24/have-efforts-for-womens-political-participation-in-kuwait-failed/ Accessed September 20, 2021.

According to Maktabi, the exclusive right to vote given to Kuwait's female citizens has prompted an internalization of the patriarchal laws on citizenship. She also believes that views on how best to develop women's rights have divided Kuwaiti activists in this area.[46]

One issue that divides women in Kuwait is the right to pass their nationality to their children regardless of their father's nationality. In the Assembly, the Committee on Legislative and Legal Affairs approved a proposed amendment to citizenship laws that would allow women to pass their nationality on to their children, but this amendment has not been enacted.[47] Certainly this amendment is a sensitive issue and concerns many who were born within a family where the father belongs to a stateless group of residents, the so-called *bidun*, and a mother is of Kuwaiti citizenship. The *bidun* of Kuwait, who comprise between 100,000 and 400,000 individuals, do not have Kuwaiti citizenship.[48] Effectively stateless, the *bidun* consist of several groups of people living in Kuwait, with different histories. What unites them is their exclusion from the social and economic rights enjoyed by other citizens.

The authoritarian and hierarchical nature of Kuwaiti society has perpetuated historical divides. Among citizens, two groups that have become markers of identity are the *hadar* and the *badu*. *Hadar* refers to those with an urban background belonging to a society founded on trade – broadly speaking, "townspeople" – while *badu* denotes those who have a more rural and tribal family history, i.e. the group commonly referred to as "Bedouin". Certainly, this division is not so evident in today's Kuwaiti society, but over time it has been transmuted into identities that are used to mobilize individuals politically. Another layer consists of the tribes that are seen as *asil*, "pure" or "noble". They are understood as being of noble and illustrious descent, and have played an important role economically, socially and

---

46 Maktabi 2017

47 Kuwaiti women are not the only women in Arab countries who are discriminated against where the right to pass on their nationality to children is concerned; see http://www.middleeasteye.net/columns/how-citizenship-laws-blatantly-discriminate-against-arab-mothers-99518507 and http://news.kuwaittimes.net/website/kuwaiti-women-able-pass-nationality-children-niqashna-debates. Accessed May 23, 2018.

48 In short, the term "*bidun*" refers to the Arabic *bidun jinsiyya*, "without nationality" or as Beaugrand (2018: 1) says it is "(...) better translated as 'paperless people.'" For a study on the *bidun* and their position in Kuwait, see Beaugrand 2018 and 2020.

politically. One can find *asil* and non-*asil* persons and tribes among the *hadar* as well as the *badu*. Although established in tradition, these identities are reconstructed and reconceptualized today by Kuwaitis in a close relationship to the everyday politics of society.[49]

Defining who is Kuwaiti and who is not is a complex matter, since status, politics, history and contingency play a significant role. The fluidity of identity, status and tribal boundaries is evident in the genealogy of Abd al-Aziz Saʿud al-Babtain's family too. In October 2016, Abd al-Aziz recounted to me how his tribal ancestors moved from today's Yemen or southern Saudi Arabia about 650 years ago to the city of al-Kharj located about 75 kilometres south of the Saudi capital Riyadh. They belonged to a large tribe with many branches by the name of Qahtan or Qahtani.[50] Abu Saʿud's branch is known as the ʿAydhi. He also pointed out the official status of the Qahtan tribe as one of the more respected of the officially recognized Arab tribes. According to Abd al-Aziz, it was in the mid 19th century that the al-Babtain family left al-Kharj and moved to a place called al-Rawda about 180 kilometres northwest of the city of Riyadh. However, facing conflicts around Najd, people left the region and went to, for example, Cairo and Damascus for work. The context was the ongoing wars and conflicts during the second half of the 19th century between, among others, the Al Saʿud and the Al Rashid over control of the interior area of the Arabian peninsula, an area known as Najd. Due to the uncertain situation in Najd, the al-Babtain family moved to the city of al-Zubayr, southwest of Basra on the border between Kuwait and Iraq. At this point in history, Abu Saʿud recounted, the states of Kuwait and Iraq did not exist. This narration of his origins shows how deeply ingrained tribal identity is in Abd al-Aziz and presumably in many other Kuwaiti nationals. The awareness is important not only for reasons of national identity.[51] It is an identity that transcends

---

49 For more on the *hadar*, *badu*, *asil* and non-*asil*, see Azoulay 2020 whose work on tribal politics and the different groups in Kuwait analyses these groups thoroughly. See also Alebrahim 2019: 31–33, al-Nakib 2014 and Longva 2009.

50 The tribal designation Qahtan refers to Arabs from the southern Arabian Peninsula, especially Yemen. In the traditions of Muslim caliphates this tribal affiliation is strongly associated with a pure Arab identity.

51 The genealogies of tribes and families are important since they determine the status and power of a person, and in contemporary society they certainly determine an individual's potential for pursuing a career as a state official or in the private sector.

national borders, upholds social status and maintains relationships as well as creates new ones. Abd al-Aziz al-Babtain appears to feel at home, and to prefer spending as much time as he possibly can, on his farm in Saudi Arabia located close to the Kuwaiti border.

A second war in the Gulf

After the First Gulf War, in 1993, a new border between Kuwait and Iraq was demarcated by the United Nations. This new border expanded the territory of Kuwait, endowing the state with an additional port and several oil wells. However, the new border had to be guarded by US troops to fend off Iraqi border incursions until 1994, when Russia mediated between the two parties and the United Nations and other international actors pressured Iraq into officially recognizing Kuwait's independence and the new borders as they had been defined. The conflict with Iraq did not end there, however, and as a result the state of Kuwait became the flashpoint for the Second Gulf War of March–May 2003.

The war lasted for a little more than a month, after more than 200,000 soldiers from coalition forces, primarily composed of US troops, were sent to Kuwait in preparation for it. Kuwait played a significant role as the platform for a major part of the invasion – and indeed it was from Kuwaiti soil that the invasion was launched in March 2003. The decision to go to war with Iraq saw the largest ever anti-war protests worldwide, with some 6 to 10 million people taking part in demonstrations in up to sixty countries over the weekend of 15–16 February.[52] The largest gatherings took place in Rome, where there were more than 3 million protesters, and also in Madrid and London, where around a million people took to the streets in each capital city. The war had profound effects both regionally and internationally, the most serious of which was the destabilization of Iraq, a fact attested by many commentators at the time. In December 2006, Iraq's former leader, Saddam Hussein, was hanged in Baghdad for crimes against humanity. His execution closed a chapter in Iraqi as well as Kuwaiti history.

For Iraq and Kuwait alike, the war had severe environmental consequences, and the period of recovery was protracted in all regards. The

---

52 See http://news.bbc.co.uk/1/hi/world/europe/2765215.stm.

environmental devastation notwithstanding, the financial strength of Kuwait enabled the country to continue being the highest ranked among Arab countries in the Human Development Index between 2001 and 2009.[53] Although today Kuwait's position in the index has slipped somewhat, with Bahrain, the United Arab Emirates, Saudi Arabia and Qatar catching up, the emirate still ranks highly in comparison to the other countries in the Gulf and among other Arab countries in indexes and reports, such as, for example, the *Global Gender Gap Report*.[54]

As I will discuss in the following chapters, it is often said that Kuwait has a certain freedom that is not shared in other Gulf countries. Turning to the media to gauge the extent of freedom of expression in the emirate, reports from Freedom House signal concern,[55] with criticism focusing primarily on the restrictions imposed upon the media. Journalists and bloggers cannot criticize the amir, and the government tries to maintain control of the media, including the blogosphere. My personal experience is that Kuwaitis within Kuwait speak very openly about the situation in their country in general and are permitted to do so, yet explicit criticism of the ruler constitutes a red line. Having said that, compared to my experience of other Gulf countries, Kuwait is more open, and this is evident in casual conversations you may have with citizens from all walks of life, even in situations when there is no pre-existing relationship of trust.

Since Kuwait, like so many other states in Africa and Asia, has a young population – it is estimated that just over 40 per cent of the population is under the age of 25 – official attempts to curb social media may backfire. In this context, one can understand the thinking of Abd al-Aziz Saʿud al-Babtain when he set out to focus on what he calls a "cultural intervention" as an approach towards closing gaps in society by promoting a common culture. As used here, the term "culture", manifested through the Arabic language and an Arab identity, signifies the glue that binds the generations within a society. Abu Saʿud has expressed concerns about the state of

---

53 See, for example, http://hdr.undp.org/en/composite/trends. Accessed May 8, 2017.

54 *The Global Gender Gap Report* is an annual report designed to measure gender equality issued by the World Economic Forum, see https://www3.weforum.org/docs/WEF_GGGR_2021.pdf. Accessed December 15, 2021.

55 See https://freedomhouse.org/report/freedom-world/2017/kuwait. Accessed October 30, 2017.

culture in this sense, especially as contemporary life among the young and the centrality of consumerist culture in Kuwait provides at best an ephemeral and fragile form of social cohesion where men and women spend their leisure time in shopping malls buying luxury commodities such as beauty and grooming products, clothing and electronics. This is different from his ideal and from the way he presents himself.[56]

Studying Kuwait and Abd al-Aziz al-Babtain

Unquestionably, the businessman and poet Abd al-Aziz Saʻud al-Babtain has lived a noteworthy life. Although he is not a typical Kuwaiti, belonging to the emirate's business, cultural and philanthropic elite, his life trajectory provides interesting insights into contemporary Kuwaiti society and culture as well as the rise of a class of entrepreneurs and businesspeople throughout the Gulf states. From relatively modest beginnings as a young man, he built his own wealth and cultivated his interests in Arabic language, poetry, culture and the dialogue between people – interests he has shaped into a legacy with international reach. Had he been born in any Western European country and made a similar career, it could be fairly assumed that most Europeans, or for that matter North Americans, would have heard of his achievements and read about his and his family's dealings in the mass media. In the present book, as noted briefly above, the aim is to present and discuss the life of Abd al-Aziz and to place him and his life story in the context of the developments of modern Kuwait.

About 12 years ago, I was contacted by Dr Faruk Abu Chakra, a colleague and friend who was working at the time at Helsinki University. He suggested I join a group of academics from the field of Arabic, Islamic and Middle Eastern Studies who were about to meet in Kuwait. The meeting concerned the planning of a conference to be held jointly in the Danish capital Copenhagen and Lund in Sweden. The details of the topic were to be discussed, but the overarching idea was to arrange a conference with perhaps 300 participants reviewing the theme of dialogue among civilizations. We were planning to spend two days in Copenhagen and one day in Lund – the travel time between the two cities is less than an hour, and, in my mind, crossing the Øresund bridge between Denmark and Sweden

---

56 On Kuwait's consumer culture, see Bagnied and Cader 2016 and Hammond 2007: 124.

twice during the conference was a very apt symbol for the principal theme of the conference. However, what prompted me to join the group and travel to the meeting in Kuwait was not so much the theme of the conference. While recognizing the need for a "dialogue among civilizations", my view is that conferences on this theme rarely have a long-lasting impact either on the status of communication or the interaction between people – regardless of whether that interaction takes place at the level of the individual or on the more abstract plane of civilizations.

Instead, what intrigued and attracted me was the simple fact that I had never previously visited Kuwait, and my knowledge of the country was limited, to say the least. In addition, I very much looked forward to meeting the principal organizer of the conference, Abd al-Aziz Saʿud al-Babtain, and becoming acquainted with the Cultural Foundation that bears his name. Hence, I joined Faruk Abu Chakra and travelled to Kuwait. Since this first journey I have travelled several times to the country. My interest in learning more about Kuwaiti society led to this book project.

This book does not pretend to offer a thorough and comprehensive account either of any historic phase or the current state of Kuwait. There are several very well-researched studies on the history as well as of the contemporary development of Kuwait available today, such as Rivka Azoulay's *Kuwait and Al-Sabah: Tribal Politics and Power in an Oil State* (2020), Abdulrahman Alebrahim's *Kuwait's Politics Before Independence: The Role of the Balancing Powers* (2019), Farah al-Nakib's *Kuwait Transformed: A History of Oil and Urban Life* (2016) and Mary Ann Tétreault's *Stories of Democracy: Politics and Society in Contemporary Kuwait* (2000). There are also works in Arabic such as Ahmad Mustafa Abu Hakima's multi-volume *Tarikh al-Kuwait* (1969-). Later Abu Hakima also published *The Modern History of Kuwait 1750–1965* (1983). Studies of this kind and more general overviews of Gulf countries or the Middle East constitute the framework for this book and give it a context. My aim has been to include many resources in English in the bibliography for further reading. Most publications of the al-Babtain Foundation are published simultaneously in Arabic and English. References are in this book given to the versions in English.

This study is based on earlier studies of Kuwait and on an individual perspective with a focus on life story and interviewing and presence as a method. Life history has usually been chosen in academia to illustrate processes of social change in the manner that it has been presented above, in the form of a chronology of the development of Kuwait paralleled with the life story of Abd al-Aziz al-Babtain. This study situates one individual's experience in a long-term perspective from early adolescence to full maturity and uses them to provide insights into the history and development of contemporary Kuwait, while at the same time drawing on Kuwaiti history to throw light on aspects of Abd al-Aziz's personal history as a businessman, philanthropist and poet. As a general rule, this method enables individuals to make their voice heard. During my stay in Kuwait in October 2016, there were not many moments in which I had the opportunity to sit down with Abu Sa'ud and personally converse with him. Beyond interviews and conversations at al-Babtain Foundation and in his *diwaniyya*, I joined him for various meetings and when he was interviewed for a television show.[57] Apart from the opinions and stories he shared with me in the conversations we had, my observations of these moments provided me with additional insights about his life as well as about segments of Kuwaiti society. Interviews with his associates and friends constitute complementary material alongside texts that have usually been produced by the al-Babtain Foundation and articles and interviews with him presented in various media.

Narrative methods have a long tradition. As commonly understood, to narrate is to create meaning and to talk about one's own life is usually a reflective and creative process in which the conceptualization of meaning is the unifying factor. To converse with an experienced and renowned person such as Abd al-Aziz is challenging, since he has answered questions about his life many times. The purpose of the book in this regard was not to discuss whether statements are objective portrayals of events – the "true" history – but rather, to converse with Abu Sa'ud and understand his experiences as reflections about and depictions of his personal life story. Behar (1990) chooses to use the concept "life story" rather than "life history" and thus emphasizes the creative and subjective part of the narration. In line with Behar's approach, one can understand Abu Sa'ud's narration of his personal and tribal heritage as an example of when an account of a life history analytically becomes a life story.

In this project the life of the businessman and poet Abd al-Aziz al-Babtain is a situated example from a participatory perspective and extracts

---

57 Interviews were mainly in Arabic and with some of the staff at the Foundation interviews and conversations were also conducted in English.

from Abu Saʿud's life are transmitted from him and the al-Babtain Foundation through linguistic and text-based communication. Studies such as Roy Mottahedeh's *The Mantle of the Prophet* (2008) and Dale Eickelman's *Knowledge and Power in Morocco* (1992) can be seen as sources of inspiration for the current study. They succinctly portray development, change, tradition and society by studying the life of two individuals and the interplay between an individual and a society. The young mullah in Mottahedeh's study and the central figure in Eickelman's research become actors through which the authors sketch vivid portraits of the developments of Iranian and Moroccan society, respectively. The representation of Kuwait in this book is linked to Abd al-Aziz Saʿud al-Babtain's life story, his experiences and his strategies, contextualized within the general development of Kuwait since the 1930s. Yet the difference is the access to the source. I have not been able to do fieldwork and come close to Abu Saʿud in the same way as Eickelman carried out his fieldwork in Morocco, nor have I been able to spend hours, like Eickelman and Mottahedeh, interviewing an individual like Abd al-Aziz in order to generate empirical material from interviews to build upon while writing this text. In my visits to Kuwait I have recorded several interviews and taken notes during meetings and conversations not only with Abd al-Aziz, but also with other persons working in the Foundation or who are close to the Foundation. I have also participated in two of the larger conferences organized by the Foundation – one in Dubai and one in Kuwait City. In addition, the foundation has kindly provided me with access to material produced by them and copies of all books and other forms of print media concerning the Foundation and Abu Saʿud.

Another reason for the choice of life story is to give a voice to individuals who previously have not been acknowledged in research. In the case of Abd al-Aziz al-Babtain, he has been the subject of a great deal of scrutiny in different forms, such as *Festschriften* and other texts appraising his achievement, and his efforts to increase awareness about the Arabic language, peace studies and culture in general. These books belong to another genre than academic studies.

The businessman and poet Abd al-Aziz al-Babtain is certainly an example of what would commonly be termed an entrepreneur. The more modern use of the terms "entrepreneur" and "entrepreneurship" is associated with ideas presented by Joseph A. Schumpeter (d. 1950) linked to his ideas on economic development in the first half of the 1900s.[58] In Schumpeter's understanding the acts of an entrepreneur, and entrepreneurship, are linked to social contexts such as, for example, discussions on capitalism and democracy. In the footsteps of Schumpeter, Magnus Forslund portrays the characteristics of entrepreneurship.[59] In his perspective, an entrepreneur and entrepreneurship are linked to an individual's capacity for innovation, engagement, participation in networking, personal or organizational status, openness to ambiguous situations, the construction of facilities, the ability to adapt his or her opinion, mobilization of resources and the search for new arenas.

Connected to the qualities of the entrepreneur as an individual is a deeper dimension of entrepreneurship. This refers to entrepreneurship as a collective or discursive process in which everyone involved shares a set of values. One example is organizations in which common values arise, providing a foundation for innovation. Many of the more general presentations of the characteristics of an entrepreneur connect to Abd al-Aziz and his career as a businessman in Kuwait and internationally. Abu Sa'ud is presented in this book as an entrepreneur in accordance with the description above, but the terms "entrepreneur" and "entrepreneurship" will also be discussed to comprehend his context – primarily in Kuwait – and his engagement with the promotion of Arabic language and Arabic culture. Connected to the life Abu Sa'ud has created for himself is the notion of him coming of age alongside the state of Kuwait – with both the individual and the state being shaped by, and shaping, a moment in history. Interestingly, this twin-track focus provides insights to how Abd al-Aziz and the Kuwaiti state relate to the identity they define as "Arab", the role and function of Islam, as well as the conceptualization of the term *umma* ("nation") as a broader idea made sense of as eternal and symbolic, creating solidarity between people and extending beyond the borders of nation states. Often in this context, the nation acquires a father-like reference for constructions of interwoven individual, as well as collective, identities. These constructions of identity are relational and contextual. Hence, conceptualizations of the father-like "nation" may shift. Significant for the understanding of the self-actualization of Abd al-Aziz and the state of Kuwait is to locate agency

58 See Schumpeter 2017
59 Forslund 2002

and context in Abu Saʿud's ambition to promote Arab language, culture and his ideas on peace.

Questions on life story, identity and Arab identity are discussed in relevant sections of the book, but will also be reviewed in the concluding parts. The chronological outline of the text and the corresponding empirical material concerning the history of the life of Abd al-Aziz carry certain limitations since the focus is on the contemporary and on him as a person and his context and not his family. However, the conceptualization of the term "Arab" and "Arabic" plays a significant role as well as Abu Saʿud's understanding of his tribal identity.

In addition, one further objective of this work is to examine the businessman and poet's own understanding of his life: scrutinizing the process of conceptualizations and analysing their context in order to better make sense of his thinking and world view, regardless of whether these understandings of the world are "true" or "false".

In February 2022, Kuwait celebrated its 61st Independence Day, in addition to the 31st anniversary of the end of the Gulf War and the liberation of Kuwait from Iraqi occupation. Narrating the history of Kuwait certainly poses the question of how one should regard classical academic statements on "continuity" and "change", and the relationship between the two. This will be further discussed in the final part of the book, but it is certainly tempting to take the position that in reviewing the modern history of the country, the past has no sway over the future.

Moreover, in the case of Kuwait's political and financial developments, such a statement almost translates into a norm. However, the idea of a continuity certainly exists in regard to views about a tribal heritage and common values in the society linked to tribal traditions. Consequently, for Abd al-Aziz and his endeavours, in a broader understanding, to enhance, develop and promote Arab culture, the future is difficult to predict, but there is also a pool of shared notions to build upon.

In the end, at the heart of the book is an attempt to interweave the life story of businessman, poet and philanthropist Abd al-Aziz Saʿud al-Babtain with the history of the state of Kuwait – a remarkable country that has undergone a major transformation in the preceding century.

2

ARABS, TRIBES, THE DESERT AND OIL: BACKGROUND AND KEY THEMES

The notion of being Arab

In the preface to a book celebrating the output of the Foundation of Abd al-Aziz Sa'ud al-Babtain's Prize for Poetic Creativity, Abd al-Aziz states:

> The creation of a foundation that attends to Arabic poetry and celebrates the Arab poets was one of my dearest and most urging dreams. It all started the moment I realized the unique value of poetry in building past, present and future nations. (...) Establishing the Foundation was not a cultural luxury, nor was it a demonstration of financial capabilities or mere stubborn insistence on realizing a dream. Rather it was a determination to reinstitute the role of poetry in the life of our nation, as poetry has always been one of the most distinguished Arabic literary forms. (...) Our passion for poetry as Arabs, was not groundless, it emerged from what poetry has been – and always will be – a presentation of Arabic life itself. Poetry for Arabs is a means of satisfying the self, the soul and even the body. He inhales from poetry whatever pleases the self, elevates the soul and delights the ear.[1]

Referring to the activities of the foundation established in Cairo – a city which in the preface he calls the "(...) great Arab cultural capital",[2] Abd

---

1 See *Years of Cultural Output* 1989–2015: 3
2 See *Years of Cultural Output* 1989–2015: 3. One part of the larger al-Babtain Foundation named the Sa'ud al-Babtain Kuwaiti Scholarship for Postgraduate Studies has since 1974 granted scholarships to students to study at al-Azhar University in Cairo. Of these scholarships, 100 are granted on an annual basis to Iraqi students; see

al-Aziz establishes a strong bond between poetry and the Arab, but also with the Arabic language and the notion of an Arab nation. The preface ends with the logo of the Foundation over-written with a statement attributed to the second caliph, Umar ibn al-Khattab (585–644), "Order your dependents to learn poetry, for it is the guide to Moral Highness, correctness of opinion and the knowledge of offspring."[3]

The strong connection in the quotation attributed to the second caliph Umar between poetry, Arab identity and perhaps humans in general lends poetry the support of a religious authority, and thereby Islam, counteracting any suggestion that the Prophet Muhammad condemned poetry and poets. Abu Sa'ud considers poetry – classical Arabic poetry in particular – to be an essential part of Arab life. "Arabness" is conceptualised as a distinctive and timeless identity intimately related to poetry, and not as a more fluid identity whose meaning is contingent upon conceptualisations in time and place. Abu Sa'ud's emphasis on poetry can be seen as a deepening of the definitions usually associated with terms like "Arab" and "Arab nation". Whereas the classical approach to "Arabness" refers to persons who speak Arabic, share notions about an Arab history and identify with the language as well as a perceived "Arab culture", for Abd al-Aziz it is language, literature and poetry that combine to make up Arab identity. Hence, the Foundation promotes the classical and literal poetry and not a vernacular Arabic poetry (*al-shi'ar al-nabati*).

Viewed from another perspective, being an Arab is understood as belonging to an ethnic group deriving from a geographically clearly defined Arab world. But this description is coloured by the encounter between the imperial powers, primarily Britain and France, and the many parts of the world that were colonized by those powers in the 18th and 19th centuries. This encounter would (re)define Arabness not as a thing in itself, but in relation to other identities.

The history of the "Arabs", like the history of so many colonized peoples,

---

Years of Cultural Output 1989–2015: 5.
3 For a confessional writing of history concerning the life and personality of Umar bin al-Khattab, in which the quotation appears in a slightly different translation to that given above, see al-Sallabi undated: 376. The caliph Umar is also said to have ordered his governors to promote the knowledge of Arabic since "it rejuvenates the mind and increases virtue", Chejne 1965: 454.

is a long and involved tale of struggles and responses to a dominant power in the era of European imperialism. This experience shaped human existence at many levels and moulded a people's understandings of the rulers in power, as well as kindling long-running, identity debates on the elements that comprised the heart of the subjugated cultures. Many of these debates continue to rage – for example, the many discussions of the various implications for Muslims concerning interpretations of Islam. Looking back, the British and French mandates in former Ottoman areas promoted new interpretations, intellectual debates and understandings of Islam that influenced everyday life among Arabs. Interpretations that both accommodated and rejected new influences in Muslim societies were stimulated by exposure to an entire colonial apparatus of officials, colonial officers and educators and the institutions they set in place.[4] In this example as in so many others, any understanding of Arab identity is powerfully connected to the other – in this case, the perception of British and French identities and values.[5]

Discussions about the identity of the Arabs and their qualities and virtues as a collective have been a recurrent theme in the history of what constitutes the Arab world in the present day. In a more contemporary sense, the term "Arab world" does not only refer to countries where a majority of the population is Arabic-speaking, but more to an abstract community that in most cases uses Arabic as a means of communication. The discussion is concerned with "Arab" identity, irrespective of where these "Arabs" live in the world. Individuals in Beirut, Jeddah, London and small towns across Sweden or the US might consider themselves part of an Arab world. Consequently, in as much as the so-called Muslim world today is a cognitive universe to some, rather than a physical geographical reality, the "Arab world" is a mental construct that does not necessarily follow the borders of any country or can easily be defined as something belonging to an imaginary "East" or "West".[6]

---

4 For an illustrative study of receptions and interpretations related to new and modern things in Muslim societies in the late 19th and early 20th century, see Halevi 2019.

5 The term "Arab" is conceptualized in a context and linked to understandings of terms like "French", "English" and other terms depicting otherness like the word *ajam* used in Kuwait to describe Iranian migrants. On the *Ajam* in Kuwait, see Azoulay 2020: 19f, 55f and 59f, and Alebrahim 2019: 183.

6 For a discussion on the "Middle East", see Voll 2011.

However, historically speaking, references to being Arab or a speaker of the Arabic language as markers of belonging are not unique. The word has been in use for more than 3,000 years. Well-known religious scholars and learned individuals in the history of Islam such as al-Jahiz (776–868/869), Ibn Taymiyya (1263–1328), Ibn Khaldun (1332–1406) and al-Suyuti (1445–1505) have all discussed the role of language in society and the close connection between the Arabic language and the designation "Arab". Contemporary scholars, such as Savant and Webb (2017) in their introduction to the translation of *The Excellence of the Arabs* written by Ibn Qutaybah (828–889), point out the complexity of the history of the Arabs and note that earlier scholarship tended to construe the Arabs as a homogenous group of tribal people that since ancient times had lived on the Arabian Peninsula. The point Savant and Webb make is that this approach is perhaps deceptive and that the conceptualization of the word "Arab" is more complex. In the earliest times "Arab" may have been a reference to nomads and settled people, but tended to be a term that denoted outsiders: it did not refer to any form of broader belonging resembling the way in which the term "ethnicity" is conceptualized today. According to Savant and Webb, the idea of "Arab" in the form of expressing group solidarity and a self-identification occurs around the turn of the seventh century. Certainly, the experience of settling in newly founded cities like Kufa and Basra played an important role in disseminating a common Arab and Muslim identity among the conquerors, in contrast to the conquered people among whom they had settled.

The idea of being Arab developed over the first two or three generations after this point as a means of separation from the conquered people in the areas that today constitute the Arabian Peninsula, the Eastern Mediterranean region and Iraq. Hence, in the eighth century, to be an Arab was to belong to a community, and in fact a very select community, as very few of the subject populations in the newly conquered areas had converted to Islam. Arabness and Islam were associated categories and Islam was an ethno-religion akin to Judaism. All Arabs were potentially Muslims and for others to become Muslims they were required to become Arabs. Indeed, in its early history, Islam was an Arab religion and converts were obliged to take on an Arabic tribal identity.[7]

---

7 For more thorough discussions on Islam, Muslim and tribal identity in early history,

The complexities of the situation in the seventh and eighth centuries need not concern us here, but what I wish to stress is that it is not self-evident how to conceptualize the term "Arab". Neither is there a possibility to consider "Arabs" as a permanent and homogenous group of people in the history of people.[8] There is no one definition that applied in those earliest times, just as there is no one means of "measuring" or defining Arabness that applies later in history. In the 18th and 19th centuries, the designation "Arab" in some contexts referred primarily to Bedouins, and other markers were regional or civic, such as being Shami or Beiruti.

The al-Babtain Foundation, dedicated to contributing to the preservation and development of Arab culture, focuses especially on how literature and poetry shape the way Arab identity has been regarded in history, as well as how it can be formed currently and in the future. Abd al-Aziz Sa'ud al-Babtain has long revered poetry and seen poets as having special qualities different from other people.[9] In many publications describing the life achievements of al-Babtain, he states that he believes poets carry a message for humanity and culture in general. According to Abu Sa'ud, poetry refines people's values.[10] Protecting, supporting and helping give voice to poets and poetry in Arabic is central to the al-Babtain Foundation's mission.

In my conversations with Abd al-Aziz Sa'ud al-Babtain, the question of Arab identity has been a recurrent topic, whether consciously or unconsciously. In his narration of his own tribal history, he describes the tribal movement and how his early relatives migrated 650 years ago from the north of what is now Yemen and the south of today's Saudi Arabia to a city southwest of the capital Riyadh. The group comprised about 50 families,

---

see Morony 1984 and Wakeley 2018.

8 For current research and critical appraisals concerning the study of the "Arab" origin in history, see Webb 2017 and Donner 2010.

9 In the "Preface" to the *Al Babtain Dictionary of Contemporary Poets* Abu Sa'ud states that poets are the only persons that can embody what he describes as the "(...) inner fact among nations", a knowledge about one another to serve as the foundation for discussions between civilizations; see http://www.albabtainprize.org/default. aspx?pageid=43. Accessed August 12, 2018. al-Babtain has also stated "As I learned more about poetry and poets, I became convinced that poets are different from other people." See Atzori 2014: 36f.

10 This was said in a conversation I had with Abd al-Aziz Sa'ud al-Babtain October 17, 2016.

and Abd al-Aziz emphasizes their tribal context. They belonged to the Qahtani or Qahtan tribe, a tribe with several branches. Abu Saʿud says that the people who moved belonged to a branch of the Qahtani called al-Ariba (*al-Arab al-Ariba*).[11] He states that al-Ariba means "original" or "indigenous". Hence, in his opinion, he and his ancestors are the original or, as is sometimes stated, "the pure Arabs" – a group that had its homeland in Yemen. Another factor in the notion of the original Arabs is the *al-Mustar-iba* Arabs. This term describes Arabs who came from outside the Arabian Peninsula, but learned Arabic and are believed to be descendants of Ismail, son of Abraham, who helped his father build the Kaʿba in Mecca. There is also a third group in this genealogy, the *al-Arab al-Baʿida*, (literally "the defunct Arabs"), referring to old, but lost, Arab tribes. The point here is not to judge if the notion of the descent of the Arabs is historically correct or not. Rather, it is to note that Abu Saʿud narrates a classical conception of the appearance of the Arabs in history, and gives voice to an understanding of Arab history that is not uncommon in Kuwaiti society.

Irrespective of when the term "Arab" came into usage and at what time something that in today's terminology can be described as "an Arab iden-tity" appeared in historical sources such as Ibn Qutaybah, the areas of the early Arab conquest in today's southern Iraq are important in the history of Kuwait. This region, the land between the Euphrates and Tigris rivers, is often referred to as the cradle of civilization. It was here where, for the first time in history, people stopped moving, settled down and cultivated the land. The Shatt Al-Arab waterway is located on the southern border between the states of Iraq and Iran, and slightly west of where it flows today is the area which today is occupied by the state of Kuwait.

Tribal history and the founding of Kuwait

For centuries, the Arabian Peninsula has been the home of Bedouin nomads who travel the land in search of pasture and water. In the classic 1975 study of Nomadic life in Saudi Arabia *Nomads of the Nomads: Al*

---

11 This distinction is classical and appears in the translation of Ibn Qutaybah cited above. In the glossary of the book it is stated that Qahtan is the name of the "legendary ancestor of the 'Southern Arabs', and a name synonymous with Yemen in Muslim genealogy"; see Savant & Webb 2017: 266.

Murrah Bedouin of the Empty Quarter, Donald P. Cole describes the importance of nomadic life for tribes and tribal identity, even if the homeland of a tribe is settled for reasons of access to power and being part of politics, or to come closer to a more sedentary tribal population. Similar examples of upholding tribal identity and ideals, but at the same time to a large extent being settled, can be seen in Andrew Shryock's study *Nationalism and the Genealogical Imagination: Oral History and Textual Authority in Tribal Jordan* (1997). In this book the author investigates the transition from oral to written history in a tribal context. In addition, it offers a portrait of developments of tribal identity and politics in Jordan, and provides a regional perspective on how histories, lineages and pedigrees are constructed in a tribal environment.

As with much of the region, Kuwait's history and its roots are deeply tribal.[12] The modern state of Kuwait began as a small fishing village on the coast of the Persian (or Arabian) Gulf. It was founded by Bedouins from inland who decided to settle on the coast once they found they could sustain themselves by living off the ocean instead of the desert. As time went by, they learnt the occupations of seafaring and pearl-diving and through these activities they eventually transformed the small fishing village into a bustling trading port. Despite the immense shift in Kuwait's fortunes in the last century alone, and despite the gleam of modernity that now defines much of the state, it is notable how significant tribal identity remains for the people of current Kuwait – regardless of whether they are settled or not.

For Abd al-Aziz Sa'ud al-Babtain, Arab and tribal identities are part of a living heritage and he readily recounts the story of his tribal pedigree. To some extent, he embodies the modern Arab and tribal identity. On most of the occasions I met him or attended meetings with him, he was on his way to or from his farm or mansion in Saudi Arabia. He has a special identity card that grants him the right to cross the border between Kuwait and Saudi Arabia. Despite the life and legacy he has built for himself in Kuwait, there is a certain sparkle in his eyes when he speaks about the farm in Saudi Arabia. His fond memories of the animals, the sunrise and the desert climate perhaps can be understood as topics linked to, and a reflection of, his ideals and what he perceives as genuine traditions inherent to a tribal

---

12 For a study devoted to tribal politics and power in Kuwait, see Azoulay 2020.

identity. The scene, cast and theme of his life inland in Saudi Arabia are signifiers of a tribal past that is less easily accessed in Kuwait, a country where
the Bedouins who once roamed the inland deserts have largely renounced
their traditional ways in favour of a more settled life.[13]

During the mid-17th century, the Bani Khalid, an Arab tribe originating
from Najd, was an important tribal confederation. The Bani Khalid were
at the peak of their powers, having succeeded in wresting control of the
eastern shoreline of Arabia, from Basra in the north to the area of contemporary Qatar in the south, by expelling Ottoman forces. More or less
the entire area that would later constitute the modern state of Kuwait was
under the firm control of the Bani Khalid, who essentially laid the foundations of present-day Kuwait. Prior to the Bani Khalid's conquest of this
area, minor settlements had existed in the bay just south of Shatt al-Arab.
In the 1670s the Bani Khalid constructed a small fort in the bay, in Arabic
a *kut*. This structure became central to their control of the region, and
the word *kut* became a diminutive for the future name of the sheikhdom
and state.

Beyond simply functioning as a centre of power, the creation of a fort
in the bay offered people in the village protection from potential raiders.[14]
The *kut* became the centre of a growing community, and this community
attracted trade and provided stability to a growing number of people from
around the region over the ensuing decades. Its growth was particularly
strong during times of inter-tribal conflict and environmental challenges.

A significant phase of development of the land that would later become
Kuwait occurred in the late 17th century, when the inland of Arabia was hit
by a drought that persisted into the early years of the following century. The
drought forced the Bedouin tribes of the Najd region to seek other lands
that could sustain their herds and livelihood. A subgroup of the Aniza or
Anaiza tribe of the Najd decided to settle the east coast of Arabia. Enjoying
good relations with the Bani Khalid through a tribal confederation and a
client relationship, these migrating families from the Najd settled in the
area that is currently known as Kuwait.[15] The migrants benefited from a

---

13 In addition, a considerable part of his family resides in Saudi Arabia and in the
country al-Babtain has several family-owned businesses.

14 al-Awadi 2014: 591

15 al-Awadi 2014: 591f. The tradition holds that the ruler, or in the official

strong linkage to Bani Khalid's hegemony, which provided a foundation of security that allowed the group, and notably the three families of al-Sabah, al-Jalahima and al-Khalifa, to develop business relationships and trade and develop a more maritime-based economy in Kuwait.[16]

Following the death of their sheikh in 1722, the power of the Bani Khalid was weakened as internal and external struggles ensued. This allowed for the growth of local powers, and the three dominant families of the Bani Utba, the al- Sabah, al-Jalahima and al-Khalifa, established their authority over the economic and political life of the area constituting the contemporary State of Kuwait. The al-Sabah family rose to prominence through its control of the port city's administration, and Sabah bin Jabir was chosen as Kuwait's sheikh in 1752.[17] This was a pivotal development in Kuwait's history, with the position of the ruler being hereditary within the al-Sabah family up to the present.[18] However, the ruler was dependent on the merchants, and his position was conditional upon promoting and safeguarding the merchants' interests. This dependency made the merchants an important group in the society and the relationship between the ruler and merchant families came to define Kuwait's politics for a long time.[19]

Under the rule of the al-Sabah family, Kuwait grew increasingly prosperous, and by the end of the 18th century the city was trading with the British-controlled northwestern Indian subcontinent, mainly exporting horses, pearls and dates. External factors were the key drivers in Kuwait's early growth and outward expansion. Political instability and high rates of taxation on goods in the nearby Ottoman-controlled city of Basra drove

---

terminology of today's state, the amir, is chosen by the family, see Tétreault 1991: 575.

16 Hijji 2010: 5. The three families or clans supposedly formed a federation named Bani Utba (Utub in plural) or al-Utub when they moved to the Gulf area.

17 Azoulay (2020: 23) says that it was an agreement between influential families within the Bani Utub that made the ascent to power possible. Abdulrahman Alebrahim states that there is no evidence for when Sabah bin Jabir was given the leadership by Kuwaiti notables; see Alebrahim 2019: 8.

18 Casey 2007: 26–28. The history of this period is vague and unclear. However, for an account of Kuwaiti history from early 18th century to independence in 1961, see Azoulay 2020 and Pillai & Kumar 1962: 108–116. For a marginally different account, see Alebrahim 2019: 7f.

19 In the 19th century an important source of income for the ruler was the tax he collected from the merchants; see Azoulay 2020: 23ff and Alebrahim 2019: 8f and 10f.

merchants to unload their merchandise in Kuwait's port, quickly propelling the small sheikhdom's expansion into a major trade destination.[20] And looking to the north, the regional decline of the Ottoman Empire in the second half of the 18th century allowed for Kuwait to develop its commercial presence relatively undisturbed by its behemoth of a neighbour.[21] Yet even as they benefited from the Ottoman Empire's decline, the al-Sabah family sought friendly relations with both Kuwaiti tribes and neighbouring ones since they shared a common enemy, the Wahhabi tribes of the Najd.

In 1871 the sheikh was given the title of *qaim maqam* or *qaimaqam* by the Ottomans,[22] meaning "provisional governor" or "sub-governor", and in 1875 Kuwait was incorporated into the Ottoman administrative region of Basra. The effect of these shifts was limited, however, with the al-Sabah sheikhdom continuing to have autonomy over internal affairs, but yielding to Ottoman sovereignty where foreign policy was concerned.[23]

Ottoman suzerainty over Kuwait continued until Sheikh Mubarak al-Sabah (r. 1896–1915) gained control over the area in 1896; he was the first ruler to enjoy supreme unchallenged authority.[24] Suspicious of increasing Ottoman interference in Kuwaiti affairs, he sought to gain the protection of the British Empire. At the same time, Mubarak was appointed *qaim maqam* by the Ottomans in 1897.[25] Although Britain had offered protection to the other "trucial states" in the Gulf, they were cautious not to upset the Ottomans and so had declined a similar undertaking with Kuwait. But

---

20 Al Hijji 2010: 5f, 8

21 Casey 2007: 28

22 Tétreault (1991: 571n) claims that there is no evidence that Kuwait paid a tribute to the Ottomans and that the idea that Kuwait was incorporated into the Ottoman Empire is therefore tenuous. However, in the *Gazetteer of the Persian Gulf,* John Gordon Lorimer (d. 1914) stated that the Kuwaiti ruler of the time, Sheikh Abd Allah (d. 1896), had a close relationship with the Turks from the end of the 1860s to the early 1890s; see Lorimer 1915: 1014.

23 Finnie 1992: 7f, 12f. Already in 1968, al-Baharna notes that the link between Kuwaiti sheikhs obtaining their administrative powers from authorities in Basra provides the foundation for later claims by the republic of Iraq that Kuwait is an integral part of Iraq; see al-Baharna 1968: 250.

24 Alebrahim 2019: 8, 12. For a detailed account pointing out that there are many interpretations by historians, Kuwaiti as well as others, on the reasons for the coup of Mubarak and the development of his rule; see Azoulay 2020: 48ff and 53ff.

25 al-Sabah 2014:10

in 1899, with concerns mounting over what was deemed to be an excessive Ottoman role in Kuwaiti affairs, the British obtained a secret bond from the Kuwaiti sheikh in exchange for British protection.[26] The agreement of 1899 was negotiated by Mubarak without consulting the merchants and it effectively gave Britain control over the sheikhdom's foreign policy, while Kuwait maintained its autonomy in domestic affairs.[27] Accordingly, from this time until the outset of World War I, there was a great ambiguity around British commitments to Kuwait, while the Ottoman Empire kept affirming its claims over the northeastern part of the Gulf. The outcome of the war gave an end to these conflicting ambitions, and Kuwait formally came under British protection, while the former Ottoman provinces to the north formed the basis of the future Kingdom of Iraq.

During this period of upheaval and difficulties, combined with the decline of the Ottoman Empire, Sheikh Mubarak maneuvered Kuwait strategically,[28] managing to create a degree of independence domestically and establishing a client/patron relationship between Kuwait and Britain.[29] He is also sometimes portrayed as the founder of the modern state of Kuwait. Consequently, it was under his reign that the first school and hospital appeared, and a charitable society was set up to send students abroad. The sheikh displayed considerable diplomatic skills in surviving domestic, tribal and regional, as well as international, power struggles. On the other hand, he displayed a ruthless side by murdering his two brothers, Jarrah and Muhammad, when he seized power in 1896.[30]

The Ottoman Turks and European countries like Britain, Germany, France and Russia were competing over influence in the region.[31] In addition, Sheikh Mubarak consolidated his governance by promoting trade; from this strengthened position he sought support from merchants and

---

26 al-Awadi 2014: 593 and Rogan 2009: 176

27 Alebrahim 2019: 20f and Loewenstein 2000: 104

28 For a detailed discussion of Mubarak's rule see Azoulay 2020: 48–57 and Alebrahim 2019: 12–28.

29 Tétreault 1991: 567–579

30 For the claim that Mubarak murdered his brothers, see Azoulay 2020: 55, Alebrahim 2019: 13, and Tétreault 1991: 570.

31 Tétreault's (1991: 576n) statement that before the rule of Mubarak, "There seems to have been no tradition of state repression of politically active individuals in Kuwait until the reign of Mubarak", is also worthy of note.

introduced new taxes on trade and property and customs duties in order to finance more extensive bureaucracy.[32] He also created alliances with different groups in Kuwaiti society such as Bedouin tribesmen, who became loyal supporters of the ruler. However, the general context of the developments which took place in the small state of Kuwait at the time is not unique, and can also be seen in other locations during this era, where people strove to become independent from foreign rulers, and assert their independence by creating educational systems, advancing healthcare provisions and founding new nation states. Thus, even if Sheikh Mubarak was indisputably an eloquent and competent politician, he was also a man of his age.[33] More explicitly, as regards the Kuwaiti ruler's strategy of upholding security and autonomy, this was seriously compromised by the experience of the country as a British client state.[34]

Escape from the Najd

Historically, regions grow and shift through a combination of push- and pull-factors. In the case of Kuwait's early years, population growth was driven less by people desiring to come to the sheikhdom on the coast, but more by people seeking to escape from elsewhere. For most of Kuwait's early inhabitants, that place was the Najd, the parched, unforgiving central region of modern-day Saudi Arabia.

It was challenging for anyone in this area to establish a sustainable life-style and to survive. The desert environment, particularly around the Najd, did not provide an abundance of resources. Even for nomadic tribes, who migrated from one area to the next in search of better sustenance or safer conditions, life on the Arabian Peninsula was relentlessly harsh. This was probably the primary reason for inhabitants in the area to turn towards the sea in search of better opportunities – for survival, trade and community – and improve their living conditions in a suitable geographical location. Those nomads who relocated quickly settled down and created a

---

32 Crystal (1989: 437) states that the rule of Mubarak was, like the one of Abdullah in the neighbouring Qatar, "personal and autocratic".

33 See al-Sabah 2014 for a positive and idealizing, but detailed, perspective on the role of Sheikh Mubarak al-Sabah in the establishment of Kuwait.

34 Tétreault 1991: 566

better economy for themselves, with the earliest arrivals reaping the great-est rewards.[35]

Abu Sa'ud's ancestors arrived in Kuwait in 1855, a century and a half after the first families had migrated to the coast from the Najd. Abu Sa'ud's pater-nal grandfather Abd al-Aziz lived with his parents and siblings in al-Rawda in Najd, 180 km north west of Riyadh. The family had moved there from the city of al-Kharj, where they had been for hundreds of years. However, life in the Najd was a constant struggle for survival in a land depleted by war, poverty and drought.

Abu Sa'ud recounts the incident that spurred his grandfather, then 14, and his 16-year-old brother Ibrahim to leave the Najd. It was a morning when their father, Abd al- Rahman had received several guests and sent his sons to fetch fresh dates from a stand of palm trees nearby. "My grandfa-ther, the youngest, Abd al-Aziz, carried the basket, as the traditions in Najd and in Kuwait require the youngest to respect the oldest", recalls Abu Sa'ud. When they arrived, his elder brother told Abd al-Aziz to climb the palm tree and cut the *al-aquq*, a small date typical of the area. The young boy did as he was bidden, and after he climbed back down, his brother ordered him to carry the dates to al-Rawda, about 700 metres away. It was at this point, Abu Sa'ud recounted, that the trouble began.

Abd al-Aziz replied, "I have done my duty. I carried the empty basket and climbed the palm tree. The rest is your duty." Ibrahim said, "No, I am your elder brother, and I order you to carry them." Abd al-Aziz then replied, "Then why did my father ask you to come with me? It was to help each other."

This quarrel resulted in the two boys leaving the basket where it was and returning to al-Rawda without the dates they had been sent to fetch. When they arrived back in al-Rawda empty-handed, their father beat them severely and promised that when the guests left, he would give them a second beating to teach the boys a lesson. At that moment, as family lore has it, the two boys resolved to settle their differences and agreed to leave Najd and seek their fortunes elsewhere – in a life free from poverty, hunger and beatings.

Most people who left the Najd at this time headed either for Arish in the Sinai, or to Cairo or Damascus. Some also made for al-Zubayr, a

---

35 Salih 1991: 46

mashyakhah (a small independent political tribal congregation ruled by a sheikh – effectively, a minor sheikhdom)[36] about 11 km southwest of Basra that did not belong to Ottoman Iraq or any other country, where new arrivals could grow dates on the margins of green lands and cooling rivers. The inhabitants of al-Zubayr formed an independent community, which had its own freely elected leaders and largely managed its own affairs. Still other escapees from the overpopulated Najd headed for Kuwait. Much of Kuwait's early population came from the Najd, and would have identified with the despair and frustration that fuelled Abu Sa'ud's grandfather's and great-uncle's quest for a better life.

Caravans leaving the Najd were typically announced 10 days in advance, so that travellers could register their names, make their arrangements and prepare for the journey to Kuwait, al-Zubayr, Al-Ahsa or Damascus. At that time, caravans were the only way of escaping from the Najd, since travelling in large numbers ensured protection from predators – be they humans or animals such as wolves, leopards and tigers. Bandits were known to attack small groups leaving the Najd, but by assembling caravans of around 100 or even 150 people, those seeking a better life were able to provide some measure of security for their journey, at least.

Abu Sa'ud tells of how the brothers, Abd al-Aziz and Ibrahim, decided to make their escape after hearing of a caravan going to Kuwait on a Thursday morning. But their plan was almost derailed when they were informed that the caravan could not accept them without their father's consent. Fearful of being handed back to their father, the two hatched a plan to slip out of the Najd undetected.

"They decided to follow the caravan walking without joining it, stopping where the caravan stopped and moving when it moved. By the time two days had passed, the people of the caravan realized the boys were shadowing them, but by that time it was impractical to turn back and return them to their father", recounts Abu Sa'ud. His grandfather and great-uncle had successfully made their escape.

---

36 In historical accounts, in Iran and Iraq during the 10th and 11th centuries, the term *mashyakhah* (pl. *mashayikh*) denoted a group of community elders or leaders; see Mottahedeh 2001: 124 and 156f. The term *mashyakhah* could also be used to describe collections of religious scholars. For an account of this kind of scholarly network, see Senturk 2005: 98f.

This story told by Abd al-Aziz is also a narrative of lineage and migration. In the story the *nasab* ("lineage") of Abu Sa'ud is traced to the Najd – an area that is the geographical centre of the Arabian Peninsula. It is a prestigious lineage that connects Abd al-Aziz and his family to a Kuwaiti merchant elite which claims to be of pure Arab and Najdi descent. This elite is Sunni and Arab and becomes a political entity in the history of modern Kuwait. In the 20th century, it established itself in opposition to Shi'a merchants and embraced Arab nationalism. Most of its members, like Abd al-Aziz al-Babtain, gave their support to the ruling al-Sabah family.[37]

Desert, depression and downturn

The Kuwait in which the al-Babtain brothers arrived in the mid-1850s was a vastly different world to the one they had left behind in al-Rawda. On the coast, near the *kut*, living conditions had adapted from the well-established and long tradition of Bedouin life in the desert to a lifestyle that was shaped by proximity to the sea. In these new conditions, people began to engage in maritime activities, such as pearl-diving, boatbuilding, fishing and trading with ships arriving from the coast of India, East Africa and the Red Sea. The young men, alone and without family connections, followed the path trodden by migrants before them, taking menial jobs and slowly working their way up in this new world.[38]

While life by the sea allowed some to become rich, it did not necessarily change the societal and hierarchical structures, patterns and habits among Kuwaitis. Life for many, if not most, was a constant struggle to survive, though arguably less harsh than back in the Najd. Success would finally beckon in the next generation. Ibrahim had a son named Abd al-Muhsin, who was a teacher at al-Mubarakiyya school in 1926 and later in the 1930s became Sheikh Abd al-Muhsin al-Qadi, the principal judge. Meanwhile Abu Sa'ud's grandfather, Abd al-Aziz, became father to Sa'ud, his father, who began the family's tradition of commerce by opening a small shop at the old al-Manakh market, close to al-Safat, where he sold dates and barley.

---

37 For more on the Arab and Sunni merchants in Kuwait of Najdi descent, see Azoulay 2020:60–63.

38 For a brief description of the pearl-fishing industry and the labour force in the early 20th century, see Alebrahim 2019: 15–17.

Abu Sa'ud told me a story that illustrates how difficult it was for a young man to develop a business and generate profits in the early 20th century. His father, Sa'ud, had borrowed money in order to grow his business, but the structure of the loan, whereby 55 per cent of the profit would accrue to the lender and 45 per cent to Sa'ud himself, made it difficult to generate any significant income. To put this all in context, a typical family in Kuwait earned around US$180 per year in the 1920s.[39] This was low even at the time, making it difficult for families to make ends meet.

"Around this time", Abu Sa'ud went on, "a rich Kuwaiti – in other words, someone with ten thousand rupees to his name – approached my father and said, 'What if you were to travel to Saudi Arabia and bring back sheep to sell in Kuwait? You take 45 per cent and I take 55 per cent.'"[40]

Though it was on the same profit-sharing terms as before, Abd al-Aziz's father seized this opportunity, which he thought would be more rewarding than selling from a shop. Sa'ud closed down the shop and journeyed to an area of Saudi Arabia commonly known as Jariah, or the Upper Village, about 150 km from the borders of modern-day Kuwait.

"He arrived in Jariah during Ramadan, though as a traveller he was permitted not to fast and to make up those days later", Abu Sa'ud said. "Introducing himself at a stranger's house, Sa'ud was greeted and offered a coffee. The aroma of the coffee drifted out of the house and was instantly detected by a bystander, who ran up to a piece of high ground and began shouting, 'Fellow Muslims, there are impious people in that house, breaking the fast!'"

Yet despite this incident, Sa'ud managed to purchase sheep and return to Kuwait. However, he struggled to sell them. Not only did he fail to turn

---

39 Salih 1991: 47

40 The value of a rupee in the 1920s was dependent on the type of rupee. There were local forms of the currency issued by rulers on the subcontinent as well as an Indian and a British rupee. After World War I the Indian rupee was linked to the price of silver (around 1924, a rupee was about 1 shilling and 5 pennies). In addition, from the outbreak of the war until 1930, the value of the rupee was instable; see Bagchi 2000: 62ff. The rupee of the Republic of India (INR) was on the day of independence in 1947 pegged to 3,30 INR equals US$1. Hence the value of the ten thousand rupees mentioned above are difficult to judge more than it appears as enough to define a rich man. For an overview of the currencies used in the early 20th century Kuwait, see al-Sabah 2014: 124f.

a profit but, with the sheep unsold, he did not even manage to recoup his initial outlay. He felt depressed after the rigours of travelling and embarrassed at his own shortcomings as a businessman. The sting of failure was not enough to prevent him from trying again, however. An acquaintance advised him to take his flock to the British military base about 7 km north of al-Zubayr and try to sell them there, so Sa'ud duly set off with his sheep. He reached al-Zubayr, and not only sold the sheep through a contractor, but also found there a close-knit community of people who like him had originally come from the Najd.

Abu Sa'ud recalls his father many years later recounting the tale of his early failures and first taste of commercial success, describing his own feeling after meeting this community at al-Zubayr as "relieved". The tale of the father's early failures and determination to press on would have parallels not just with the son's early years in business, but with the experience of Kuwaitis and Kuwait in general at this time.

Sa'ud al-Babtain, the father of Abd al-Aziz returned to a growing Kuwait and slowly expanded his commercial activities. The 1920s and 1930s were a time of rapid population growth, even though incomes were low. As Kuwait's population grew, so did its need for some of the structures and mechanisms of governance, developing institutions for a legal system, education, finance, and infrastructure. Those mechanisms were, in many cases backed by the al-Sabah family who understood the significance of consultation with other leading families. In this new context, Kuwait was shifting into a society with a ruling body that governed the local population in return for taxation. Early tax revenues were obtained primarily from activities such as fishing, pearl-diving and boatbuilding, but these were small enterprises, generating around US$40,000 of revenue in 1938, a very small sum compared to the affluence of contemporary businesses in Kuwait.[41]

In the era before oil was discovered, Salih describes how Kuwaiti society comprised three distinct groups: the governing al-Sabah family, merchants and individuals who like Sa'ud were engaged in labour.[42] The exercise in

---

41 Alebrahim and Salih discuss the implications of the establishment of a Shura Council with appointed members in 1921, and the first written Charter as a foundation for legislation; see Alebrahim 2019 38–47 and Salih 1991: 47.

42 Salih 1991: 47. Alebrahim makes this type of distinction more complex and includes, for example, religious scholars, intelligentsia, an emerging educated class,

Portrait of Saʻud al-Babtain, father of Abd al-Aziz al-Babtain. © the author.

power was primarily in the hands of the al-Sabah family which elected its leaders based on accomplishment, but the al-Sabahs also governed in consultation with diverse interest groups within Kuwaiti society.[43] At this time, Kuwaiti society was subject to a customary style of rule founded on tribal models – a mode of governance that would today be considered autocratic. The al-Sabah family received taxes from the population of Kuwait, and in return the state offered various services, essentially protection and minor administrative undertakings.

In the early 1930s, Kuwait was hit by the global financial downturn following the Wall Street Crash of 1929, which made life even more difficult for most of the country's inhabitants. The crash of the US stock market and the ensuing worldwide economic crisis had general systemic repercussions. One consequence was a decreased demand for luxury goods all over the world, but especially in North America and Europe. This had a direct effect on the economy of Kuwait.[44]

The luxury goods that Kuwait – and several other Persian or Arabian Gulf economies – most depended upon were pearls, and the demand for them, primarily in Western Europe and North America. In the 1920s and 1930s, this mainstay of Kuwait's economy was hit by a drastic slump in global demand for pearls. Additional factors affecting sales of pearls from Kuwait were the invention of cultured pearls around this time and especially the rapid growth of the Japanese cultured pearl industry.[45] Before long, the new, more efficient and cost-effective Japanese methods of cultivating pearls began to have a serious impact on traditional oyster-pearl diving in the Gulf.[46]

The effect of the slump in the pearl-diving industry was felt throughout virtually the entire Kuwaiti economy. Owen and Pamuk refer to reports from a British political agent living in Kuwait, who reported witnessing widespread starvation and beggars appearing for the first time on

---

people of various professions such as pearl divers, villagers and Shi'a-Muslims. He also points out how groups or belongings overlap; see Alebrahim 2019.

43 Salih 1991: 47

44 Owen & Pamuk 1999: 82

45 For a partly personal portrait of pearling in the Arabian Gulf from the early 1900s to the collapse of the sector in the 1930s, see al-Shamlan 2001.

46 The establishment of the industry producing an artificial pearl caused a tradition that may be as old as 4,000 years to collapse; see Bowen Jr 1951: 161f and Crystal 1992: 2.

the streets of Kuwait City. In addition, there were reports of a number of pearl-divers dying of malnutrition.[47] The fledgling sheikhdom's fragile economy, barely a century old, had proved highly vulnerable to global economic forces.

The shipping business was also beset by problems in the late 19th and early 20th centuries. By the turn of the century, Kuwait was prospering as a mercantile nation, with the largest commercial fleet in the Gulf by 1860.[48] However, the early 20th century posed significant challenges to Kuwait's economy as trade was repeatedly hampered by political events on a regional and international scale.

The first sign of the troubles facing Kuwaiti traders was the British blockade of the port in 1918. This was carried out in an effort to halt trade to the Ottoman Empire since merchandise could be transferred overland from Kuwait.[49] The defeat of the Ottoman Empire later that year brought some respite, and trade again flourished in Kuwait until Ibn Saʻud (1876–1953), the leader of Wahhabi tribes in the Najd and founder of the Kingdom of Saudi Arabia, sought to annex Kuwaiti territory in 1919 and the area was raided by the Ikhwan, a group of fighters nominally operating under Ibn Saʻud. In 1920 the raids developed into attempts to overrun the entirety of Kuwait, but this ambition was halted after the British intervened. The dispute between Ibn Saʻud and Kuwait's Sheikh Salim al-Mubarak al-Sabah (r. 1917–21) ended with Salim's death and the conference at Uqair in 1922.[50]

The disputes and negotiations leading to the Uqair agreement can also be set within in a wider context. The fall of the Ottoman Empire, the victory of the Allied powers in World War I and the establishment of mandates through a covenant of the League of Nations were all developments

---

47 Owen & Pamuk 1992: 82

48 Hijji 2010: 8

49 Tétreault 1991: 13. See also Alebrahim 2019: 21.

50 Sheikh Salim al-Sabah was replaced in 1921 by the tenth ruler of Kuwait, Ahmad al-Jabir al-Sabah. He ruled the country from 1921 until his demise in 1950. The conference in Uqair lead to the signing of the Uqair protocol. This document outlined by the British representative Sir Percy Cox gave almost two-thirds of Kuwait to what later became Saudi Arabia, but also transferred Saudi Arabian land to Iraq and established the current borders of the countries involved; see al-Baharna 1968: 264ff and Lauterpacht, Greenwood, Weller and Daniel Bethlehem (eds) 1991: 46ff.

that impacted on the formation of the Middle East in the 20th century. Negotiations and agreements between the Allied powers in San Remo in 1920 discussed a British mandate in Iraq. The signing of the Treaty of Sèvres meant that Turkey renounced all the territories outside the frontiers defined in the agreement. A similar arrangement was agreed upon in the Treaty of Lausanne from 1924. Consequently, local treaties between actors on the Arabian Peninsula can be understood as part of a process in which the victorious colonial powers sought to maintain control, but also as a process in which the world was being reordered in terms of borders and nation states. Certainly, the mandate established by the British in the three *wilayats* (districts) of Mosul, Baghdad and Basra had consequences, and still has, for the borders of Kuwait.[51]

The agreement the British negotiated between the parties at Uqair constituted the foundation for the neutral zone between Kuwait and Saudi Arabia, a zone that was eventually abolished and divided by an agreement between the two countries in 1970. Yet the oil resources from onshore and offshore fields are still shared between Saudi Arabia and Kuwait. Fundamentally, the agreement set the borders of the future Kuwait, which at the time amounted to the loss of more than half of the sheikhdom's territory. On top of this loss came another hit: after the conference, Ibn Sa'ud imposed an economic blockade on Kuwait, effectively halting most of the desert trade to the port.[52] The blockade lasted until 1942 and had a significant impact on the Kuwaiti economy, according to Hijji, even causing starvation in the area.[53]

The Saudi Arabian economic blockade of Kuwait was not the only financial problem of the time. It was more or less contemporaneous with the global economic crisis and subsequent depression, and the collapse of the pearl-fishing industry. Against this backdrop, the country had few goods to export and restricted access to the Bedouins for selling of imports. Accordingly, the blockade limited the access to trade with Bedouins living in the desert regions since they usually moved across border lines. By the

---

51 For a review of the status of Kuwait in light of various early treaties and agreements, see Pillai & Kumar 1962: 112ff.

52 Tétreault, 1991: 13–14

53 Hijji 2010: 128. Also, from the stories that Abd al-Aziz told of his father, it is clear that some trade nevertheless did cross the border.

mid-1930s, Kuwait's economic situation and commercial prospects were close to disastrous.

The game-changing discovery of oil: the opportunity for entrepreneurship

Kuwait's fortunes changed forever on 23 February in 1938, when oil was discovered in the Burgan oil field in the southeast of the country. However, Kuwaitis had for some time known their country held some oil reserves, while Bedouins had long been aware that bitumen existed in the desert.[54] After the discovery of oil in Iran in 1908 and the creation of the Anglo-Persian Oil Company (later the Anglo-Iranian Oil Company and eventually British Petroleum), the British Political Resident enquired of the Kuwaiti ruler Sheikh Mubarak if an oil concession was possible. Later, in 1913, geologists appointed by the British Admiralty visited the area of Burgan to carry out a survey. The result of the investigation was not unfavourable, but the outbreak of World War I put developments on hold. In the 1920s the exploration for oil on the Arabian Peninsula continued. Many surveys were made, and various competing companies were involved in the discussions about concessions. In 1933, two of the competitors, the Anglo-Persian Oil Company and Gulf Oil, put their rivalries aside and registered a joint venture in London, the Kuwait Oil Company (KOC). The offer made by the new company to the Kuwaiti ruler, Sheikh Ahmad al-Jabir al-Sabah (r. 1921–50), was accepted and the first oil concession was signed in December 1934 awarding production to Kuwait Oil Company Limited.[55]

One persistent myth surrounding Kuwait's oil wealth concerns Harold Dickson, a colonel in the Kuwaiti civil service from 1929 to 1936. During this period, Dickson personally advised the sheikh of Kuwait and had established for himself a reputation as a soothsayer. In 1937, by which time he was officially retired but was continuing to act in an advisory capacity, Dickson dreamt that he and his wife were living in the desert at the site of an oil field.

---

54 Khouja & Sadler 1979: 17
55 The stories of how oil entered into the history of Kuwait are sometimes told differently in regard to the years given for what happened between 1911 and 1914. However, the differences do not change the content of the story; see Kouja & Sadler 1979: 17 ff., Brennan 1990: 103f and Sorkabi 2012.

In the dream, a storm blew up, revealing a hidden ancient tomb beneath the cavity of a *Sidr* tree. Inspecting the tomb, Dickson and his wife discovered a young woman wrapped in a rotten cloth lying on a slab of stone. The couple decided to remove the cloth and were preparing to rebury her when the woman suddenly awoke. Immediately, they washed, clothed and fed the woman, who gratefully gifted them an ancient copper coin. She warned them that "wicked men" would attempt to kill and bury her, and that Dickson should seek aid from the sheikh and the British government. Almost immediately, an armed mob arrived. Defending the woman, Dickson killed the leader of the group, who in Dickson's dream looked like a Persian, and drove off the mob. Once awake, Dickson sought the advice of a locally respected Bedouin female dream-reader by the name of Umm Mubarak. The dream reader claimed that the woman and her valuable coin symbolized the wealth of an undiscovered oil field located near the tree and that the mob represented the locals who opposed oil drilling. Umm Mubarak recognized the *Sidr* tree Dickson spoke of and located it in Burgan. Subsequently, Dickson advised the sheikh and the Kuwaiti Oil Company to drill in the area, and as has been noted above, in 1938 the company duly discovered one of the world's most plentiful crude oil deposits.[56]

The 1934 oil concessions had been given to the Kuwait Oil Company, jointly owned by what later became British Petroleum Oil (BP) in Kuwait, and by Gulf Oil, an American company.[57] These two companies each owned 50 per cent of the shares. Oil concessions are contracts for companies to search for and extract oil within a defined area. The rights to do so are given by a state or private body in return for a fee. Territory in Kuwait is the land of the state and the ruling family. At the beginning of the oil exploration era, drilling and export operations were carried out by foreign companies which negotiated contracts and were granted concessions. In return, they paid the Kuwaiti government, primarily the rulers, for the right to prospect and drill for oil, and export it from the country.

Despite its size, the effect of the Burgan discovery would take several years to materialize. The Second World War put commercial production

---

56 This story about Dickson dreaming of oil is included in Moss 2009: 126ff. It is also documented by Dickson in his book about Bedouin life in Kuwait and Saudi Arabia; see Dickson 1949: 332ff.

57 For a record of the negotiations about oil concessions, see Chisholm 1975.

on hold, and it was not until the war's end that production was to begin at any speed.[58] In June 1946, Sheikh Ahmad al-Jabir al-Sabah inaugurated the export of Kuwait's first crude oil shipment.

Between 1946 and 1988, oil revenue grew from US$500,000 to US$6 billion.[59] The revenue created many opportunities for the ruling family and the population. From a political and financial standpoint, the rulers spent some of the rapidly expanding oil revenues in developing Kuwait. In general, a new infrastructure was created and the form of welfare system the citizenry of Kuwait enjoys today was crafted.[60] At the time Kuwait was also anticipated to be a country placed on top of the largest oil reserves in the world. Salih states that the reserves were estimated to be in the region of 70 billion barrels of oil; this can be compared to the United States which at the same time was estimated to have reserves of around 40 billion barrels of oil.[61]

After the Second World War, oil exports increased significantly in Kuwait. In the post-war period, the world became politically more stable, and there was certainly a growing need for reconstruction and industrial development in several countries devastated by the war. Cities, villages, buildings and roads in several of these countries had suffered enormous damage, and to rejuvenate their economies they needed to rebuild the infrastructure. This reconstruction required oil, both as a source supplying energy, but also for the derived petroleum products used in different types of production. On a more or less global scale, societies were transformed into oil-dependent ones. This was a development encouraged by the use of energy and a shift of social organization in which financially stronger societies, especially in North America and Europe, came to be identified with modernity.[62]

---

58 Owen & Pamuk 1992: 87

59 Salih 1991: 48

60 The welfare system of Kuwait will be further discussed in chapters 4 and 6. Yet for a thorough discussion on the development of the infrastructure and the consequences thereof, see al-Nakib 2016.

61 Salih 1991: 48

62 I follow here Giddens's (1990) understanding of modernity as a mode of social life, primarily a more flexible society, not bound in time and space, that opens several choices for the individual instead of as in earlier societies in which most choices were predestined in their outcome.

It was impossible to satisfy the global demand for oil through the exploitation of resources found in larger countries such as the US or the Soviet Union. The search for oil was a global and lucrative business which led to an increased supply of crude oil in the 1940s and the 1950s from the Middle East, mainly Algeria, the Arabian Peninsula, Iran, Iraq and Libya. As a result, the rulers of Kuwait pursued a rapid increase in oil revenues after the Second World War in order to participate in the global crude-oil supply chains. The first barrels of Kuwaiti oil were exported in 1946 and from the first payment Kuwait received £200,000, a sum that could be considered insignificant. In the early years of the oil industry the government, primarily the rulers, of Kuwait signed rather unfavourable agreements with foreign oil companies. The adverse terms become clear in the light of the amount of money the oil companies themselves were making at the time. Consequently, in 1951 the Kuwaiti government renegotiated the contract with the Kuwait Oil Company. The new agreement gave the Kuwaiti government 50 per cent of the company, thus greatly boosting the state oil revenues. In comparison, in the year 1951, production of 28 million tonnage of oil had generated around £7 million for the Kuwaiti government and the 1952 production of 37 million tonnage generated revenues of around £50 million for the rulers of the country. This steady growth in revenue due to new agreements enabled the government to implement a series of development projects, and to embark upon the development of a welfare state – one exclusive to the citizens.

The production of oil would continue to grow on a yearly basis after 1946. It was reported that in 1961, the production of oil had reached 86 million tonnes. A year later, at the time of independence, it had reached 97 million tonnes providing revenues of around 160 million Kuwaiti dinars for the rulers and the government to spend.[63] Effectively, the oil was an asset belonging to the state. However, the Kuwaiti government did not have the resources, skilled labour or the overall capacity to conduct oil exploration and drilling operations. To carry out operations linked to the oil business would have required competent workers and engineers and advanced equipment, which did not exist at that time in Kuwait. The state could not

---

63 *Kuwait Today: A Welfare State* 1963: 70f. This text provides the figures above. It should be noted that it is produced by the Ministry of Guidance and Information (*Wizarat al-irshad wa al-anba'*) in Kuwait.

produce, take to market and profit from its newfound asset without undergoing certain changes of its own. For this reason, the discovery of oil and the emergence of Kuwait as an oil-exporting state marked the start of a new phase in the country's history, one that would see sweeping changes across nearly every aspect of life, from infrastructure and the economy to the daily life of the population and the culture and politics of the country as a whole.

These momentous developments may have spelt the end of the story of depression-era Kuwait and the harsh existence of Kuwaitis like Abu Saʿud's grandfather and father. However, they also marked the beginning of a radical new chapter in the history of Kuwait. The financial changes opened the door for merchants, entrepreneurs and individual citizens to take advantage of the new circumstances. Nor were these transformations in Kuwaiti society solely confined to the country's economic development. They went hand in hand with major changes in social and political structures, development, which were to lay the foundations of modern Kuwait.

3

SETTING THE SCENE: THE FOUNDING OF MODERN KUWAIT

Early years of the oil industry: political and economic changes

The political and economic shifts that Kuwait underwent in its early years as an oil state are best understood in the context of the years leading up to the discovery at Burgan. Years of economic stagnation and persistent financial mismanagement by the regime had left the state facing significant challenges in the 1930s.

Before the oil industry was established, the al-Sabah family ruled in an intimate, carefully balanced relationship with rich and prominent groups of merchant families who were customarily consulted before important decisions were made. According to Rivka Azoulay, Farah al-Nakib and Abdulrahman Alebrahim, the exercise of power operated via a balanced relationship between the socially, financially and politically significant families and the rulers. New political institutions also developed from the end of the 19th century. In such a system the al-Sabah ruled, but could be held accountable by the dominant business families. In her comparative study of Qatar and Kuwait, Jill Crystal states that Kuwait had a much stronger merchant class in the period before the advent of oil. Moreover, the arrangement was founded on the merchant families' financial support for the governing body and its expenditure through taxes. This way of organizing the management of the society gave them a role through which they could influence state affairs. However, this kind of balanced relationship came to an end with the emergence of the oil industry.[1]

Born in the mid-1930s, Abd al-Aziz al-Babtain grew up in the 1940s in a world where the balance of power was rapidly shifting. On a global level his

---

1 See Azoulay 2020, Alebrahim 2019, al-Nakib 2016 and Crystal 1990.

childhood was coloured by the Second World War and political changes, but also by the increasing pace at which dependency upon petrochemical products was advancing. It was also a time of flux within Kuwait, which saw major changes in traditional power relationships. These changes opened up new career opportunities for Kuwaitis, especially in the later 1950s and 1960s.

Problems also became apparent in the functioning of the state – problems that were to have a significant effect on the shape of the state for generations to come. Among other things, Kuwait lacked sufficient healthcare facilities, educational establishments and a police force. The small group of Kuwaitis involved in trade and commerce particularly resented corrupt customs officials and monopolies that only permitted members of the ruling family to open shops. The oil concessions and the staggeringly large revenues from oil exports rendered the need for financial and political support from the merchant families obsolete. Contracts concerning concessions and oil production were signed directly with the ruling family. Consequently, the income also accrued to the ruling family, thus making it the responsibility or prerogative of the ruler to distribute wealth amongst the population.[2]

As the tides of change began to reshape the economic landscape of Kuwait, political changes followed suit. One of the key reasons noted in Michael Herb's account of why Kuwait among the Gulf monarchies has a particularly strong National Assembly is that the rulers of Kuwait were chosen. They did not conquer the country. Moreover, Herb observes that the rulers were relatively weak in the 1930s because internal discord and the loss of support of the British prompted them to establish a broader coalition of allies.[3] However, Herb also argues that the coalition formed in the 1930s excluded the merchant class and formed an enduring and absolutist dynastic monarchy.[4] In the interwar period, political tension as well as social and economic changes also accounted for the growth of a political and more structured opposition that organized secret meetings and clubs,

---

2 al-Nakib 2016: 91
3 117 Herb provides a list of reasons for why Kuwait has a powerful National Assembly and refers to different statements from several scholars proposing a variety of answers to the question; see Herb 2016: 8, 10.
4 Herb 2016: 20

as well as public protests. An increasing presence of new institutions such as libraries and theatres and new technology such as radio, cinema and printed media also paved the way for new knowledge and political development.[5]

In order to ease the political tension, the opposition, supported by the British Political Agent, compelled the sheikh to establish a legislative council in the summer of 1938. The council consisted of 14 men and was elected by representatives of the leading merchant families. In relation to the constitution, it was given far-reaching legislative, judicial and executive powers. In addition to legislative powers and control over the budget, the council's president also embodied the executive powers of the state, including its foreign policy. This shift of authority unsettled the British, and although they officially refrained from intervention in the internal affairs of the country, in accordance with the 1899 agreement, they did nevertheless grow increasingly concerned at the sweeping powers with which the council had been newly endowed.[6]

Despite British unease, the council passed several reforms that significantly increased the effectiveness of the country's administration. It endorsed the opening of new schools and the construction of the sheikhdom's first hospital, among other major infrastructure projects. It also abolished a number of onerous restrictions that had been imposed on commerce, dismissed a number of corrupt officials and did away with the ruling family's monopoly on opening stores.[7]

Before long, the actions of the council also aroused the opposition of the ruling sheikh's long-time chief secretary, Mulla Saleh. He attempted to undermine the council's influence, and in response the council called for his dismissal. This call, in turn, angered Kuwait's large Shi'a community – approximately 18,000 people out of a total population of some 65,000. As a Shi'a Muslim, Mulla Saleh was regarded as the community's foremost representative in the regime. His religious affiliation was also at variance with the overall make-up of the council, since all its other members were Sunni Muslims, with 12 of the 14 council members originating from one specific branch of the mercantile class. The issue of the council, already politically and religiously complicated, was further exacerbated by the fact

---

5 Crystal 1989: 429 and Alebrahim 2019: 49ff
6 Alebrahim 2019: 66ff and Salih 1992: 68–78
7 Salih 1992: 81–83

that the sheikh, who was sceptical of the council's role to begin with, began to view it with even more suspicion. As their solution to a previous problem seemed to be in imminent danger of becoming a problem in its own right, the British moved to bring about a compromise. The result was an agreement in which Mulla Saleh, a long-term confidant of the ruler and a prominent Shi'a, would be placed on indefinite leave. This decision was part of a broader exclusion of the Shi'a community with the suppression of its representation in various councils and ignoring their demand for Shi'a schools.[8]

According to the oil concession of 1934, the ruler of the country was the sole beneficiary of the revenue from the concession granted to the Kuwait Oil Company to explore for oil and a share of the future oil revenue. Yet despite the numerous benefits of Kuwait's new injection of capital, the new source of income brought challenges, too. It changed the former structure and role of the al-Sabah, namely by reducing Sheikh Ahmad's dependency on duties that were once collected by the ruler and distributed among the ruling family. In 1938 the state had no financial structure to deal with the new source of income. A new law was passed and the recently established legislative council was the body designated to control the state budget. It requested in the same year that the ruling sheikh sign over his personal control of oil revenues to the authority of the council. He accepted the request, which alarmed the British, who were worried it would give the council too much political and financial influence. Thus, the issue of the distribution of the oil revenues and the council's, at least theoretical, authority concerning the foreign affairs of Kuwait led the British to suggest that, like the ruler of Bahrain, Sheikh Ahmad should keep one-third and give two-thirds of the oil incomes to the state, in this case the council.[9]

The ruler of Kuwait was annoyed since he disliked the idea of transferring power to the council and also disapproved of the dismissal of his chief secretary by the council. The British were alarmed at the council's ambition to control oil revenues and the army.[10] The loss of support for the council from the British representative and the encouragement of the expression of opposition to the council among religious conservatives and Bedouins

---

8 Salih 1992: 83–87. For a detailed account of the legislative council of 1938, see Alebrahim 2019: 62–73.

9 Salih 1992: 87–90

10 Tétreault, 1991: 576 and Alebrahim 2019: 69ff

on the part of the ruling sheikh, along with other oppositional parts of the society such as disadvantaged merchants and the Persian and Shiʻa communities, gave the sheikh an opportunity in late 1938 to challenge the authority and influence of the council. Another factor influencing this challenge on the part of Kuwait's ruler was the division in interests and identities and how the events in 1938 gave the ruler an opening to build alliances with various groups. Azoulay states that, "[It] provided a crucial moment in the consolidation of the authority system of the Al-Sabah through patronage and divide-and-rule-logics that would be perpetuated with the discovery of oil...".[11]

In late 1938, Sheikh Ahmad decided to dissolve the council. When news of the council's imminent dissolution reached its members, they barricaded themselves in the citadel of Kuwait City along with their supporters. This act of defiance was ultimately the council's undoing, as it made it possible for the sheikh and Britain's representatives to compel council members to enter into negotiations. The final negotiations resulted in the council being elected by a larger electorate, but also in a reduction of its functions to that of an advisory board to the ruling sheikh.

In December 1938, a larger electorate duly elected a new council. However, in February 1939, Sheikh Ahmad tabled a new constitution formally changing the function of the council from a legislative to an advisory body, but this was rejected by council members, so the ruler dissolved it again.[12] According to Salih, the council was finally suspended in 1940,[13] ending a brief and early period of a form of political representation in Kuwait. The sheikh did not support reform, and in the end his power was thereby strengthened.[14] However, the six-month-long existence of the council did spawn a movement able to produce an articulated and organized opposition to the ruler, and this movement consisted of the foremost merchants. The opposition was also fuelled by a transnational element, the

---

11 Azoulay 2020: 60

12 Tétreault, 1991: 577 and Alebrahim 2019: 82f

13 The presentations of the history of the legislative council are somewhat different in regard to details in Azoulay 2020, Alebrahim 2019 and Salih 1997. However, in this context the point is the importance of the period and the changes it purported in the Kuwaiti society.

14 Salih 1992: 90–97. Also note the comment by Tétreault that reform only happened when bottom-up pressure was applied; see Tétreault 2011: 73.

Iraqi media and by movements promoting Pan-Arab nationalism.[15] Like other coastal states of the Gulf, Kuwait had rapidly evolved into a country that would become enormously wealthy and politically important. But these countries also led the way in welfare services provided for citizens and in income per capita.[16]

Although Sheikh Ahmad and al-Sabah family had taken control of state institutions, the ruler's authority was still compromised by financial mismanagement. The latter was to change in 1946 when oil revenues increased dramatically after exploration began in earnest after the Second World War. At the same time as the world was becoming more dependent on oil, Kuwait was finding more of it – prompting the British to seek greater influence in the area, as Kuwait's importance to Britain changed with the discovery of oil. This small country on the Persian or the Arabian Gulf and its port in Kuwait City turned from a point of communication with Britain's Southeast Asian colonies to a strategic source of oil.

By 1950, Kuwait's oil production sat at around 350 million barrels per day. Kuwait and its neighbours had transformed from traditional tribal societies living off fishing, livestock herding and pearl-diving to states producing oil gas and petrochemical products.

Another aspect of the transformation of the country was the new role that it (and the other Gulf states) played in the international economy. The states not only needed to have a well-functioning bureaucracy for national purposes, but also had to be able to compete and promote their interests in an increasingly global marketplace. For Kuwait, the key partner in the international economy was Britain, and relations changed as soon as oil appeared on the scene. For years, Britain had been concerned that the ruling family was investing too little in Kuwait's development, particularly in its ailing and still ineffective administration. To address this, they called for Sheikh Ahmad to employ the services of British financial advisors to direct his rule. This also served another goal: to strengthen British control over the vital oil supply and, by extension, over the development of the country.

Sheikh Ahmad and his successor Sheikh Abd Allah al-Salim al-Sabah, who was appointed as the new ruler in 1950 after the death of his cousin, shunned the repeated requests from the British. They refused on the

---

15 Crystal 1989: 429. See also Alebrahim 2019: 62ff.
16 Owen & Pamuk 1999: 208

grounds that the appointment of British financial advisors would arouse domestic opposition.[17] The refusal of the two sheikhs was also a sign of the decreasing influence of the British Empire and of British ambitions to intervene in the country's internal affairs. A parallel development was that, for the British, Kuwait became more important as a strategic partner than an economic one, even if these interests sometimes overlapped as in the case of oil production. In the 1950s it became clear to most Kuwaitis that the situation had changed. Resources, namely oil exports, were going in new directions, from Kuwait to Britain rather than the opposite direction. As a result, Kuwaitis saw themselves as entitled to oil revenues, and most inhabitants were uneasy with the protectorate status of their country. The new ruler, Sheikh Abd Allah, was not a client ruler installed by the British, and events in the world such as the Suez crisis increased the support for Arab nationalism and anti-British sentiment. Kuwait no longer needed British support to keep its own house in order: Sheikh Abd Allah proved ready to take a more active role in the country's development and moreover appeared to be a more effective administrator than his predecessor. He engineered a shift in Kuwait's role, from a British client to a state reliant on oil income for its independence as well as domestic administration.[18]

Oil revenues enabled Sheikh Abd Allah to lay the foundations of an extensive welfare state. The idea of a welfare state, the generous provision of government benefits to Kuwait's citizens, was combined with an ambition to garner domestic support for his rule. Perhaps that is the case in any political context, but it is also a question about the role of the state. In the case of Kuwait, it took the form of an authoritarian state in which welfare was treated as a commodity. Citizens were provided with welfare benefits and offered their loyalty in return, allowing rulers to govern with ease – a very different approach to, say, a state dependent on tax revenues, which do not accrue obligations of loyalty to the government.

Kuwait's new-found wealth and the welfare state it facilitated brought about a major shift in the sheikh's as well as the country's relationship with Britain. Previously the sheikhs of Kuwait had been dependent on British support to ensure the continuation of the rule of the al-Sabah family when faced with opposition at home. However, as domestic support could now be

---

17 Loewenstein 2000: 115f
18 Tétreault, 1991: 578

generated by extending welfare benefits to the country's citizens, the ruling sheikh's dependency on the British dwindled.[19] The end of the old order was made official through the termination of the Anglo-Kuwaiti Treaty of 1899 in June 1961. The country became independent and the first elections to the parliament were held in 1963. In addition, Sheikh Abd Allah was appointed the first amir of the independent state of Kuwait.[20]

It is not easy to find elsewhere in the world states that, like Kuwait and the other countries of the Arabian/Persian Gulf, are economically entirely dependent on one natural resource.[21] Kuwait and other states sharing the condition of financial reliance on one natural resource are commonly referred to as "rentier states". This term implies that the dependency not only affects economic life and decision-making, but also has political and societal implications, such as the formation of state institutions and patriarchal political structures.[22] As has been stated in earlier studies, the governance of a rentier state is not solely about control; it is also about managing and generating wealth.[23]

---

19 Tétreault 1991: 579

20 Amir is in this case a title and it follows a long tradition of naming rulers in decision making or leading positions as amirs; in the primary example, the title *amir al-mu'minin*, usually translated as the "Commander of the faithful" referring to a title that the Prophet Muhammad according to Muslim history writing gave to the fourth caliph Ali ibn Abi Talib (d. 661). This title is also in usage today in different contexts such as under the rule of the Taliban in Afghanistan, as well as being a title bestowed on the king of Morocco. Current usages of the title amir may evoke associations with Islam's early and normative history and with authority legitimizing the power of an amir.

21 According to *Kuwait: Land Ownership and Agricultural Laws Handbook* (2011: 11) the natural resources of Kuwait are petroleum, natural gas, fish and shrimps. The handbook also states that the water resources are negligible, and the country contains no arable land, no permanent crops and no forests and woodland. However, 8 per cent of the land is for permanent pastures. In regard to the land the category "other" is 92 per cent. This category of "other" refers to land covered by desert.

22 In the academic study of Gulf countries, the rentier state theory is much discussed; one question concerns whether the theory explains how states have developed and how they can progress. The special issue of the *British Journal of Middle Eastern Studies* (Yamada and Hertog 2020) is exclusively devoted to a discussion of rentierism. See also the overview of the discussion in *The Politics of Rentier States in the Gulf*, 2019.

23 Dresch 2013b: 21

The harsh natural environment and the paucity of resources in general made it difficult for the population as well as the state of Kuwait to support and maintain their livelihoods through the exploitation of resources other than oil.[24] Certainly, the desert climate with its limited rainfall and resource-poor soil has made agriculture practically non-existent in the country. Consequently, the natural environment has made it nearly impossible to build an economy founded on any other industry than oil, and associated chemical products derived from crude oil and petroleum. In addition, the financial opportunities for individuals compared to other economic activities also worked in the favour of the oil industry. Put simply, there was a lot more money to make from working in any oil-related business. In the 1950s and early 1960s, it was estimated that 90 per cent of the income of the Kuwaiti government came from oil exports and the petroleum industry.[25] This percentage was more or less the same for most of the oil-producing countries on the Arabian Peninsula.

All these political and economic shifts, which began in the 19th century and lasted until Kuwait's independence, heralded a powerful new wind of social change. The income from concessions and oil production altered the social and political circumstances in the country. The increased wealth and the established agreements with the rulers served to consolidate and centralize power.[26] Furthermore, the creation of administrative institutions under the British protectorate was part of a bureaucratization process in former colonial areas. It restructured administration to mirror the models of European nation states – a development which also occurred in many parts of the world in the first half of the 20th century. It was a transition from one society to another that created relatively little resistance.[27]

The ruler of Kuwait until 1950, Sheikh Ahmad al-Jabir al-Sabah encountered great difficulty in redistributing wealth in a fair and proper manner to his people, and proved to be resistant to reform in general.[28] The British,

---

24 In *Kuwait: Land Ownership and Agricultural Laws Handbook* (2011: 14) it is estimated that the petroleum reserves of Kuwait accounts for about 9 per cent of the world reserves. And petroleum constitutes nearly half the GDP and 95 per cent of the export revenues.
25 *Kuwait Today: A Welfare State* 1963: 65
26 al-Nakib 2016: 91
27 Crystal 1989: 441
28 Loewenstein 2000: 107

who were still active in Kuwait at this time and played a significant role in the country's internal and external affairs, encouraged him to create a more efficient administration. In the opinion of the British, Sheikh Ahmad needed to create a formalized budget to control the economy and to increase spending on projects that would benefit the population of Kuwait. However, this did not happen. Instead, a good portion of the oil revenues ended up in the offshore bank accounts, primarily of the ruling family.[29]

As we will presently see, the developments in Kuwait financially as well as in the form of the welfare state certainly created opportunities for Abd al-Aziz Saʿud al-Babtain. However, even though he benefited from the state's welfare services, his success was by no means a foregone conclusion when he embarked upon his career as a businessman in the 1950s. The economic reality for many people in Kuwait was still harsh, and oil revenue had not yet trickled down into society at large. As part of a larger societal shift, Abd al-Aziz worked for the government in his youth, while at the same time selling cigarettes door to door. According to a friend, he faced bankruptcy several times before his business became established and started to make a decent profit. The al-Babtain family is also an example of a family that did not belong to the traditionally wealthy and influential merchant families or to a tribal elite. Instead, they came from a modest background, but being Arab and among those who had migrated from the Najd in Saudi Arabia, the family benefited from the social changes in Kuwait and shifting political allegiances. They developed into a successful family which became an integral part of the new alliances being forged by the country's rulers in order to consolidate their power.

As al-Nakib emphasizes, Kuwait had now changed from a country where the ruler governed in concert with the wealthier and more influential business families to a country with a patriarchal form of governance. Local businesses were also to a greater extent becoming a part of a global economy – a form of connectivity beyond national borders arose that influenced society in general. The governing powers were henceforth vested in the ruling family, a development that signalled a change in the relationship between the ruler and his subjects. The inhabitants of Kuwait became citizens of the state.

---

29 Loewenstein 2000: 117

Property, the State, Islam and Arabism

A justification for the shift that augmented the power and fortune of the al- Sabah ruling family, and also their function as rulers, has to do with their relationship to the land. This can be seen in the ways that laws governing land ownership evolved. These laws are also an example of state formation in Kuwait and an illustration of how Islam is incorporated into the legal framework of the state, but also of how this integration of religion and legislation helps underpin the new role of the al-Sabah family as the country's rulers.

Under the heading "Property in Islamic Law", in *Kuwait: Land Ownership and Agricultural Laws Handbook* (2011), a mix of references to legal texts, scholarship in the academic discipline of Law and Quranic quotations are utilized to discuss property ownership in Kuwait. In relation to the Quranic verses quoted, the conclusion in the text is that the physical land is part of God's creation. God is the ultimate owner of land, and humans can possess and own land in a form of trusteeship. According to the handbook, this act of delegation is central to ownership, and access to property implies that humans should recognize the will of God. In the handbook, this condition for ownership gives the state of Kuwait the authority to evaluate whether land is deemed to have not been used properly by its owner. In this capacity, the state is a guardian of God's laws. Consequently, the state can, by reference to God's laws, appropriate land and force owners to give up their right of possession. At the same time, the text stresses the sanctity of private ownership and, therefore, that it is encouraged and permitted provided it is beneficial to the wider community.

In the handbook, it is also stated that there is no clearly defined field of Islamic land law or property law. The handbook refers to Ottoman land law from the mid-19th century, but concludes that, for example, contemporary land property and housing rights are dependent on the Quran and the Sunna of the Prophet Muhammad. One problem which is thereby highlighted is gender empowerment and how to clearly interpret the Quran on this point. The suggestion in the handbook is to constantly refer to the Sunna, namely the body of legal and social custom that is believed within Islam to contain the normative words and deeds of the Prophet Muhammad and his closest contemporaries. As in the jurisprudence (*fiqh*) of the branches of the Islamic law, these words and acts become an interpretative source for legal discussions. Furthermore, the principles of analogy (*qiyas*), consensus (*ijma'*), consensus of opinion primarily among the legal scholars of the time and independent personal reasoning (*ijtihad*) are seen as tools that are to be utilized in legal discussions on private, public and state property. By reference to statements of Muhammad that humans are partners in three things, "water, fire and pasture", the handbook states that some Muslim scholars have concluded that the privatization of water, energy and agricultural land is not permitted. According to this reading of the law, public property therefore becomes state property. Various natural resources become state property, and the handbook also stipulates that property which is unclaimed, unoccupied or uncultivated can be deemed to be state property. In relation to the figures cited above which indicate that only 8 per cent of the land is cultivated for pastures, it becomes evident that land and natural resources are construed as the property of the state in Kuwait.[30]

The paragraphs above concerning property are based on the Maliki school of jurisprudence in Islamic law. Therefore, from the general statements concerning ownership there may be variations in the other legal schools of Sunni- and Shi'a-Islam. Interestingly, in the handbook, "Islam" is an actor and thus has legal agency. That is, "Islam" is, for example, ascribed an opinion in statements such as "in Islam property is (...)", and at the same time the idea in the text is to comprehend the meaning of Islam in relation to contemporary legal issues. Perhaps the discussion in the text of the handbook is an example of how modernity in the form of legal debate and the need for laws relating to property and ownership merge with the earlier legal traditions. The basis of this integration is the need for national and international laws, but also the view that Islam is the true revelation to humankind, and so cannot be omitted from a discussion if one believes that religion embraces all realms of human life. In the end, the conclusion concerning property and ownership is that the role of the state is substantiated by a legal argument and endorsed by references to a religious tradition. State concessions and oil revenues become a source of income for the state and the rulers of the state. They are the owners of the natural resources of the country, but also of the land. The references to Islam underline that it is incumbent upon them to distribute wealth, but also that they have the opportunity to distribute wealth, fairly and equally among the citizens of Kuwait.

---

30 The paragraph above is a summary of *Kuwait: Land Ownership and Agricultural Laws Handbook* 2011: 31ff.

Kuwait's transition from a maritime-based economy centred on ship-building, seafaring, fishing and pearl-diving to an oil-exporting country led to the virtual abandonment of these former occupations. Like Abd al-Aziz al-Babtain, many Kuwaiti citizens sought employment in government departments and offices or in the newly established oil industry. The new jobs were more attractive as they offered job security and a larger income.[31] The renunciation of traditional forms of work in Kuwait was another factor conducive to the consolidation of political power with the ruling family. The state had now emerged as the country's largest employer, and a consid-erable portion of the Kuwaiti population was dependent on the state for their income, having effectively been rendered clients of the state.

As Kuwaitis became dependent on the government, there was little interest in political reform as long as the government provided the means to maintain and raise their standard of living in general. In addition, Abd al-Aziz al-Babtain has stated on many occasions that he is not interested in politics, and that he simply dislikes it. The statement concerns domestic "politics" conceptualized as an activity carried out by political parties and politicians, which as a result of their disagreements destabilizes the country and thereby jeopardizes the well-being of society at large. In his case it is also a notion of politics in which terms like "democracy" does not always carry a positive value. Connected to the assumption concerning political reform and the change within the Kuwaiti society is also the idea of the rulers or the state being the legitimate providers of welfare to its citizens – a role for the state and the rulers motivated and justified by references to Islamic traditions. However, as we have seen, the government of Kuwait led by the al-Sabah family initially found it difficult coping with the rapid social change which took hold of the country after the establishment of the petroleum industry. Before the oil boom, the state had been seen as patri-archal in nature, but not as a government ruled by an autocratic despot.[32]

The British became ever more concerned about the mismanagement of the country's finances under the rule of Ahmad al-Jabir al-Sabah. There were reports of mounting hostility and an increase in anti-Ahmad sentiments within the population of the country.[33] Ahmad al-Jabir was not particularly

31 Lawson 1985: 16
32 Salih 1991: 52
33 Loewenstein 2000: 109

interested in following the British ideas of reorganizing the economy of Kuwait, and there was likewise little hope during his reign of a restructuring of the country's financial system. Growing antagonism between various special-interest groups and the ruling family could have destabilized the political situation. However, this never happened, and by the time Sheikh Ahmad died, the country had already begun to enter the period commonly known as the Golden Era (1946–1982).

The changes in Kuwaiti society that began in the early 20th century included the development of administrative institutions along European lines. The interpretation of the Maliki legal school reviewed above underlines that bureaucratic and political changes in Kuwaiti society and the shifting status and role of the ruler become justified or even necessitated by interpretations of Islam. In this regard, "Islam" becomes a legitimizing force for change and not the opposite. This understanding reflects the official view since the documents are produced by the government, and the reference to a handbook produced by state authorities is a sign of how Islam has been "nationalized" and incorporated into the logic of the state.

The institutionalization of Islam made the religion into an entity that was subject to organization, control and interpretation by the state. In the case of Kuwait, this was accompanied by a desire to control and interpret the notion of the meaning of Arabism and the "Arab" in general. In the later stage of the Ottoman Empire and throughout the 20th century individuals and movements promoting various forms of Arabism or Arab nationalism have been prominent in many of the independent Middle Eastern states that emerged, especially in the aftermath of the Second World War. The ideology of Pan-Arabism saw all Arabs as being part of one nation (*watan*), an idea that was often rhetorically dependent upon Islam. It aimed to unite all Arabs irrespective of their religious affiliation. Another related and contemporary movement was the Arab nationalism promoted by individual nation states and frequently formulated as a form of Arab socialism. From the early 20th century onwards, Arab leaders began to posit various paths to Arab unity, which in some cases resulted in the formation of independent unions of states such as the one forged between Egypt and Syria (1958–1961). The union was named the United Arab Republic (UAR), and the ambition of the leaders of its two constituent countries was to expand it into a pan-Arab state. The UAR lasted only three years and was fraught with problems. The dominance of Egyptian officials over Syrians, difficulties in establishing a workable procedure for effective government and financial mismanagement were among the reasons why the UAR broke up. However, Arabism and the idea of Arab unity was also apparent in the creation of organizations such as the Arab League, formally the League of Arab States, founded in Cairo in 1945 to bring Arabic-speaking countries closer to each other and to strengthen their independence and sovereignty. It perhaps goes without saying that a significant amount of time, effort and political capital have been invested in the cause of Arab unity, with very little in the way of tangible results. The political leaders of Arab-dominated countries have struggled to jointly address and promote the cause of unity.

While discussions and projects founded on the idea of unity among Arabs may have come to nothing, there nonetheless exists among Arabs a common acknowledgment of the notion of a distinct Arab identity. In the case of Kuwait, the rulers and other representatives of the state often express a strong adherence to an Arab identity. This blend of Kuwaiti and Arab identities is also mirrored in celebrations of the state of Kuwait. For example, a message issued by Kuwait News Agency (KUNA) on the occasion of the celebration of the National Day of Kuwait on February 25 in 2001, a celebration that took place ten years after the end of the Gulf war, was headed "Kuwait remains in the heart of Pan-Arabism". The short message – a review of an editorial in the daily newspaper *al-Siyasa* – continues:

> A Kuwait daily stressed Sunday that Kuwait remains in the heart of Pan-Arabism and considered expressing loyalty and love to Kuwait and the rule on the occasion of the 40th anniversary of National Day and the 10th anniversary of Liberation Day as "established facts" for Kuwaitis. Al-Seyassah [*al-Siyasa*] newspaper said in its editorial entitled "Kuwait Deserves its Glory" that we do not have to repeat that we are Kuwaitis and Arabs (...).[34]

This statement is, of course, from a later period in history and is also linked to the Iraqi occupation of Kuwait, a specific event that certainly shaped historical memory. However, it symbolizes the development of a notion in which the country itself, "Kuwait", is given agency connecting

---

34 See https://www.kuna.net.kw/ArticlePrintPage.aspx?id=1146809&language=en. Accessed February 25, 2017. The English translation is by KUNA.

to pan-Arabism. Moreover, it intricately links a national Kuwaiti identity together with a perception that Kuwait and Kuwaitis belong to a broader conception of being distinctly Arab that transcends national borders.[35] In the 1950s and the 1960s, this version of nationalism was a force to be reckoned with in Kuwait as well as in other countries. At the same time, the promotion of a nationalism of the nation-state is amalgamated with the supranational or transnational vision of pan-Arabism.[36] Other components to be considered in forming a nation-state, and that were in play around the time of Kuwaiti independence, were ethnicity, tribal politics, clientelism and religious affiliations, especially to Sunni Islam, but also to the Shi'a branch of Islam. In the emerging state of Kuwait, these potential primary loyalties, or multi-layered identities, had to be managed and delicately balanced to become part of a fluid definition of "Kuwaitiness".

The emergence of the State of Kuwait: from Sheikh Mubarak to Sheikh Abd Allah

Modern state-building in Kuwait is usually attributed to the reign of Sheikh Mubarak bin Sabah al-Sabah,[37] the seventh ruler of the al-Sabah family. Sheikh Mubarak, also called "the Great", consolidated power within the al-Sabah dynasty and established a hereditary system that kept political power within the ruling family.[38] During his reign, Sheikh Mubarak centralized power within the government, creating a structure that would ultimately be the foundation for the future state of Kuwait. After his death in 1915, he was briefly succeeded by Jabir II al-Mubarak al-Sabah, who died in 1917 and was replaced by Sheikh Salim al-Mubarak al-Sabah. However, in their short reigns, these successors failed to develop a state capable of coping with the political and social change that began to unfold within the country.

---

35 See Ozkirimli 2017 for an overview of theories and discussions about nationalism. See also Philips 2012: 20ff for an overview of discussion on Arabism and state nationalism.
36 Philips (2012: 21) claims that countries in which the political rhetoric of a (pan) Arab identity has been integrated in the state identity have been reasonably resilient.
37 For a review of the life of Sheikh Mubarak, see al-Sabah 2014. For more general views on the importance of Sheikh Mubarak for Kuwait, see Pillai and Kumar 1962: 110 and Tétreault 2001: 203.
38 Tétreault 1991: 203

Between 1940 and 1956, several state institutions developed in Kuwait. The establishment of municipalities, a police force, a security apparatus and a succession of key government departments such as Education, Health and Finance along with a Shura council and an *awqaf* (charitable endowments) department transformed the country, and adjusted the state of Kuwait to the new financial and social realities.[39] However, it was not until the death of the tenth ruler of Kuwait, Sheikh Ahmad al-Jabir al-Sabah, in 1950 that real change in the structure of government took place in Kuwait. After Sheikh Ahmad's death, the reign of Sheikh Abd Allah al-Salim al-Sabah (r. 1950–65) witnessed a massive development drive that would change the country forever.[40] Under the rule of his predecessor, the growing demand for political and social change had not been addressed, leaving many in the population feeling sidelined and ignored, as they did not benefit from the new oil wealth to remotely the same degree as the country's rich elite or the ruling family. This situation would subsequently change, as Sheikh Abd Allah realized that if it continued, it would be devastating for Kuwait.

Sheikh Abd Allah al-Salim al-Sabah was a reformer with ambitious and utopian plans for Kuwait's future.[41] He recognized the need for social change and realized that a reorganization of the government was crucial if he was to stabilize the political situation in the country. He responded to the request of the population for reform by initiating an immense state-led modernization drive affecting both society and state. These developments shaped contemporary Kuwait. It was during this period that the government invested in the creation of a welfare system supporting citizens from the cradle to the grave. This shrewd move effectively deprived the political opposition of much of its support and momentum.[42] In conjunction with the religious imperative to support the population and distribute wealth, this strategy further increased citizens' dependency on the government as it became clear that if the state could provide a high standard of living and increase the wealth of Kuwaitis, relatively few would oppose the system.

---

39 Alebrahim 2019: 88. The Ministry of *Awqaf* and Islamic Affairs oversee religious affairs in Kuwait and controls religious institution. It supports information and the cultivation of Islam in general.
40 al-Nakib 2016: 5. See also Alnajdi's (2014) thesis on the reign of Abd Allah al-Salim al-Sabah and the transformations during his time as ruler.
41 al-Nakib 2016: 5
42 al-Nakib 2016: 6

The welfare system that emerged in Kuwait under Sheikh Abd Allah differs from the welfare systems that exist in, say, Western Europe, in that it is financed exclusively from the country's enormous oil revenues. Unlike most other states outside the Gulf region, the Kuwaiti government never needed to implement a taxation system. Kuwaiti citizens are exempt from paying taxes, and by extension, from financing state expenditure even today.[43] This lack of responsibility for financing the state through taxation meant that citizens do not have a natural voice in political affairs. Rather, the government and ruling bodies conduct all state affairs on behalf of the people, further consolidating power within the ruling elite. The welfare system is legitimized through the religious duty of the rulers as part of God's creation and a trusteeship by God – a responsibility or almost a contract in which the rulers are obligated to divide wealth and support the citizens of Kuwait in, ideally, a fair and equal manner. Obligation in the eyes of God, rather than accountability to citizens, is therefore the ideological basis of Kuwaiti welfare state. Certainly, tribal politics, interests linked to the rulers and relationships founded on religious affiliation have conditioned how this wealth was apportioned, and that has not always been fair and equal.

Developments in Kuwait in the 1950s were not focused solely on broader political, administrative and institutional matters. The physical layout of the country changed, and these transformations also influenced everyday life. Farah al-Nakib (2016) points out that after 1951 land ownership became an important issue in Kuwaiti society. Put simply, land that had been acquired in the 1920s for insignificant sums could be sold in the 1950s for up to 12,000 times its original value. The price of land thus skyrocketed during a time of rapid development and a small private property market. In her study, al-Nakib outlines the numerous development plans and land acquisition schemes that were implemented in Kuwait City and in the country as a whole in the 1950s. The shift was dramatic, and the country's new physical infrastructure – with new roads, dependency on cars, boulevards, roundabouts, new office buildings, parking spaces, high-rise buildings and almost no residential areas in the heart of Kuwait City – radically changed the way

---

43 Owen & Pamuk 1991: 207. The current talks on taxation in Kuwait will be discussed in chapter 6, but new taxation methods have been proposed; see *Arab Times* March 29, 2016 and http://www.arabtimesonline.com/news/tax-alternative-vat-studied/. Accessed June 22, 2016.

of life in the city. The city became segregated as foreign workers attracted by the oil and service industry of the country occupied particular neighbourhoods, away from the urban and, mainly, suburban quarters where Kuwaiti citizens tended to live.

The country changed in many different yet interrelated ways. The changes in finance, state institutions and the physical structure were accompanied by changes in legal structures, with the introduction of a new legal system in 1961, in addition to demographic changes which saw a large proportion of the heterogeneous labour force become non-Kuwaiti by the early 1960s. These changes also affected the Kuwaiti population and their family relationships as well as their norms and values.[44]

As we have seen above, the early years of Abd al-Aziz al-Babtain mirror some of the changes that were taking place in Kuwait at large. Apart from mentioning the familiar fact, well known from short biographies of his life, that at an early age he was already an avid reader of Arabic poetry, it should be noted that he was literate, a skill that was by no means universal at the time.[45] He had learned to read in the formal school system developed from 1936 onwards, where he received an education that had not been available to Kuwaitis of the generation before him.[46] In 1945, when Abd al-Aziz was aged nine, there were 17 schools in Kuwait. In an interview with Daniel Atzori (2014), Abu Sa'ud talks about his childhood and recalls that his older brother Abd al-Latif collected Nabatean poetry, and that from the age of eight, in the 1940s, he was employed serving tea, coffee and water in the *diwaniyya* at nights. It was around this same time that he developed a deep appreciation of the rhythm of poetry.[47] In the same interview, Abd

---

44 For various aspects of societal change in Kuwait from the 1950s to the early 1980s, see Hijazi 1964, al-Moosa 1984, al-Thakeb 1985 and Shah 1986.

45 See the biography published by the Foundation, *Abdulaziz Saud al-Babtain: Biography & Cultural Achievements* 2017.

46 Al-Mubarakiyya school was established in 1912 and aimed to train administrators for business. In 1921 the al-Ahmadiyya school was created and offered courses in English. The next step was the creation of girls' schools with curricula focusing on Arabic, Quranic studies and home economics; see Nyrop et al. 1977: 131 and Alebrahim 2019: 24–26

47 He also stated that his father was a poet who wrote Bedouin or popular (*nabati*) poetry which contributed to Abd al-Aziz's passion for poetry and literature; see *Abdulaziz Saud al-Babtain: Biography and Cultural Achievements* 2017: 42.

al-Aziz also revealed that his passion for poetry grew, and, encouraged by his elder brother and his father, he wrote his first poem at the age of 11. He studied different poets such as classical Arab ones like Umar Ibn Abi Rabi'a (644–719) and Jamil ibn Ma'mar (659–701; also known as Jamil Buthayna), as well as more contemporary poets like Mahmud Taha (1909–1985). Abd al-Aziz recounts that he grew up in modest circumstances and he was unable to complete his education since his family needed him to work and earn money. His first paid employment, in 1954, was as a secretary in the al-Shuwaykh secondary school library. This gave him access to books other than poetry. Abu Sa'ud is acutely aware of the humble nature of his upbringing and that he never completed his education, and has pointed this out on several occasions. This personal experience may well be the prime mover behind his ambition to help young Arabs and Muslims receive an education through the al-Babtain Foundation. Abd al-Aziz also seems to regard his desire to read as a characteristic shared by all humans and to believe that people can be encouraged to share this common attribute. It is a question of education and cultivation.[48]

The education he received and his Kuwaiti citizenship (citizenship here understood as a category appearing in correlation with the progressive emergence of a nation-state after the late 1940s) allowed Abd al-Aziz to obtain a position in a ministry in 1955, at the age of 19. From then until 1962, he worked in the payroll department of the Ministry of Education.[49] Between 1956 and 1962, Abu Sa'ud had four day-time jobs. In the morning he worked at the Ministry of Education, in the afternoon he was trading in a shop he had acquired in a village near Kuwait City, in the evening he studied and he also ran a household. At the time Abd al-Aziz was thinking about his financial situation and was not entirely certain that his future lay in trading. He felt that his shop was destined to be a failure and so began to think about new ways to earn a living. His first entrepreneurial scheme was to offer a service providing goods to grocers so that they did not have to leave their shops and travel by taxi to the city to buy commodities. This service was well received by shopkeepers, and the money that Abd al-Aziz earned enabled him to buy a second-hand car and expand his business to

---

48 Atzori 2014: 36f. Abd al-Aziz's more personal narration of his early life will be further developed in chapter 7.

49 *Abdulaziz Saud al-Babtain: Biography & Cultural Achievements* 2017: 7

other villages. The relationships Abu Sa'ud was building through his new business created trust between him, his company and other companies. He was approached by them and concluded profitable agreements making him their agent in Kuwait and Saudi Arabia. From the very beginning of his business career, the bond with Saudi Arabia has always been strong, and family members, like some of his brothers, have been living and working for the family business in the kingdom. In time, Abd al-Aziz's lucrative role as an agent for various companies made it possible for him and his expanding company to set up shops in various Mediterranean ports as well as in Afghanistan in Kabul.[50]

The Kuwait that developed from the 1940s and into the 1950s and 1960s clearly opened new possibilities for entrepreneurial individuals like Abd al-Aziz. Education was one new possibility, as was the opportunity to work in recently established government departments and the oil industry. Improved standards of living, revenues of the state and new structures in society provided fertile ground for entrepreneurship. In a way, Abu Sa'ud's early life and his first steps in commerce are similar to other stories of successful entrepreneurs and businesspeople, but one must bear in mind that Abd al-Aziz's success, like that of so many other entrepreneurs, was dependent on societal change, but also in the case of Kuwait, on the promotion of domestic entrepreneurship by the rulers and the opportunities extended by them to their subjects in return for their support.[51]

Transformed by wealth: changes for government and citizens alike

From 1946 onwards, as Kuwait received immense revenues from oil exports, its citizens became increasingly wealthy, and there was a growing demand for more exotic or luxurious goods that had not hitherto been available in the country. To satisfy consumer demand, Kuwaiti merchants began importing goods from foreign countries in large quantities. This shift in the marketplace touched a political raw nerve, raising fears in the government that foreign companies could become increasingly influential in

---

50 Atzori 2014: 37
51 I am here referring to the scholarship that discusses a more narrative and discursive approach to entrepreneurship; see Hjorth and Steyaert 2004.

Abd al-Aziz al-Babtain and the car that helped revolutionize his
business, late 1950s. Courtesy of the al-Babtain Foundation.

Kuwait's economy and political arena. To protect and promote the business interests of Kuwaitis and to preserve their own political capital, the
government, led by the ruler Sheikh Abd Allah al-Salim al-Sabah, passed a
law which stipulated that foreign companies operating in Kuwait had to be
jointly owned by a Kuwaiti national. This ensured that every company from
abroad seeking to conduct business in Kuwait would have do so in conjunction with a Kuwaiti national, who would co-own on a fifty-fifty basis the
subsidiary of the foreign company that was operating in Kuwait.[52]

In passing this legislation, Sheikh Abd Allah ensured the survival and
continued pre-eminence of Kuwait's established business families. He succeeded in creating a business climate in which merchants could expand,
grow and even diversify their businesses. Broadly speaking, the aim of this

52 al-Nakib 2016: 92

policy and others like it was to safeguard the wealth of affluent Kuwaitis so that the benefits of that wealth could be spread throughout the economy. Sheikh Abd Allah recognized that at this time in Kuwait's history, perhaps for the first time, citizens could profit from the thriving business sector that was feeding off the revenues from the oil industry and become increasingly wealthy. The ruling bodies saw this trend as significant, and defensive policies were thus enacted in order to promote and support wealth-creation in Kuwait, to the end of securing the loyalty of a growing class of modern entrepreneurs.

By the late 1950s, the old merchant class that had once dominated the Kuwaiti business sector had abandoned its old occupations and become wealthy entrepreneurs. Many companies that were still engaged in the traditional activities of seafaring, trade, fishing, pearl-diving and shipbuilding struggled to survive at this time thanks to deteriorating economic conditions and an almost total reorientation of the economy towards the oil industry. The few companies that survived did so by adopting a practice that would henceforth come to characterize Kuwaiti society, namely the use of low-cost foreign labour.[53] Compared to the multitude of public sector and oil-industry jobs that were opening up, traditional occupations were seen as demanding and gruelling. Upwardly mobile Kuwaitis preferred to seek work in the new sectors – government or the oil industry – where they could expect greater financial rewards, decent job security and easier working conditions. With few Kuwaitis able or willing to do yesterday's jobs in a fast-changing world, companies imported workers from Oman and Iran. Cheap foreign labour slashed the costs of running a business, driving profits back into the black. But critically, in the post-oil era, those working in these traditional Kuwaiti occupations were, in fact, rarely Kuwaiti.[54]

Beyond the new practice of importing cheap labour, the advent of the oil industry profoundly altered the structure of the labour market. With

---

53 For an early study of the development and outcomes of labour migration to Kuwait, see Shah 1986.

54 The data that Salih cites relates to non-Kuwaitis in different vocations who had been continuously resident in Kuwait for five years or more. In 1965 they represented 44.7 per cent of the labour force. See Salih 1991: 50. Shah states that in 1965 non-Kuwaitis, irrespective of how long they spent in the country, constituted 77 per cent of the total labour force; see Shah 1986: 822.

significant oil revenues flowing into the public purse, the public sector grew rapidly and soon represented a disproportionate share of the labour market. Practically speaking, more and more jobs were in the hands of the government or the ruling family. In search of a share of the oil wealth, Kuwaitis gravitated towards these jobs.[55]

In the economic system that developed in these first years of significant oil wealth, a growing number of affluent families took up senior positions in the central administration, eventually becoming major shareholders of government corporations involved in the oil business. This opportunity for richer families offered the government the chance to balance the power relationship between the rulers and the old influential merchant families. In this new system, the state favoured the old merchant families and allowed them to secure highly paid and politically important jobs.[56]

From the point of view of the rulers and the state, the advantages of such an arrangement were twofold: it guaranteed that the merchant families would be loyal to the rulers, and in conjunction with this created an entrenched state of dependence whereby these families were wholly reliant on the state for their income.[57] This was an important strategy on the part of the ruling family, which had to carefully manage this relationship in order not to neglect old and influential merchant groups, especially since they had ruled in tandem with them since before the discovery of oil.

---

55 Lawson 1985: 16
56 Azoulay 2020: 69
57 Lawson 1985: 16. See also Salih 1991: 48.

4

KUWAIT ON THE WAY UP: THE WORLD OF AL-BABTAIN

A fertile business environment

By the mid-1950s, Kuwait's ruling al-Sabah family was relying on a calcu-lated strategy. The aim was to make the old merchant families increasingly affluent, but give them limited access to power[1] and weaken their capacity to bring about political change. The strategy worked. In the late 1950s and especially the early 1960s, commercial undertakings in Kuwait were thriv-ing, particularly the export and import industry, construction projects, the property sector and the health services.[2] The businesses involved in these activities were managed and owned by the merchant families, who had by now established themselves as an increasingly prosperous entrepreneurial and business community. As the ruling family had intended, their hold on power was just firm enough to keep them comfortable and to ward off any serious political challenges. Over the coming years, the government and the ruling al-Sabah family worked to open trade and finance opportunities to generate even more profits for Kuwait's expanding community of entrepre-neurs and merchants.[3]

Abd al-Aziz Sa'ud al-Babtain would become one of the new young merchants seeking profit and opportunity in this fast-changing chapter of Kuwait's history. Although Abd al-Aziz's parents were living in al-Zubayr

---

[1] This was not a new strategy considering how earlier rulers acted and how powers have been balancing against each other in, for example, the 1930s; see Alebrahim 2019: 74.
[2] Salih 1991: 48
[3] For a detailed discussion on the ruler and the ruled relationship in Kuwait, see Azoulay 2020.

in southern Iraq, according to the tribal tradition of the time, women in late pregnancy moved into their parents' homes to give birth. It was customary for them to stay there for 40 days before rejoining their husbands. Since the parents of Abu Sa'ud's mother did not live in al-Zubayr, she asked permission to go and give birth in her uncle's house in al-Mirqab in Kuwait instead, and there Abd al-Aziz was born.[4]

As already mentioned, Abd al-Aziz was not a member of a prominent merchant family, but his life story runs almost perfectly in parallel with the history of modern Kuwait. In 1945, at the age of 9, he left his parents' home in al-Zubayr and returned to Kuwait with his uncle Abd al-Muhsin al-Babtain. The young Abd al-Aziz came of age as Kuwait's oil revenues began to trickle and then flood into state coffers. His understanding of how public and private sectors work was shaped by the policies of the ruler Sheikh Abd Allah and the al-Sabah family. His hunger to strike out on his own and build businesses was likely kindled by the heady environment of wealth-creation, growth and entrepreneurship that defined Golden Era Kuwait in the 1950s.

As befitted a book lover, Abu Sa'ud's first job was as in the library at the al-Shuwaykh secondary school. But even as a young man, it was clear that his aspirations lay beyond the library walls. "I was ambitious and I wanted to work as a tradesman", Abu Sa'ud recalls.[5] It was a time of rapid urbanization in Kuwait, and he soon spotted an opportunity. "I saved my salaries over the years 1954, 1955 and 1956, and I convinced a relative to open a sanitary shop, selling plumbing supplies." Abd al-Aziz states that "I grew up in a modest family. My father was neither rich nor poor, but I could not complete my studies because my family needed me."[6] He lived with his extended family, so earnings made from his work in the library and from trading could be saved.

The relative he persuaded to open a shop was initially reluctant, cautioning Abu Sa'ud that the family had no experience with this type of business. But another partner was found, a man named Samir Lubnani. He had the relevant professional know-how to teach his partners. Abu Sa'ud placed a

---

4 Interview with Abd al-Aziz October 17, 2016.
5 The quotations in the following are from conversations with Abd al-Aziz carried out at the Foundation in Kuwait on October 17 and 18, 2016.
6 Atzori 2014: 37

high premium on such experience. Lubnani joined the business without investing any of his own capital, but on the understanding that he would share his knowledge. "The total business capital was 200,000 rupees, I paid 20,000 and my relative paid 180,000. We started the work, and my share was 10 per cent of the profits and 10 per cent of the losses. My relative's share was 75 per cent and Samir's was 15 per cent."[7]

Abu Sa'ud's development from a first-time entrepreneur into a wealthy businessman was not without difficulties. Like so many entrepreneurs, he suffered a number of failures on the road to success, funding his efforts by working several jobs – like many entrepreneurial Kuwaitis, at least one of which was in the public sector – and studying alongside his work.

> I was doing three things at the same time between 1956 and 1962: I was an employee in al-Ma'arif (at the Ministry of Education), in the afternoon I was with Abd al-Aziz al-Rumayah in the new business, and I was study-ing at night, as I was pursuing my studies.[8] ... Al-Rumayah was critical of me working in several fields and as I was young and as every young man, I did not accept any hurtful word. After a few months, I came to Abd al-Aziz al-Rumayah and said, "Please check my account. If there is any profit, I do not want it, I want only my share of the capital". He responded, "Why 'Abd al-Aziz!?" I told him, "this was my final deci-sion". He tried to convince me to change my mind, but in vain. He hurt me, however it was a trivial thing, if it happens today, I would have for-given him. At those days, I was a youth full of himself. I regarded Abd al-Aziz al-Rumayah highly and considered him as a father, but could not have changed my mind. Then he sent me some amount of money that included the profits, but I refused to cash the cheque and said: as long as there are some profits, which I do not want, I want only my share of the original capital. I would like to mention how I managed to accumulate my first 20 thousand rupees. At that time, I had only 10 thousand, I took

---

7 As has been stated above, the rupee of the Republic of India (INR) was on the day of India's independence in 1947 pegged to 3.30 INR to the US dollar. In 1959 the Gulf rupee was introduced and pegged to the British pound, with 13.33 rupees to the pound. The Gulf rupee was replaced by the Kuwaiti Dinar introduced after independence 1961.

8 As can be seen from above, in the interview with Atzori (2014: 37), Abu Sa'ud cites his responsibilities towards his family as a fourth profession.

7 thousand as a loan from my employer, the educational authority and I borrowed another 3 thousand from Abd al-Aziz al-Rumayah to make the 20 thousand, my share. I repaid my debts as I was working and opened a shop in Tunis Street.[9]

The story told by Abd al-Aziz above about his initial experiences as a businessman is not unique. In the 1960s, an entire class of entrepreneurs was establishing small businesses in Kuwait that would flourish and make the owners increasingly wealthy.[10] Abu Sa'ud was among them.

Anyway, I opened my own shop; however, I noticed that it did not make any profit. I used to sell foodstuffs, tobacco, i.e. I was a kind of retailer. I forgot to tell you that before starting the partnership with Abd al-Aziz al-Rumayah, in the second half of the 1950s, I had a partnership with a Palestinian friend and we had a small women's clothing store (Novote) on al-Mubarakiyya Street. After a year, my father asked me, "Have you opened a shop in addition to your job?" Then I exploited the ignorance of my father of the business of Novote and his passion about trade and said to him, "Yes, I trade with Novote." He said, "Ma sha' Allah, congratulations! But what does it mean, trading with Novote?" Of course, I was not able to lie to my father, therefore I said, "Women's clothing!" He said, "Please leave it this very afternoon!" I did my best to convince him about the possible profits that I could get, but his answer was, "Please this is a female job, so do not work in it as you are a young man. Please try to get your money before the end of the year."

Abd al-Aziz continued, "I then sold the shop to a Kuwaiti cousin of mine, who was blessed by Allah and his trade flourished. Meanwhile, I opened a new shop, and stayed for six months without selling anything. I had to pay 250 rupees as a monthly rent, in addition to 150–200 rupees in salary for a person I hired to work in the shop. You know, I had to work in al-Ma'arif in the mornings for about 450 rupees; however, my shop did not attain a 450 rupees turnover (I am not speaking about profits, just

---

9 The story related in this and the following extract were told by Abd al-Aziz in conversations October 17 and 18, 2016.
10 Lawson 1985: 17

turnover). It meant that this was my third failure in business; however, with the blessings of Allah, I was able to make this failure a springboard for later success."

After being successful in business as a distributor of goods to shops in smaller villages outside Kuwait City, Abd al-Aziz started, as has been briefly mentioned above, to become an agent for various foreign products that were coming on to the market in both Kuwait and Saudi Arabia at that time. In conversations with Abu Saʿud, he described in detail how he was approached by Albert Abila, a Christian Palestinian residing in Lebanon and an influential businessman, who was the concessionary agent of the Kent tobacco company in Kuwait, and how they made an agreement in which Abd al-Aziz promoted Kent cigarettes. This took place in 1959 and the agreement was verbal. In 1963, Abu Saʿud terminated the agreement and instead became the agent for Marlboro. This was a highly successful venture and in 1994, Abu Saʿud's company was granted the franchise for selling Marlboro cigarettes in Saudi Arabia. In our conversation, Abd al-Aziz states that he knew the harmful impact of cigarettes on health and the link between smoking and a range of diseases, but he could not relinquish this business. To some extent, he claims, he was in a similar position to Alfred Nobel, "He invented dynamite. To compensate for its harmful effects, he established the Nobel prizes".[11] For Abu Saʿud, the knowledge about the damaging effects of smoking and the profits he made on cigarettes became the spark to found a scholarship in his name for students without financial means to pursue their studies.[12]

For entrepreneurs, a critical aspect of success is the ability to read the culture around them and anticipate people's needs – almost before people can articulate those needs themselves. Abu Saʿud made his fortune selling and distributing goods to people who, a generation earlier, could not have afforded those goods. The greatly improved standard of living evident

11 Conversation with Abd al-Aziz, October 17, 2016.
12 The work of the al-Babtain Foundation with various scholarships and other initiatives will be further discussed in chapter 6. This particular one is a scholarship for students that have completed their undergraduate degree and can prove that their families do not have the means to support their further studies. It gives an opportunity for students who are Arab nationals to study for a master's or PhD degree in the US, United Kingdom or France. In the 1990s, the scholarships were expanded and were also awarded to non-Arab students from Muslim-majority countries.

in 1950s and 1960s Kuwait, and the economic conditions that shaped it, were a necessary precondition for his own success. Another important circumstance was, as Crystal states, the political continuity in the transition from one society to another.[13] In this sense, Abu Sa'ud was a product of his environment and age. But even in those early days, he was also an agent of change working to shape that environment, cultivating tastes for new, unfamiliar goods and establishing a culture of entrepreneurship which in some regards challenged traditional ideas.

The financial services rush

The discovery of oil, and the monetization of that discovery through state concessions, unleashed a wave of revenue that shrewd leaders channelled into a business boom that benefited key constituents – Kuwait's merchants. Companies were launched and expanded and entrepreneurs thrived in the coastal state where, scarcely a generation before, what few industries there were struggled to make a living.[14]

The economic growth that took place in Kuwait after the Second World War did not occur in a vacuum. Companies in the oil industry relied on other service providers to carry out support and service functions such as banks and retail. As a result, businesses and entrepreneurship developed, and Kuwait witnessed the emergence of a dazzling array of financial instruments to sustain and promote economic life. As early as 1946, with large capital revenues from the oil industry moving around the market, the country was in need of a financial system fit for purpose to handle economic transactions, investments and banking activities.

It was not that Kuwait had no financial sector: commercial banking had existed before the oil era. In 1941, the British Bank of the Middle East was granted permission to establish a branch in Kuwait and started operations in the country.[15] But commercial banking really took off after 1946, at the

13 Crystal 1989: 427

14 Crystal (1989) examines primarily the political conditions for the transition from one society to another and compares the transitions in Kuwait and Qatar. A complementary view on developments in Kuwaiti society but focusing on the tension between social development, particularly in terms of women, and maintaining tribal organization is Tétreault 2001.

15 After the end of the concession of the British Bank of the Middle East in 1971 the

same time as oil production increased and the government was, for the first time in its history, reaping the benefits of significant revenues.

To begin with, the British Bank of the Middle East was initially the sole provider of commercial banking services, but by the early 1950s it had three competitors, despite having expanded from one to four branches to meet the massively greater demand for banking services to Kuwaiti individuals, companies and the government.[16] In conjunction with this development and to further meet the demand for banking services from Kuwait, in 1952 the government established the National Bank of Kuwait and the Kuwait Commercial Bank.[17] In order to strengthen and stabilize the economy, the Dinar of Kuwait was issued as the currency of the country in 1961. Prior to the issuing of the currency, the Central Bank of Kuwait was established in 1959.[18]

After Kuwait became independent in 1961, several Kuwaiti-owned banks were established, among them the Credit and Savings Bank in 1965 in order to support domestic projects, agriculture and housing, and in 1973 the Industrial Bank of Kuwait to support industrial financing and the Real Estate Bank of Kuwait to fund property development. By 1978, Kuwait had seven commercial banks operating in the country, a figure that was still the same in 2004.[19]

Beyond banking, there was also a growing need for financial services to help the government and wealthy Kuwaitis invest in foreign markets and in Kuwait itself. From a state perspective, these financial activities were particularly important as the state viewed reinvestment as a significant driver of the growing economy. Kuwaitis' need for the means to carry out this inward investment further boosted the level of banking activity – a cycle that continues to this day. Despite periods of depressed oil prices and a current global shift away from fossil fuels, Kuwait's banking industry has constantly expanded since the 1950s, making Kuwait not just a significant

---

bank took a new name, the Kuwait Bank, and 60 per cent of the bank's capital was purchased by Kuwaitis; see Molyneaux and Iqbal 2005: 126.

16 *Kuwait Today: A Welfare State* 1963: 82

17 *Kuwait Today: A Welfare State* 1963: 82. According to Molyneaux and Iqbal (2005: 126) the establishment of the National Bank of Kuwait in 1952 was undertaken by a group of Kuwaiti families.

18 Molyneaux and Iqbal 2005: 126

19 Information on the establishment of banks is from Molyneaux and Iqbal 2005: 126.

exporter of oil but also a major financial actor on the global stage.

Money brings money, and for Abd al-Aziz al-Babtain it was vital that the necessary financial institutions and systems were in place while his business were growing. After establishing himself as an agent for tobacco companies in Kuwait, he started to look for new business opportunities. In the 1970s land was cheap and Abu Sa'ud decided to venture into property. This soon became a lucrative business. Today the family of al-Babtain, through several companies, has property interests in Amman, Damascus, Geneva, Kuwait City, New York, Saudi Arabia and the United Kingdom. The small company grew quickly from the 1960s and 1970s into a business that also invested in consumer goods. He and his company became the agents in Kuwait and several other countries for global corporations such as Nokia, LG, Panasonic and Samsung. Under the umbrella of the al-Babtain Electronic Company, he also manufactures electronic appliances in South Korea for the market in Kuwait and the Arabian Peninsula. Another business venture concerns the import of agricultural products to Kuwait and other Arab countries. He also owns farms in Saudi Arabia and in Iraq, mainly for the cultivation of dates. In this early expansion of the businesses of Abd al-Aziz, the support of the government, providing the necessary structures, and the development of the financial sector were instrumental. Hence, the growth of Abu Sa'ud's businesses can in a national context be seen as an example of the rise of a new financial elite.

In sum, the launch of the oil industry and the increasing oil revenues required a structural change in the structure of the Kuwaiti economy. The government had to establish a system capable of handling financial transactions and affairs and of promoting the country's business sector. This has served the country well, but Kuwait's dependency on oil as the primary driver of economic growth has been a concern since the advent of the oil industry. The government had been looking for other means to secure revenues for the state and its people. This exclusive reliance on oil exposes Kuwait and the Gulf states in general to the potential of high volatility. In addition, wealth and increased prosperity saw some money channelled into speculative activities on the small local stock market, and indeed, as already noted in chapter 1, a small market crash occurred in 1977.

Changes in the supply and demand chain or fluctuations concerning pricing of oil and gas products are factors that have serious consequences for the Kuwaiti economy. Kuwait's rulers as well as other leaders in Gulf countries took these elements of risk seriously, and economic diversification became one of the strategic goals for the Gulf Cooperation Council (GCC) after the fall of oil prices in 1986.

A society in flux: citizenship laws, limitations, difference and identity

Oil has been the catalyst for immense social change in Kuwaiti society, not least at the level of basic demography.[20] Before the explosion of the oil industry, most Kuwaitis were relatively uneducated and low-skilled. In one of the first national censuses, taken in 1957, it emerged that the Kuwaiti workforce included just two doctors and eight accountants – an astonishing deficit of skilled workers.[21] In those early years of the oil industry, Kuwait was utterly ill-equipped to staff the infrastructure required to process and sell its great national asset. Kuwaitis lacked the expertise required to operate oil and gas fields, build an industry around petroleum products, and handle the export of oil. This meant that from the beginning of the oil industry, Kuwait had to import skilled labour from foreign countries.

Beyond workers to staff the oil and financial industries, the government also needed to employ people to run the administration of the state: police officers, soldiers, doctors and many other roles vital for the everyday functioning of the state and country. While it was straightforward to import workers for, say, the services sector, police officers had of necessity to be recruited from within Kuwaiti society. As citizens began to reap the benefits of oil revenues, a split developed between the highly paid jobs in both the public and the private sector that were available to Kuwaiti citizens, and the jobs available to foreigners – jobs that were often lower paid or considered less prestigious. As early as the 1940s, Kuwaiti society became highly bureaucratized, with nationals working in government institutions and corporations, and the less glamorous jobs left to foreigners.[22]

The mass import of foreign workers provided the labour necessary to keep Kuwait's oil fields, operations and exports running, and, by extension,

---

20 For examples of early studies of social and demographic change in Kuwait, see al-Moosa 1984, al-Thakeb 1985 and Shah 1986.
21 Owen & Pamuk 1999: 208
22 al-Nakib 2016: 95

to keep revenues flowing into the state coffers, but it also posed a political challenge. These non-citizens, many of whom eventually settled in Kuwait for years on end, posed a challenge to the government's welfare state model. The increase in migrant workers sharply increased the number of people who could access the benefits of the welfare system, raising the possibility that the welfare system might be watered down to cope with the greater demands on it. The key question at the heart of the issue was who should be eligible for state benefits – all those who contribute through labour, or just Kuwaiti citizens?

There had been foreign workers in Kuwait since before the arrival of the oil industry, but never in any significant numbers. Migrants seeking employment first started to enter Kuwait in large numbers in the early years of the oil industry. These people came primarily from nearby countries, such as Iran and Oman. Thanks to the burgeoning oil industry, many saw Kuwait as a place where they could get a secure job, earn a decent salary and build a future. The benefits ran both ways: these foreign workers were the lifeblood of Kuwait's large oil concerns, and their labour supplied much-needed revenue to the government's coffers. But citizenship was the only way to take full part in the country's new-found wealth, and once these foreign workers realized the great benefits of the oil-funded Kuwaiti welfare system, many applied for citizenship. This raised concerns within the government, which saw that a sudden increase in the numbers of Kuwaiti citizens would seriously impair the efficacy of the welfare system. The government therefore took measures to restrict citizenship eligibility.

The first limitation on becoming a Kuwaiti citizen was put in place by the government in 1948 with the passing of the Nationality Law. This was an attempt to control the anticipated influx of future foreign workers and restrict their rights to gain citizenship. Those people eligible for citizenship after 1948 were Kuwaiti families who had lived in Kuwait since 1899, children born in Kuwait to Arab or Muslim fathers and people who had lived in Kuwait for at least ten years. The latter were granted the right to become naturalized citizens.[23]

After the Nationality Law was passed, the government anticipated that workers from foreign countries would not stay longer than their contract required. When the particular project they were engaged on was over, the

23 al-Nakib 2016:94

expectation was that they would return to their countries of origin. Furthermore, there was a sense that this process would be repeated for a few years until a tranche of Kuwaiti citizens became highly enough educated to perform the tasks previously done by foreigners.[24] However, things did not turn out this way. Many workers chose to stay in Kuwait, which offered them better living standards and prospects for the future than their home countries. Many also knew that they could live a much more comfortable life if they managed to get citizenship and become recipients of state welfare. For these people, the aim was to stay on for a decade and become naturalized.

Regional factors also came into play. Often a person's unwillingness to return to their home country was exacerbated by geopolitical instability in the Middle East and on the Indian subcontinent. When workers' home countries were riven by conflict or even just shaken by political upheaval, the prospect of staying on in Kuwait, where workers had steady incomes and reliable security, began to look a lot more appealing. As wages in Kuwait rose to the point where they far outstripped what a person might have earned in their home country, workers had yet another reason to wish to stay. All of this led the Kuwaiti government to implement further, more restrictive policies concerning the rights to Kuwaiti citizenship.

In 1959, the government passed a new law that defined citizenship in a much narrower sense. The law stated that "original" Kuwaiti nationals were those individuals who belonged to families that had settled in Kuwait before 1920.[25] Children of Arab or Muslim fathers born in Kuwait were no longer eligible for citizenship, and the earlier possibility of naturalization became much more restrictive. The law was further subject to amendment in 1960, when it explicitly sanctioned the naturalization of only 50 foreign workers per year.[26] This was a sharp, sudden decrease in the number of people eligible to gain citizenship, compared to the situation in 1948. For foreign workers hoping to naturalize, the doors were pretty much shut. But for the government, working from a position of trying to limit the number of mouths the welfare system might have to feed, this policy was a success: a system was now in place that would not compromise the welfare system

---

24 al-Nakib 2016: 94
25 Freeth 1972: 13
26 Salih 1991: 50

or the lucrative future of Kuwaiti nationals who would continue to enjoy the economic benefits of the oil industry. Alongside this came a law reserving certain jobs for Kuwaiti nationals. In a job market in which the public administration was expanding rapidly, this meant that many Kuwaitis were almost entirely dependent on the state – a dependency that weakened any demand for political change within the country.

The question of identity came to the fore again in 1961, when Kuwait gained its independence from Great Britain and a new Kuwaiti government took full control of the country's policies.[27] Consequently, the British protectorate formed by the Anglo-Kuwaiti agreement from 1899 was annulled, and Sheikh Abd Allah al-Salim al-Sabah, the 11th ruler of Kuwait, became the first amir of the new State of Kuwait. The Anglo-Kuwaiti agreement of 1899 had provided an assurance to the then-ruler of the country, Sheikh Mubarak, and his successors, that Kuwait would be defended against outside aggression, but also that the British would not interfere in Kuwaiti internal affairs. A consequence of the treaty was that the British government took control of the country's foreign affairs, and the British Representative became the equivalent of a minister of foreign affairs. However, British jurisdiction was put in place from 1925 on, running in parallel with national jurisdiction.[28] On the face of it, this provision was a violation of the agreement, but it was approved by the ruler.[29] British courts were abolished in 1961 as part of an ongoing process of modernization of the Kuwaiti National courts initiated in 1959 and Kuwait's independence.[30] Independence ended the British political control of Kuwait, though Britain continued to maintain relations with the new state of Kuwait in the same manner

---

27 The Iraqi leader of the time, Abd al-Karim Qasim (d. 1963) protested, stating that his country considered Kuwait a part of the *wilaya* of Basra and, hence, a part of Iraq. British troops were sent to Kuwait in response to a request from the amir Abd Allah al-Salim al-Sabah; see Tétreault 1991: 582. See also Hijazi 1964: 435 and the article about the political and legal status of Kuwait at this time by Pillai and Kumar 1962.

28 National law was a combination of tribal and Islamic law and the Ottoman Civil Code. The National law embraced persons considered Kuwaitis, from independent Arab states, Iranians and citizens from Gulf states protected by the British. The British jurisdiction embraced mainly British and Commonwealth citizens; see Hijazi 1964: 429.

29 Hijazi 1964: 428f

30 Hijazi 1964: 433

as it did with other post-colonial states. At the time of Kuwaiti independence, a Treaty of Friendship was signed between the British and Kuwait.[31] Business relationships were maintained, and new ones established, and in the early 1970s Kuwait became an important actor in the financial markets in the City of London.[32]

According to Article 4 of the constitution of 1962, the country is "(...) a hereditary Amirate held in succession in the descendants of the Mubarak Al-Sabah".[33] Complementary to the constitution was the passing in 1959 of the aforementioned Nationality law. This law builds on a decree from 1920 and has been amended several times since it was enacted. Since the 1970s it has been more restrictive, but in the constitutional sense, a Kuwaiti is an individual who qualifies as an original Kuwaiti and, hence, is legally regarded as such. From 1961 on, the construction of a Kuwaiti identity become linked with the exigencies of statehood. Construction refers in this context to a process in which terms such as, for example, "Arab", "Arabism", "tribe", "Islam", "Muslim", "family" and "nation" were conceptualized and sometimes endowed with conflicting or competing meanings.

Outwardly it was also important for Kuwait to establish its identity as a new state and create an international profile that made it distinct from other states. As early as July 1961, just a month after independence, Kuwait became a member of the Arab League on the condition that the British troops supporting the new state withdraw from the country. The Iraqi claims on Kuwait, which deemed it to be part of the region of Basra, were settled in an agreement in 1963 which defined the border between the two countries. The Iraqis also received financial compensation of US$80 million from Kuwait.[34] In addition, Kuwait took an active role in foreign policy through its membership of the United Nations from 1963 and as a founding member in 1960 of the Organization of Petroleum Exporting Countries (OPEC). Through the oil revenues, Kuwait developed aid programmes

31 Hijazi 1964: 434. For a more detailed review of the context of the Friendship agreement and the relation the British at this period in history, see Pillai and Kumar 1962: 114f.

32 Tétreault 1991: 583

33 For the constitution of Kuwait from 1962 in English, see https://www. constituteproject.org/constitution/Kuwait_1992.pdf?lang=en. Accessed September 25, 2018.

34 Tétreault 1991: 582

initially directed to Arab recipients, but later with a broader ambition. Another way of establishing Kuwait and strengthening the status of the new state was to direct economic assistance to countries and organizations defined as Arab and at war. For example, aid was given to the Palestine Liberation Organization (PLO) in its struggle against Israel and later to Iraq in the Iran–Iraq War (1980–1988).[35]

At the time of independence, steps had already been taken to safeguard Kuwaiti nationals' privilege, to control the oil industry and profit from its benefits. But the motivation for the country's ever more stringent nationality laws also went deeper than this. The presence of thousands of foreign workers did not just dilute the rewards of the country's oil reserves. It also affected Kuwait's national make-up, adding ethnic and cultural variety where previously there had been a far greater homogeneity. Among the ruling elite, there was a fear that the national identity of Kuwait was threatened. In its opinion, integrating foreigners would change the very fabric of Kuwait. Thus, policies were designed with the aim of preserving Kuwaiti culture and identity and segregating citizens from foreigners.

Restricting citizenship meant that the government had a more homogenous group of people to provide for and govern. From the perspective of the ruling family, foreign workers may have had a political agenda that would challenge the government's own plans, and if they were granted citizenship they might start to press for change. The government of Kuwait preferred to rule over a smaller number of citizens whom they presumed to know well and to create an environment in which they could control a more homogenous Kuwaiti population and keep close control over any risk of political instability.

The restrictions on the granting of citizenship were followed by the government taking even firmer political control of the population by restricting the right to vote and excluding foreigners from top positions within the administration. In the mid-1980s, senior executive positions in the public sector were reserved for Kuwaiti citizens, as were the purchase and sale of land.[36] Skilled foreign workers in fields such as education, law, medicine,

---

35 Tétreault 1991: 583f, and for an overview of the history of Kuwait's policies on assistance and charity to foreign countries, see Leichtman 2017 and discussion about the work of the al-Babtain Foundation in chapter 6.
36 Salih 1991: 49f

KUWAIT ON THE WAY UP

engineering, finance and the military were excluded from the decision-making processes. Arabs comprised almost 60 per cent of the non-Kuwaiti labour force in 1980, while Asians made up approximately 30 per cent. Among the Arabs, Palestinians with Jordanian passports were the most numerous group, while the broad category "Asians" covered people from a variety of countries such as Bangladesh, Pakistan, Sri Lanka, the Philippines, Nepal and Indonesia.[37] Kuwaitis were thus not only separated from migrants by virtue of their socio-economic prospects, but were also now legally a completely different class with distinct legal advantages over non-citizens, regardless of whether those defined as foreigners were skilled or unskilled labourers.[38]

The government's defensiveness and restrictive policies towards foreigners served to separate Kuwaitis from the increasing body of migrant workers. This process was further streamlined in the 1970s and the 1980s, resulting in a divided society where Kuwaitis had exclusive access to high-status jobs and the abundant generosity of an oil-revenue-funded welfare system, while the growing number of migrant workers, regardless of how long they had lived in the country, had restricted employment opportunities (confined mainly to working in service-sector jobs or manual labour) and enjoyed only limited, if any, social and political rights. This divide between Kuwaiti citizens and foreigners was not just evident in employment and in engagement with the state, but also at street level, specifically regarding which groups of people lived in which neighbourhoods. Although nearly every city on the planet shows the same patterns of like attracting like, and people settling in communities close to those they perceive as their own kind, in Kuwait (especially in the wake of the series of laws limiting citizenship) this phenomenon was even more pronounced. In the late 1950s and early1960s Kuwaitis became segregated from the rest of the population by settling in certain residential areas designated as reserved

---

37 For further details on the non-Kuwaiti labour force between 1965 and 1985, see Shah 1986.

38 The position of those defined as Kuwaitis in Kuwaiti society is also mirrored in the statement by Lawson that, "Four of the clans that the British resident considered among the most influential during the 1920s supplied two-thirds of the government's cabinet members during the 1960s and 1970s. These same four clans provided almost one-third of the directorships of the country's largest shareholding companies in the same period." See Lawson 1985: 16.

exclusively for Kuwaiti citizens.[39] Two types of residential areas began to emerge: one designated for Kuwaitis and one for immigrants. The residential areas assigned to foreigners, especially poorer economic migrants, were of a lower standard than those for Kuwaitis. Housing for the non-Kuwaitis was far from luxurious, indeed in some cases almost slum conditions. Often, these neighbourhoods were, and still are, overcrowded, unlike those reserved for Kuwaiti nationals. In most cases, this stark contrast in living standards prevented Kuwaitis from embracing the concept of mixed residential areas, as some believed it would lower the tone of the neighbourhood they lived in.[40] The foreigner/national divide went beyond the socio-economic realm. The best way to illustrate this is with the case of some of the higher-quality housing various Kuwaiti companies constructed for foreign workers of a higher social and employment status. This type of housing was occupied primarily by migrants from Europe and North America, as opposed to Middle Easterners or workers from the Indian sub-continent. But, critically, these foreigners, despite having a higher status and standard of living in Kuwait, still lived apart from locals, even if in some instances they occupied more desirable homes than locals. According to al-Nakib, "(...) socially homogenous enclaves that differentiated between sectors of the population by background" were created and this division was not only a separation between foreigners and Kuwaiti nationals, but also between those who were referred to as "urban townspeople" (*hadar*) and those who were defined as Bedouins.[41] In addition, enclaves of business people as well as of Shi'a Muslims were created, the latter as a direct result of state relocation policies.[42] These examples of national, ethnic or religious segregation among citizens and between citizens and foreigners was not a factor of socio-economics or class only, but could also be understood as part of a drive to create a Kuwaiti society in which citizenship, social, ethnic

---

39 al-Moosa 1984: 46. In addition, Farah al-Nakib (2016) has a chapter on the constructions of suburbs in Kuwait City and the move to new residential areas. She points out (2016: 122) that this transformation of the city was in the hands of the government and that non-Kuwaitis were excluded from the new suburbs.

40 al-Moosa 1984: 51. See also al-Nakib 2016: 134–143.

41 al-Nakib 2016: 134. From a political perspective, a division also appeared since Bedouins in Kuwait were loyal to the al-Sabah rulers, but urban townspeople were more supportive of Arab nationalism; see Herb 1999: 63.

42 al-Nakib 2016: 135

and religious hierarchies were imprinted in the geography of Kuwait, with identities and status being affirmed through urban residential segregation. A parallel intention was to use space to reinforce a Kuwaiti identity in a society where most of the population were not full citizens.

According to surveys in the late 1970s and early 1980s regarding the residential situation, most Kuwaitis preferred to live with people of the same ethnicity and religious affiliation, and who were fellow citizens, rather than foreigners and other perceived strangers.[43] One survey conducted in around 1980, at the start of the urbanization era when Kuwaitis had started to move out of the city centre and into the suburbs, showed that almost 90 per cent of the Kuwaitis lived next door to fellow Kuwaitis.[44] It was a government policy at the time to keep Kuwaiti citizens together in more or less closed quarters. According to al-Moosa (1984), the underlying intention of this was to promote and consolidate a Kuwaiti national identity. The government may have also feared that if mixing between foreigners and Kuwaitis were to occur, Kuwaitis might start to lose their national identity and their sense of privilege associated with it. Ultimately, such a development might risk them becoming politicized and agitating for change, which would have posed a clear threat to the political status quo.

Researchers studying the situation of Kuwait in the early 1980s and the effects of the influx of foreigners found that only a minority of Kuwaitis opposed the policy of segregating Kuwaitis from migrants. Most people preferred to live close to their fellow Kuwaiti nationals and almost all of them rejected proposals for mixing between foreigners and nationals. However, at the same time, foreigners said they were not against the idea of mixed residential areas.[45]

The effect of these arrangements was twofold – firstly to insulate Kuwaiti citizens from political engagement, for the most part, through the pacifying effects of the state's generous welfare provision, and to create a sense of privilege among them by drawing a sharp distinction between "deserving" citizens and effectively "undeserving" foreign resident labourers. This dichotomy was reinforced by spatial and other forms of segregation.

---

43 al-Moosa 1984: 48. This also follows a pre-oil era tradition of having a tribal, Bedouin or religious preference for living in a certain area; see Alebrahim 2019: 33ff.
44 al-Moosa 1984: 49
45 al-Moosa 1984: 51

Al-Moosa also states that segregation went beyond residential patterns all the way to the level of personal self-expression, particularly in terms of how people presented themselves in their mode of apparel.[46] According to al-Moosa, in the early 1980s, the traditional white robe (*thawb* or *dishdasha*) became a symbol of being a Kuwaiti, while European or American dress was typically sported by foreigners. Accordingly, by way of distinguishing themselves, a growing number of Kuwaitis began to wear traditional Arab clothes. It soon became relatively simple to spot who was Kuwaiti and who was a foreigner. More recently the dilution of this dress-code boundary through the mixing of Arabic and English, dressing in jeans and t-shirts rather than a perceived Kuwaiti dress, eating American brands of fast food and listening to hip-hop music among Kuwaiti youth has become a way of signalling modernity and belonging to a global context often defined as "western".[47]

For Abd al-Aziz al-Babtain these developments are problematic. They do not connect the young generation of Kuwaitis to the roots of the culture and the society, and indicate the demise of an Arab and Kuwaiti culture. Abd al-Aziz himself dresses differently in various instances and contexts. In the meetings I have attended in Kuwait with Abu Saʻud, he has always been dressed in a white robe. However, pictures of him from the 1950s and the 1960s also show him in suit and tie, as well as in a white robe wearing a jacket on top of the robe. In more recent years, when he has appeared on Arab TV or when inaugurating the ceremonies awarding the al-Babtain Poetry Prize, he has been dressed in a traditional Kuwaiti robe. These events are usually held in Kuwait or in other Gulf countries. When travelling, Abu Saʻud is usually dressed in business-like fashion in a suit and tie as, for example, when visiting the Nobel committee in Stockholm, Sweden, or participating in the inauguration of the Abdulaziz Saud al-Babtain Laudian Chair of Arabic at Oxford University. In recent events in Europe under the umbrella of discussing a culture of peace, Abu Saʻud is usually dressed in a suit with a robe over the shoulders. Abd al-Aziz's personal self-expression in regard to clothing has, more or less, followed the fashion of his time and generation. In the broader Middle Eastern context, the influence of primarily European and North American dress codes since the 19th century

---

46 al-Moosa 1984: 45
47 Abdulrahim, al-Kandari and Hasanen 2009: 58f and Satti 2013: 2

Abd al-Aziz al-Babtain in the late 1960s, the modern young
gentleman. Courtesy of the al-Babtain Foundation.

influenced the society and introduced the suit as business or office attire. As
noted by Nancy Lindisfarne-Tapper and Bruce Ingham, clothing or styles
can be borrowed, copied and integrated, and be expressions of wealth or
political power or distinguish the wearer from others.[48] For Abu Sa'ud, to
wear clothing regarded as Kuwaiti and Arab in some contexts and Euro-
pean-style business clothing in others is a pragmatic choice on his part, and
an example of him adapting to different conditions. Teaming a suit with a
robe in Europe and North America also adds an element of Middle Eastern
exoticism to his appearance.

A loss of heritage? Kuwaiti culture and the *diwaniyya*

As has been the case in many other countries, abrupt socio-economic
upheaval in Kuwait radically changed people's way of life in irreversible

---

48 Lindisfarne-Tapper and Ingham 1997: 2f. For an overview and study of men's
dresses in the Arabian Peninsula, see Ingham 1997: 40–54.

ways. The transformations that affected Kuwaiti society meant that many people abandoned their traditional lifestyles as shifts occurred in popular culture and in perceptions of Kuwait and its heritage. But in Kuwait, as has been discussed above, a country where so much stress was placed on preserving the status quo, changes to mainstream culture were seen as unfavourable where the project of forging a national identity was concerned. As with nationality and housing, wherever these currents of change were felt, policies were implemented to preserve and consolidate cultural traditions. One particular aspect of cultural change, according to al-Moosa (1984), was the breakdown of family culture in Kuwait. In a broader perspective of the transformations that swept through Kuwaiti society, the invention and construction of a national heritage – a history of the country – also became part of a process of nation-building. This process is clearly evident, for example, in the inauguration of a Pearl Diving Festival. The festival provides a cultural and symbolic underpinning for the making of a nation-state and helps generate support for the political rulers. There are a number of similar celebrations of invented traditions and festivals concerning, for example, poetry and folklore. Khalaf sees them as imaginary histories, fabricated memories of a nation-state, but also as ways of counteracting the influence of a foreign or global culture perceived as threatening the indigenous local culture.[49]

As discussed in the first chapter, a longstanding tradition within Kuwaiti society is for friends, neighbours and family to assemble in the *diwaniyya* (pl. *dawawin, diwawin or diwaniyyat*). The *diwaniyya* symbolizes friendship and closeness to one's kin and to the guests of the family. Rulers have their own *diwaniyya*, where their subjects can come to express grievances, present complaints and share their opinions, and influential families have *diwaniyyat* where people meet to discuss the difficulties they face in their daily life and their thoughts about the government and politics in general. Abu Sa'ud refers to the structure of *diwaniyyat* as something of an early implementation of democracy – a place for people's voices to be heard and for the government to take heed. Abd al-Aziz's idea of democracy focuses on the freedom of expression he perceives as operating within the *diwaniyya*, and not to other factors associated with democracy such as gender

---

49 Khalaf 2008: 40–70

equality.[50] The *diwaniyya* is embedded in Kuwaiti culture and serves several purposes, from being a place of leisure where people can watch football matches to an arena for discussions about politics, and it is primarily a male space. Having said that, exceptions to this are no longer uncommon, and female as well as mixed *diwaniyyat* do exist.[51] During my visits to the *diwaniyya* of the businessman and poet Abd al-Aziz, women have been present, but they have been guests from other Arab or non-Arab countries, never Kuwaiti nationals.[52] Females have also started their own *diwaniyyat* in more recent times. Even if women rarely appear in *diwaniyyat,* strict borders between males and females in private and public urban spaces such as homes, shopping malls, universities, *suqs*, cafes and coffee shops are more difficult to maintain than before. Another challenge to the conventional role of the *diwaniyya* in society is the ability to meet electronically through smartphones, computers and an online life in general.[53]

"The government respects its value within society and many of the al-Sabah sheikhs listen carefully to the advice coming from the *diwaniyyat*", Abu Sa'ud told me. "My father used to say, 'Men are known by the status of their *diwaniyya*.'" Abu Sa'ud's comment indicates that *diwaniyyat* are differentiated socially and they can be linked to a wider political context.[54] In

---

50 It is noted by Freedom House (see for example Freedom Alerts dated February 5, 2013, and October 26, 2012) that freedom of assembly and association is guaranteed in Kuwait by law, but deteriorating in practice; see also Hafidh 2017: 99ff. It should be noted that *diwaniyyat* are mostly located in the homes of individuals and are therefore explicitly and formally safeguarded under the articles 38 and 44 of the 1962 constitution. The privacy of Kuwaiti homes has seldom been infringed by authorities, not even in times of repression of civil liberties; Hafidh 2017: 120. See also Nakib 2016: 171. However, this has happened, and security forces have entered *diwaniyyat*, see Azoulay 2020: 179.

51 See Eickelman and Piscatori 1996: 98f and Tétreault 2009: 124.

52 For a brief discussion on the role of the *diwaniyya* in contemporary times, see https://agsiw.org/the-diwaniyya-in-the-digital-age/. Accessed March 23, 2017.

53 See https://agsiw.org/the-diwaniyya-in-the-digital-age/. Accessed March 23, 2017. See also Tétreault 2009: 125f on how the *diwaniyya* culture is declining among young Kuwaitis, who prefer visiting shopping malls and cafes or sitting at home browsing online.

54 Eickelman and Piscatori 1996: 98f state that *diwaniyyat* "(...) constitute the arena for non-state activity and discussion, interlocking networks of *diwaniyyas* form the backbone of civil society."

one of our interviews in October 2016, he told me how he helped arrange a state visit to Kuwait by the Tunisian president Mohamed Beji Caid Essebsi (1926–2019). Abu Saʻud invited the Tunisian guest to stay in the two rooms in the *diwaniyya* of the influential family of al-Shamlan. The former president of Tunisia, Habib Bourguiba (1903–2000) had stayed in these very rooms during an early visit to Kuwait in 1926. President Essebsi stayed in the rooms decorated with the furniture from Bourguiba's visit. Recalling this event, Abd al-Aziz stated that the *diwaniyyat* have "(...) a great value and they are considered a unique means of expressing love, peace and solidarity between people."[55] They are part of a culture he cherishes and would like to preserve.

Despite this emphasis on the *diwaniyya* in Kuwaiti culture, urbanization in Kuwait during the 1950s meant that for many families, this tradition was left behind.[56] Smaller homes in a more urban setting were part of the issue, but underpinning the shift was the sense that things had changed. One result of Kuwait's oil rush and its attendant political and social changes was that people were no longer reliant on each other to the same extent as before, but were instead reliant on the state.

The extension of the welfare state has made reliance on informal support networks of friends, neighbours and kin less crucial, as the government is now there to provide help whenever required. This was a profound shift, from a pre-oil society where horizontal bonds meant everything, to a post-oil state where power, wealth and a sense of belonging flowed to a large extent from the government to its people. This shift "rewired" the relationships Kuwaitis had with their close kin. The new mode of interaction resembled family culture in highly developed counties, where families often isolated themselves as a nuclear unit rather than operating as part of a larger, extended family network. Driving this shift was the sense, even unconscious, of there being little need to spend as much time as before with friends or relatives to promote the needs of the larger family as a unit jointly endeavouring to improve its lot in life. This change may also have been underpinned by the decreasing numbers of Kuwaiti citizens in the labour force and in the country in general.[57]

---

55 The quotations of Abd al-Aziz above are all from an interview October 17, 2016.
56 al-Moosa 1984: 50 and al-Nakib 2016: 121ff
57 al-Moosa (1984: 46) states that in the labour force of Kuwait in the early 1980s

Among the more affluent and politically engaged Kuwaitis, however, the institution of the *diwaniyyat* survived this shift. As evidence of this, we may take, for example, Abd al-Aziz's story about the ruler of Kuwait at the time of the Iraqi occupation, Sheikh Jabir al-Sabah, taking up residence in his *diwaniyya* and using it as his office. This was a distinct honour for the al-Babtain family, confirming their strong relationship with and support for the al-Sabah rulers, but also underlined the fact that the al-Babtain family is among the country's elite. Among the leading Kuwaiti families, the *diwaniyya* is a place where you can display your wealth or social status. The pictures of famous visitors on the wall of Abu Sa'ud's *diwaniyya* are there to make the visitor aware of the importance of the owner, as is the sheer magnificence of its design and craftsmanship reminiscent of ancient al-Andalus in Spain.[58]

Wealthy and powerful families continue to build *diwaniyyat*, a symbol of Kuwaiti culture that was more than merely symbolic. In Abu Sa'ud's opinion, they are places where people meet, create and renew bonds, and work out peaceful solutions to seemingly intractable problems. He considers the institution of *diwaniyyat* in Kuwaiti society as a vehicle securing the communication between the rulers and the people, strengthening the relationship or the bond between them, while at the same time institutionalizing and formalizing the hierarchical relationship between those who rule and those who are ruled. Additionally, for Abd al-Aziz the *diwaniyya* plays a significant role as a social space for his family. This not only relates to family events such as weddings, but also to the businesses and the activities of the al-Babtain Foundation. He seems to be very proud of it and in relation to poetry festivals or discussions concerning businesses, guests are often invited to his *diwaniyya*. To listen to recitations of the Quran during warm evenings or to share a meal among the many guests are social events that follow a pattern and are linked to Abu Sa'ud not only as a champion of Arabic classical poetry and as a supporter and sponsor of education, but also as a guardian of established views on family and society. Abd al-Aziz's *diwaniyya* is a marker of identity beyond his family; it becomes an intrinsic

---

nationals comprised less than a third of the employed labour force. Owen & Pamuk (1999:209) point out that as early as 1965 the foreign labour force exceeded the Kuwaitis by 3.5 to 1.

58 For more on al-Babtain's *diwaniyya*, see chapter 7.

part of an ambition to support and defend a way of life he believes to be quintessentially Arab and Kuwaiti.

Crafting Kuwaiti citizens: the rise of a welfare state for nationals

While oil exports and the rapid increase in national revenues funded – and still fund – Kuwait's welfare system, they were not the prime mover behind the transformation of Kuwait into a welfare state.[59] Instead, that transformation was the response of a state facing powerful currents of change: it is what the state was obliged to do to consolidate and preserve itself.[60]

Across the Gulf, oil exports and increased national revenues made it necessary for states to devise new ways of governing. The governments and ruling bodies understood the imperative to transform their administrations to maintain power in the face of such powerful economic and social changes. In addition to building alliances with different interest groups, the development of a welfare system that redistributed some of the oil revenue among the citizenry was key in facilitating the development and political stability of Gulf states like Kuwait, while legitimizing the rulers, since the establishment of welfare provisions was regarded as the ruler's duty. Article 11 of the 1962 Constitution (reinstated in 1992) states that "[T]he State shall guarantee assistance to citizens in their old age, in sickness or in disability. It shall also provide them with social insurance services, social help and medical care."[61] Aside from this key article in the constitution, the leading role of the state regarding its duty of care towards its citizens is expressed in several other articles.

Before the advent of the oil industry, Kuwaiti society was poor, primarily rural and dependent on just a few small-scale industries. The economy was volatile, and both job security and incomes were not always guaranteed. Standards of living were low and socio-economic conditions were harsh. The state did not have the resources to care for the basic needs of its

---

59 In 2010, the foreign assets of Kuwait were estimated to be more than US$277 billion; see Kamrava 2013: 71.
60 See Khalaf and Hammoud 1987 for a discussion on the emergence of a welfare state in the Arab Gulf countries and especially in Kuwait.
61 For the Constitution of Kuwait, see https://constituteproject.org/constitution/Kuwait_1992?lang=en. Accessed August 23, 2018.

citizenry, so people tended to fall back not on the state but on the extended family network. This situation began to change in the 1930s and by the time the Kuwaiti welfare state was established in the 1950s, life had become markedly easier for Kuwaiti citizens.

The transition, in such a short period of time, from a poor society where people depended on those around them, to a wealthy society where people depended on the state to a much greater extent than before, came with profound implications for Kuwaiti culture and the day-to-day lives of Kuwaiti citizens. Kuwait's new-found oil wealth enabled the state to invest money into a diverse number of development projects, resulting in an era of modernization, social and economic development, and prosperity. Kuwait is today a transformed country with a state-of-the-art infrastructure and a strong welfare system, both of which benefit the state and, by extension, its citizens. Kuwaitis also benefit directly from oil wealth: today Kuwaitis are among the wealthiest people in the world, enjoying one of the highest per-capita incomes. The Kuwait Investment Authority was founded in 1953 to manage funds of the Kuwaiti government. In 1976 the Kuwait Future Generations Fund (FGF) was set up. Today, in accordance with Kuwaiti law, 10 per cent of all annual state income is transferred to the fund. FGF invests outside Kuwait and the fund also receives 10 per cent of the income of the General Reserve Fund (GRF) – the general reserve of the state of Kuwait. The incomes have been huge and the programme for citizens is extensive.[62]

The government has built a comprehensive state-financed scheme of welfare that contains a provision by the Ministry of Social Affairs for affordable housing for financially less well-off Kuwaiti citizens. In addition, the government provides financial assistance to citizens in need, loans to disabled people to start businesses, free education and free healthcare.[63]

---

62 For more information on the Kuwait Investment Authority and the different funds, see http://www.kia.gov.kw/en/Pages/default.aspx. Accessed January 16, 2019. In October 2014 the Jordanian media website al-Bawaba estimated the reserves of the two funds in Kuwait to be close to US$600 billion, see https://www.albawaba. com/business/kuwait-reserves-future-generations-hit-598- billion-616361. Accessed December 12, 2018.

63 In general, Kuwaiti society differentiates between male and female concerning duties in the family. Males are heads of households accountable for the welfare of the family, and females administer domestic responsibilities. The idea of the male responsibility towards the family is visible in the national laws in which males receive

The ruler also hands out cash gifts to citizens on occasions, such as the commemoration of Kuwait's liberation from the Iraqi occupation. In 2011, for example, to mark the 50th anniversary of independence and 20 years since the end of Iraqi occupation, amir Sabah al-Ahmad al-Jabir al-Sabah offered Kuwaiti citizens the equivalent of US$3,600 and 14 months of free food supplies.[64]

It is worth looking at three particular aspects of the Kuwaiti welfare state: healthcare, media and education. We will discuss the different ways in which state wealth and power are directed to benefit citizens, but are also used to foster a sense of loyalty towards the government and even suppress dissent. Special attention is given to education because of the link between education and the work of the al-Babtain Foundation.

Developing healthcare

Until the 1930s, before revenues from oil exports and concessions began flowing into the country, Kuwait lacked adequate healthcare provisions for its citizens. In 1910, the al-Sabah family called upon an English doctor stationed in Basra to come and help alleviate the situation. He came to Kuwait and under his expertise a hospital was built within a year.[65] According to Salih, no public hospital existed in Kuwait until 1946.[66] At that time, just after the Second World War, the government began receiving increasing revenues from oil concessions and exports and could afford to commence the construction of the welfare services it so badly needed – beginning with a public hospital.

The development of the health sector was rapid. Whereas in 1949, there was only one doctor per 25,000 citizens, ten years later, in the late 1950s, this number had risen to one doctor per 1,000 citizens. By the early 1960s, Kuwait had 10 hospitals hosting around 3,000 hospital beds and a staff of 340 doctors. There were also 37 health clinics, 128 school clinics, 24 dentists

---

the allowance from the government for children (in 2009 US$150 for every child in the family); see Abdulrahim, al-Kandari and Hasanen 2009: 59.

64 See, https://www.thestar.com/news/world/2011/02/16/life_in_kuwait_too_good_a_deal_for_revolt.html. Accessed October 4, 2018.

65 *Kuwait Today: A Welfare State* 1963: 41

66 Salih 1991: 47

and around 600 nurses operating with modern technology to provide healthcare for Kuwaiti citizens. In 1962, the ruler amir Abd Allah al-Salim al-Sabah opened up the new al-Sabah hospital, which at its time was one of the largest hospitals in the Middle East.[67] By this point, healthcare was of consistently high quality, geared towards providing citizens with adequate care on every level needed and was free for all citizens.[68] Mental healthcare was also developed early in Kuwait compared to other countries in the Middle East. The first mental health policy was introduced in 1957 and the resources invested in mental health in Kuwait have exceeded those of other Middle Eastern countries, as evidenced by the greater number of psychiatrists and psychiatric nurses in the country.[69]

The government's role in the national health expenditure is significant. In 2008 almost 77 per cent of the total expenditure on health came from the government and the remainder from the private sector.[70] For several years, the costs of the healthcare system have been called into question by leading Kuwaiti politicians, and as the 2007–2008 global financial crisis caused oil prices and production to fall and the GCC's external and fiscal surpluses to dwindle, voices calling for a rethink of Kuwait's health sector expenditure grew louder. Speaking at the United Nations General Assembly, September 25, 2013, the Kuwaiti prime minister Sheikh Jabir al-Mubarak al-Hamad al-Sabah stated that the welfare systems of the Arab Gulf states were unsustainable saying, "[T]he current welfare state that the Kuwaitis are used to is unsustainable." He also stated, "[I]t is necessary for Kuwaiti society to transform from a consumer of the nation's resources to a producer."[71] These statements referred not only to the healthcare system, but also all other benefits, from subsidized petrol and cheap electricity and water to the support of nationals receiving funds for housing and food.[72]

---

67 *Kuwait Today: A Welfare State* 1963: 47

68 See *Kuwait Today: A Welfare State* 1963: 42 and Salih 1991: 49.

69 Okasha, Karam and Okasha 2012: 53

70 Alkhamis, Hassan and Cosgrove 2013: 67

71 See https://uk.reuters.com/article/uk-kuwait-economy-pm/kuwaits-pm-says-welfare-state-is-unsustainable-calls-for-cuts-idUKBRE99R0GL20131028. Accessed January 9, 2019.

72 It was reported in January 2014 that the government proposed the introduction of a four-year reform programme to reduce the financial dependency on oil, including a reduction of some of the subsidies; see https://www.gfmag.com/magazine/

But there is more to the story: as a result of socio-political considerations, healthcare became a key tool in the government's welfare system arsenal to keep citizens content. The rapid development of a healthcare system has been vital in order to win support from Kuwaiti citizens. By serving this basic human need, doing so at a high standard, but also firmly linking the idea of welfare provision to an understanding of Islam which supports the role of amirs as rulers of the country and its citizens, the government has engendered dependence, goodwill and loyalty.

From local to global media

When Kuwait embarked upon its transition into a highly developed country, the state needed to expand the media sector.[73] Kuwait was in need of a functioning media apparatus including television, newspapers and radio, and oil revenues were utilized to fund the project.[74]

In 1951, Kuwait's first broadcasting station was launched from a small room inside a police compound.[75] A few private radio transmitters had been operating in the country prior to this, but before the founding of Radio Kuwait, to hear news of public interest people gathered in *diwaniyyat* or in cafés and listened to broadcasts from London, Berlin, Cairo or Baghdad.[76] At the outset, the new Kuwaiti broadcaster provided only a limited service, transmitting for only two hours a day. But before long these hours were extended. Radio proved a powerful tool for reaching people, and by 1958 listeners were tuning in to music programmes running throughout the evening, accessible to anyone with a radio receiver and a speaker. There was also a listeners' choice programme, where members of the public could call in and request their favourite song. In 1960, news broadcasts were added and the broadcasting hours were extended to over 16 hours. At times of

---

january- 2014/kuwait-reshaping-the-welfare-state. Accessed September 17, 2018.

73 For an overview of media development in Arab countries in general, see Gunter & Dickinson 2013.

74 Wheeler 2000: 434

75 The Kuwait News Agency (KUNA) briefly recalls the history of radio in Kuwait; see https://www.kuna.net.kw/ArticlePrintPage.aspx?id=2424349&language=en. Accessed January 22, 2019. Also see *Kuwait Today: A Welfare State* 1963: 31.

76 For a brief presentation of radio in Bahrain and Kuwait during the Second World War, see Ulaby 2010: 116f.

public emergency, such as when Iraq threatened the country in 1961, radio became an important instrument for the government to muster support and to put forward its interpretation of events. During the Iraqi occupation of 1990–1991, Radio Kuwait was relocated to the Saudi Arabian city of Dammam and played a similar role, being instrumental in generating support for the government in exile.

After the occupation, Radio Kuwait resumed its normal service and today state-run Radio Kuwait also faces competition from private radio stations, some of them online. Moreover, there are stations serving various communities in the country, as well as several religious radio channels.[77]

Kuwait's first television broadcast is usually dated to November 1961. However, Ibrahim Beayeyz states that TV broadcasting was actually initiated by a wealthy Kuwaiti merchant, Murad Bahbahani, who in late 1959 and early 1960 established a low-power TV station broadcasting cartoons and foreign films.[78] The government took over the station in 1961 and thereafter, for a long while, all television broadcasting in the country was under the aegis of the Ministry of Information.[79] In the 1970s and early 1980s, Kuwait Television advanced in terms of technology and facilities, moving to new buildings, increasing the volume and quality of productions and in 1978 creating a second channel, KTV2.

Later on, a number of private TV channels were added to the national ones. At the time of the Arab Satellite Agreement Organization (Arabsat) in 1976, Kuwait was the second largest shareholder (11.9 per cent) after Saudi Arabia (29.9 per cent).[80] The development of satellite capacity in Kuwait and the broader Middle East led to the establishment of many new channels such as the Egyptian ESC, the Saudi Arabian MBC and the

---

77 https://www.kuna.net.kw/ArticlePrintPage.aspx?id=2424349&language=en, https://www.bbc.co.uk/news/world-middle-east-14646837. Accessed January 11, 2019. Also see *Kuwait Today: A Welfare State* 1963: 32.

78 Beayeyz 1989: 15

79 The communications infrastructure in general was very limited. In 1961 an exchange was set up by British Telecom that served 200,000 Kuwaitis, and in 1965 2,000 international calls were made from Kuwait. This number had increased by 1986 to 500,000 calls. This increase in the number of calls epitomizes the development of the telecommunication structure; see Wheeler 2000: 434.

80 Sakr 2001: 9

Qatari al-Jazeera.[81] Since the introduction of locally produced and foreign satellite TV, Kuwaitis can view as many channels as any other individual in the world, and the offerings are more or less the same as in other countries.[82] Consequently, from the mid-1990s, the general access to information was high in comparison to many countries including European and North American states.[83] Some commentators also believe that the experience of the Iraqi occupation spurred the Kuwaiti authorities to update the country's telecommunications technology. This modernization programme was therefore not merely instigated to serve consumer needs, but it was also a matter of national security.[84]

Cinemas are widespread and popular in Kuwait. Cinescape, the Kuwait National Cinema Company, is a private company dominating the distribution of films in Kuwait and has built a number of movie theatres throughout the country. It is also a major distributor of films in the Middle East in Arabic, Persian and a variety of other languages from, for example, India. Cinemas play a significant role in public life in Kuwait; most movie theatres are located in shopping malls and watching a film is a popular leisure activity. The majority of films screened at the cinemas in Kuwait are produced in the United States, and this dominance is also reflected in the films screened on Kuwaiti television. In comparison with cinema, TV offers a lot more entertainment in Arabic, and several programmes are produced in Kuwait, though most are products of pan-Arab TV originating primarily from Egypt.[85] Viewers in Kuwait have had access to Netflix since 2016 and Amazon is also available, though where online shopping is concerned, customers in Kuwait have to go to the UAE address of Amazon and have items shipped to Kuwait from there.

---

81 Sakr 2001: 15. The rapid development of a broad communication infrastructure from the 1960s to the 1990s is also described in Wheeler 2000.

82 In a study on the effects of media on understanding of the female and male body, only 13 per cent of the persons in the poll stated that they watched Kuwait TV; see Mitchell et al. 2014: 77.

83 Wheeler 2000: 434f

84 Wheeler 2000: 435 and Mitchell et al. 2014: 76

85 Satti 2013: 3ff. Kuwait has a film industry and Cinescape was, for example, involved in the production of the first Kuwaiti film, *Sirb al-hamam* ("Swarm of Doves"), launched in 2018 and the first film about the 1990 Iraqi invasion produced in the country.

One of the first printed magazines in Kuwait was *al-Arabi*. This publication was – and still is – produced with the financial support of the Kuwaiti Ministry of Information. It was established in 1958 and was at the time the leading magazine in the Arab-speaking world, covering such topics as literature, society and politics. At the time of its launch, Kuwait's population was close to 210,000 people, and *al-Arabi* had some 85,000 subscribers, with average monthly sales through newsstands numbering roughly the same. Yet *al-Arabi* was a magazine sold in many Arabic-speaking countries and not just in Kuwait.[86] The first daily newspaper, *al-Siyasa*, appeared in the mid-1960s. In 1977, the publishing house of *al-Siyasa* launched a daily newspaper in English, *Arab Times*. However, the oldest newspaper in English, the *Kuwait Times*, was established in 1961. making it the oldest national news publication in Kuwait after *al-Arabi*. As in many other countries, print media suffered from the arrival of new media in the form of satellite TV and later the internet. Following the passing of a new media and press law in 2006, the number of daily newspapers has fluctuated between 10 and 20. Almost all of these have been private ventures. Many of the newspapers have adapted to the new media landscape by developing digital platforms and referencing social media in their reporting.[87]

In terms of press freedom, Kuwait is seen as less repressive than many other countries in the Middle East. Freedom House has described the situation regarding the media in Kuwait as "partly free".[88] Indeed, there is public debate on various issues relating to governance and state policies, and views in the media are diverse and sometimes critical of the state. Articles 36 and 37 of the constitution stipulate that freedom of opinion, scientific research, press and publication is guaranteed; however, these freedoms are "[S]ubject to the conditions and stipulations specified by Law (…)."[89] A new press and

---

86 *Kuwait Today: A Welfare State* 1963: 37. The size of the population is from Hill 1969: 84 and his review of the census of 1957.

87 https://www.cjr.org/analysis/why_kuwaits_news_outlets_are_ahead_of_the_digital_game.php. Accessed January 27, 2019.

88 https://freedomhouse.org/report/freedom-press/2016/kuwait. Accessed October 4, 2018. Reporters without Borders ranks Kuwait as 105th out of 180 countries in the 2018 World Press Freedom Index and points towards unclarity in the cyber-crime law in effect in January 2016 and various actions taken by the government concerning media; see https://rsf.org/en/kuwait. Accessed January 27, 2019.

89 https://www.constituteproject.org/constitution/Kuwait_1992.pdf?lang=en.

publications law was promulgated in 2006 strengthening the protection of journalists from prosecution and imprisonment and liberalizing the licensing of new newspapers. Consequently, several new dailies appeared in Kuwait in 2007, including *al-Wasat, al-Sabah, al-Jarida* and *al-Nahar,* breaking a longstanding stranglehold of the market by just five publications since the 1970s. The print media has therefore been expanding in Kuwait at a time when its very survival has been called into question elsewhere. One reason for this was the potential they afforded to a new private and financially strong elite to influence discussions in the public sphere through the ownership of newspapers.[90] Articles 19, 20 and 21 of the 2006 press law concern the proscription of certain subjects.[91] The law forbids the defamation or slander of God, the Quran and the companions, wives and family of the Prophet Muhammad. It also outlaws any challenge to, or criticism of, the amir of the country as well as any display of disdain or contempt for the constitution, judges or the judicial system of Kuwait. Libel is also treated as a criminal offence in Kuwait and a defamation case can be subject to the penal code as well as the media law. One factor hampering press freedom in the Gulf is that the absence of clear laws creates ambiguity and effectively precludes journalists from truthfully reporting, say, the actions of prominent public figures for fear of being indicted for defamation.[92]

Publishers are also not allowed to circulate texts in Kuwait that would insult public morals or infringe upon the dignity of individuals or religious beliefs. Courts can hand down prison sentences for the defamation of religion. In addition to the law of 2006, a recent law took effect in 2016 concerning cyber-crime.[93] One outcome of the new legislation was

---

Accessed September 9, 2018.

90 This idea is from Selvik 2011. In addition, he states that the establishment of new newspapers is a reflection of a more and more complex political landscape in which discussions about questions concerning identity and ideology as well as personal rivalries are played out through newspapers; see Selvik 2011: 477f.

91 http://www.dailystar.com.lb/News/Middle-East/2006/Mar-07/70398-kuwait-passes-new-law-easing-freedom-of-press.ashx. Accessed January 30, 2019.

92 Duffy 2014: 12f. Duffy's article contains a discussion on Arab media regulations in the GCC countries and also brings to attention the legislation concerning, national security, public order, criticism of rulers and public officials and moral norms.

93 Azoulay (2020: 192) states that the cyber-crime law in combination with changes of the electoral law has undermined the opposition.

that online media must apply for a government licence to operate. The law relating to electronic media contains the same restrictions as the 2006 regulation forbidding slander and defamation of Islam in general and criticism of the amir. The regulations are reflected in online censorship, arrests and imprisonment of bloggers and online activists as well as the closing of art exhibitions. In 2015, al-Watan TV was taken off air due to allegations of anti-government activity, and in early 2018, London-based blogger Abdallah Saleh was sentenced to a 25-year gaol term *in absentia*.[94] Another problem area has been the emergence in the Gulf of female music performers from the 1970s and 1980s onwards, and specifically their public exposure through live stage performances and radio or TV broadcasts. Religious conservatives in Kuwait see the rise of female stars and media culture in general as harmful to traditional values. Religious lobby groups persistently exert pressure on the Kuwaiti authorities and the organizers of public performances by women, yet they cannot prevent performances from being broadcast on satellite TV or on the Internet.[95]

Online journalism, bloggers and social and satellite media have changed not only the media landscape but also provided transnational platforms for Arabs and the Arabic language. These forms of media are not easily censored and have in many cases performed an important role in giving the public access to information. Internet usage has been high in Kuwait since the introduction of the internet in 1993. Between 1994 and 1996, there were more internet hosts in Kuwait than in Poland or Greece.[96] Close to 80 per cent of the population accessed the internet in 2016, while the usage of smartphones is, as in many other countries, now firmly entrenched within modern culture.

According to statistics from 2018, internet usage among Kuwaitis now stands at virtually 100 per cent.[97] In 2018, the network was also improved

---

94 See https://freedomhouse.org/report/freedom-press/2016/kuwait and https://rsf.org/en/kuwait. Accessed May 4, 2018. For the closure of an art exhibition, see http://www.reorientmag.com/2012/07/its-a-mans-world-interview-with-shurooq-amin-kuwaits-rebel-with-a-cause/. Accessed April 30, 2018.

95 Ulaby 2010: 119f

96 Wheeler 2000: 434

97 For internet usage in 2016, see http://www.internetlivestats.com/internet-users-by- country/ and in 2018 almost a 100 per cent internet usage, see https://www.internetworldstats.com/me/kw.htm. Accessed February 1, 2019.

technically through the use of fibre-optic cables, and is now among the fastest in an Arabic-speaking countriy.[98] The internet in Kuwait has attracted young and female users, and the country has produced popular portals.[99] The growth of a modern and diverse media scene has seen the emergence of telecommunication companies such as Zain in Kuwait. The Zain group began life in 1983 under the name "Mobile Telecommunications Company" (MTC) and was renamed in 2007. It operates in at least eight countries and has over 6,000 employees.[100]

Abd al-Aziz al-Babtain and the al-Babtain Foundation are present on social media in the form of home pages, Facebook pages and YouTube.[101] In recent years, the names of the different home pages and YouTube channels have changed. Currently most of the recently published material on Facebook and YouTube as well as the home page is primarily in Arabic. They do have a social media presence in English, but it is not regularly updated. The numbers of visitors, followers and subscribers are low, irrespective of whether the social media outlet is in Arabic or in English, while the material presented is fairly static. The content of the various social media outlets also focuses primarily on the person of Abd al-Aziz al-Babtain. During a visit to Kuwait in October 2016, the recently appointed General Director of the Abd al-Aziz Saud al-Babtain Cultural Foundation, Touhami Abdouli, stated that he planned to reorganize the Foundation's social media presence. The new web page in Arabic is an improvement, but the quality as well as the outreach in terms of visitors and subscribers is still low.[102] The current trend on YouTube appears to focus more on discussions concerning various peace initiatives rather than presentations of Arab or Kuwaiti culture and poetry. The low number of visitors to the pages and the relative rigidity of the Foundation's social media content is not unique, as several comparable

---

98 http://www.arabtimesonline.com/news/kuwait-to-have-the-fastest-internet-in-the-arab-world/. Accessed January 27, 2019.

99 Hofheinz 2007: 68, 70

100 https://www.zain.com/en/. Accessed February 1, 2019. Even if it has slowed down, the ambition to grow and conquer markets have made Gulf telecom companies strong in a global context, see Smith 2009: 31ff.

101 In July 2020 the key web page was https://www.albabtaincf.org/ and the main Facebook page was https://www.facebook.com/albabtainprize. Accessed July 17, 2020.

102 For an example of the type of content and number of viewers, see the YouTube channel https://www.youtube.com/user/albabtainprize. Accessed July 20, 2020.

institutions worldwide face similar problems. The feeling within the al-Babtain Foundation is that it is enough to be present on social media and the presence is not accompanied by a dissemination strategy. It is, however, indicative of a disconnect between what the foundation represents and envisions and the contemporary social media culture, and thus an indication of the challenges that similar conceptualizations of Kuwaiti as well as, more broadly, Arab culture face in a globalized world driven by consumer culture.

The development of Kuwait's media scene, funded either directly or indirectly by oil revenues, has not taken place in isolation. Kuwait's oil-producing neighbours experienced a similar boom followed by a wave of economic, social and cultural changes which ushered in a period of rapid development and modernization. The example of the development of Kuwaiti radio and the link between the magazine *al-Arabi* and the state are also an illustration of how the government channelled financial resources in efforts to develop the country, but also of how it sought to control or even censor the flow of information through these media channels. The development of satellite TV and the internet have made the control of media more difficult, but at the same time provided a transnational forum for discussions among Arabs on a variety of topics. It has created an arena of competition between different growing markets. Finally, the use of contemporary communications technologies to construct, consolidate and promote Kuwaiti identity in a transnational market that challenges borders presents significant challenges and is riven by inherent contradictions.

Education: schooling modern Kuwaitis

A third key example of shifts in Kuwaiti society following the discovery and extraction of oil and the transformations this brought is the construction of an education system, modelled on those in Europe and North America. The development of education in Kuwait from the end of the 19th century has been discussed above. Here, I will focus on it in greater detail, discussing the impact of the transformations of the past 80 years.

Before the advent of the oil era, Kuwait had no state-run educational system. Historically, all education in Kuwait, as in many other countries of the Middle East, was private and often linked to mosques and *madrasa*.[103]

---

103 For a description of schooling in Egypt from colonial times and for the role

Thus, at the dawn of the 20th century, the Quran schools (*kuttab*, in plural *katatib*) were the only form of lower elementary school in Kuwait.[104] The curriculum focused on training students to read and recite the Quran and memorize the sayings and traditions (*hadith*) of the Prophet Muhammad. Pupils were also trained in the skill of reading and writing Arabic, including Quranic Arabic. At a later stage, paralleling the growth of trade in Kuwait, practical subjects such as basic arithmetic and science as well as elementary book-keeping entered the curriculum. Education was gender-segregated. Girls had female teachers and their schooling was limited to memorizing the Quran. There was nothing by way of educational infrastructure. Teaching took place primarily at the home of the teacher and teachers were paid directly by the students' parents. Instructionally pupils were learning by rote and no schoolbooks were available. In addition, there were no regulations stipulating admission at a certain age or a specified length of a child's education. Children's schooling customarily lasted only for around two to three years. There was no formal graduation, but the completion of the memorization of the Quran by a student was celebrated. The longer a pupil remained in education, the more he learnt about Islamic law.[105]

In 1911–1912, a group of prominent merchants decided to build Kuwait's first school, the al-Mubarakiyya. After the creation of the Customs authority, this was the second new institution established in Kuwait. Alebrahim sees the creation of al-Mubarakiyya school as a sign of the merchants' awareness of a changing political reality. He states, "The ideology that the merchants started to follow in this period was Islamic and modernist, with an initial focus on cultural and charity activities."[106] He also notes that at the same time as the merchants were placing a premium on education, the ruler, Mubarak, seems to have had no interest whatsoever in promoting it.[107]

---

of education in the framework of building a society and the ambition of the new education systems to create a modern citizen, see Starret 1998: 23–61. For a study of several national cases, see Daun and Walford 2004.

104 Another word for the elementary school in use was *maktab*, in plural *makatib*, see Meleis, El-Sanabary and Beeson 179: 116. For types of what is termed Islamic Education and the *kuttab*, see Daun, Arjomand and Walford 2004: 17–20.

105 al-Awadi 1957: 101f and *Kuwait Today: A Welfare State* 1963: 102

106 Alebrahim 2019: 24. The interest of the merchants in charity activities is also a foundation for the development of a tradition of charity in Kuwait, see chapter 6.

107 Alebrahim 2019: 25

Initially, the al-Mubarakiyya school had no clear curriculum and students were trained in the skills in demand at that time. Primarily it taught the same subjects as the *katatib* – commerce, arithmetic and bookkeeping – but in a more systematic manner. The al-Ahmadiyya school opened in 1921, with English added to the curriculum. Under the impact of the global economic recession, this school was forced to close down in 1931 due to lack of funds.

Merchants in Kuwait established a municipality in the year 1930 and a Council of Education in 1936. In 1937–1938, the new ruling body established the first girls' school and had the responsibility of managing existing schools and the opening of new ones. These were the first steps toward modernizing the country's education system. Here too, significantly, this development was stimulated and funded by private enterprise rather than at the instigation of the ruler, who was indifferent to education.[108]

In 1936–1937, before the oil rush, wealthy merchants again initiated the next wave of change in the country's educational system by levying a tax devoted to funding the newly established Educational Council and meeting educational needs within the country.[109] The creation of the girls' school also signalled a turning point in women's education.[110] In parallel with the development of schools for boys, female education was promoted in the 1940s and 1950s and, in 1952, the first secondary school for girls opened. By the 1970s the number of girls in education accounted for some 46 per cent of the total student population.[111]

The changes in the organization of education in the 1930s and the 1940s generated a demand for teachers who could teach new subjects like chemistry, geography, history and physics. In these early days, these teachers were brought in from Palestine and Syria. The teaching of new subjects was not always welcomed, especially when particular subjects were thought to threaten traditional religious beliefs. Thus, schooling in geography lessons about the earth being round or about rainfall being caused by climatic

---

108 al-Nakib 2016: 34f, al-Awadi 1957: 102, Meleis, El-Sanabary and Beeson 1979:116 and *Kuwait Today: A Welfare State* 1963: 102

109 al-Nakib 2016; 34f

110 Meleis, El-Sanabary and Beeson 1979: 116 and *Kuwait Today: A Welfare State* 1963: 103

111 There were less than 1,000 female students in 1946. This number had increased to 3,594 students in 1951; see Meleis, El-Sanabary and Beeson 1979: 116.

factors triggered protests, especially where girls' education was concerned. Likewise, for religious reasons some also objected to children being taught how to draw animals. After a couple of years, the new system became institutionalized, however, and the protests evaporated.[112]

Once the government had recognized the importance of an educational system and had the financial resources to fund it, it began reforming it. The great importance attached to this task is clearly apparent from the amount of funding the government channelled into education. In 1946, the Kuwaiti Department of Education, which would later be named the Ministry of Education, had an annual budget of 83,000 dinars. Three years later, in 1949, that figure had risen to 500,000 dinars, and reached 6 million dinars in 1955–1956. Just three years later, in 1959, it stood at 14 million dinars.[113] This pattern continues to this day, underscoring the importance the Kuwaiti government places on primary, intermediate and secondary education and the investment it is willing to make in an educated labour force. Part of the pattern is also a determination to control education. In 1971–1972 half of public spending was on education and in the budget of 1973–1974, state education spending exceeded the budget allocated to defence and was more than twice as large as public expenditure on health.[114]

The great advances in Kuwait's educational system may be gauged by the number of students enrolled in it. Although it is difficult to estimate the population of Kuwait in the pre-oil era, we know that in 1936, when the population was around 100,000, there were some 600 students, or 6 per cent of the population. By the early 1960s, with a population of almost 300,000, the number of students had risen to 60,000, or 20 per cent.[115] Behind this surge in the number of students in formal education was a general increase in population and a series of educational reforms begun in 1954. In building a formal educational system, the authorities had to start from scratch, which was a challenge: in the early days of the oil industry, there were few Kuwaitis with sufficient education and knowledge to run the day-to-day business of the country. Finding the people tasked with setting up and running an education system from a finite pool of talent was

112 al-Awadi 1957: 102
113 *Kuwait Today: A Welfare State* 1963: 102
114 Meleis, El-Sanabary and Beeson 1979: 116
115 al-Sabah 2018: 24f and *Kuwait Today: A Welfare State* 1963: 102

a challenge. The reforms began with a review of the existing system, carried out by two Arab educational experts, and, off the back of this, a detailed plan for a new system was drawn up. As with other developments in Kuwait around this time, the reforms of the educational system were effective in the sense that the rulers had the financial resources to implement the suggestions put forward by advisors.

Following expert recommendations, education in Kuwait was restructured into a three-step programme. In the mid-1950s, kindergartens opened and enrolled Kuwaiti children between the ages of four and six. The second step had them move on to elementary school, which lasted for four years and included reading, writing, mathematics, history, geography, art, science and Arabic language. After completing elementary school, pupils entered the third phase: a four-year programme of intermediate schooling. In 1956–1957, the system changed again and established the current form of elementary level of three years, intermediate of three years and secondary of three years.[116] In a sense, the national public education system that became compulsory for children between 6 and 14 in 1965, while it was a challenge to create, aimed to offer a solution to one of the government's most pressing problems: the lack of local Kuwaiti experts. Ever since the oil money had started to flow in, facilitating rapid development, the primary hold-up had not been funding change, but finding the experts needed to deliver it. Bringing in non-Kuwaitis was a solution to a widespread lack of Kuwaiti experts, but developing a modern education system created a means by which to end that dependence on outsiders and cultivate a steady supply of local experts.

The national system of education was guaranteed according to Article 40 of the constitution, stating that Kuwaiti citizens are entitled to free public schooling. In general, Sunni citizens are favoured before the Shi'a in the context of citizenship, and Shi'as are marginalized in many areas in society. Immigrants and the part of the population called *bidun* are excluded from free schooling. Since the free school system is linked to citizenship, and therefore excludes a substantial part of the resident population, most families in Kuwait today must pay for private education.[117] Private schools were

---

116 *Kuwait Today: A Welfare State* 1963: 102 and al-Awadi 1957: 105
117 For a discussion on education and democratic development in Kuwait, see al-Nakib 2015.

established in the country primarily from the 1970s onwards. They accept pupils with or without Kuwaiti citizenship and follow different curricula, including the national one, but also the ones adopted in the American, British, French and Indian education systems, including the one culminating in the International Baccalaureate.

The benefits of such a system for the state of Kuwait were manifold: not only were the authorities able to design and deliver the education programme they deemed necessary to equip a future workforce, but in providing this for free to citizens, they cultivated gratitude and loyalty from the Kuwaiti population. Moreover, by offering high-quality state schooling, they made it less likely that private citizens or groups might identify a need for independent or non-state schools that would be more difficult to monitor. In this way, the authorities controlled the substance of the curriculum, and had the ability to play a significant role in shaping the minds of the country's next generation. In the end, education became a system reflecting and perhaps reinforcing the hierarchies and inequalities of Kuwaiti society, as the educational system became yet another space where the clear distinction between the legal status of citizen and the transient status of migrant or *bidun* was institutionalized. In addition to the ethnic, religious and other status disparities, the gender-segregated public educational system played a crucial role in reproducing and upholding gender difference and hierarchies and establishing clear gender boundaries.[118]

In this context of state provision of free education for Kuwaiti citizens, and the reproduction of a value system endorsed by the authorities, relatively little space was left for individuals who share the values of the ruling family, like Abd al-Aziz Saʿud al-Babtain, to channel their energy and resources to set up structures that would duplicate the existing provision. Abd al-Aziz thus directed his charitable activities towards creating structures that would promote education outside Kuwait, but which propagated the traditional values that underpinned the Kuwaiti education system and, as I will discuss in chapter 6, state considerations and priorities. Since the 1970s, he and the al-Babtain Foundation have initiated numerous educational projects in several countries, ranging from schools to universities. He has also financially supported individual students and funded

---

118 In the case of Kuwait and the idea of education as an instrument controlling difference, see al-Nakib 2015: 6f.

academic chairs and programmes. In Kuwait, neither he nor any of the many branches of the al-Babtain Foundation have set up schools, but on a personal, as well as symbolic, level Abu Sa'ud is involved in education in Kuwait. He is a member of the Kuwaiti *National Committee for Educational Support*, a permanent committee set up by the Ministry of Education with its own financial endowment, tasked with raising the standard of education and undertaking educational projects in Kuwait.[119] Abd al-Aziz is also a member of the Board of Trustees of the College of Arts at the University of Kuwait and has also been recognized by the latter with the award of a honorary doctorate in 2015. Although Abu Sa'ud's educational work outside Kuwait is not replicated in the country itself, the inauguration of the al-Babtain Central Library for Arabic Poetry in 2006 enabled schools and the public to visit an institution specifically dedicated to classical poetry in Arabic. In conversations, officials at the library claimed that they have regular visits from schools. The founding of the library brought further recognition of Abd al-Aziz in Kuwait, through his appointment as Honorary President of the Kuwait Library and Information Society.[120]

Kuwait's strategy for education from 2005 to 2025, according to al-Nakib, presents the cultural identity of Kuwaitis as "national, singular and static, with the notions of thought and change conceptualized as potential threats to this status."[121] She goes on to describe how "Islam" is presented in terms of a monolithic religion and value system containing eternal values to be taught in schools as a foundation for children's identity. This presumed "Islamic" identity is seen as integral to Kuwaiti citizenship, but its portrayal of Islam disregards its considerable diversity and, at a more practical level, the differences between Kuwaiti Sunnis and Shi'as and the small community of Christian citizens – all of them equally diverse. It also excludes those within the population who profess no religious affiliation.[122] As we have already noted, Abd al-Aziz al-Babtain shares the goals and the views that are expressed in Kuwait's strategy concerning education, as his thinking on the preservation and a revival of the Arabic language and Arab identity also

---

119 See http://www.ibe.unesco.org/sites/default/files/Kuwait.pdf. Accessed October 23, 2020.

120 See *Abdulaziz Saud al-Babtain: Biography & Cultural Achievements* 2017.

121 al-Nakib 2015: 9

122 al-Nakib 2015: 9f

rests on a notion of it being a singular and unique identity that should be propagated through education and serve as a bond between the people of the small country.

Immediately after independence, in the early 1960s, Kuwaiti citizens were given the opportunity to travel around the world to study at foreign universities.[123] The study-abroad programme was entirely state-financed, meaning that it was free for individual students with citizenship. Many families were reluctant in the 1960s and the 1970s to permit especially their young daughters to go to non-Muslim countries and had a preference to let female students go to other Muslim countries,[124] indicating an affinity with people sharing the same religion as they and, presumably, the same moral codes. Again, this belief in the fundamental commonality of moral codes of other Muslim societies and the need to support these and reinforce them is an underlying element in the work of Abu Sa'ud and the al-Babtain Foundation.

The creation of Kuwait University in 1966 had a significant impact on higher education in Kuwait in general. For female students, the effect was significant since 42 per cent of the first class of 418 students were women. Ten years later, in 1976, the university had developed considerably and the total number of undergraduate students in the spring semester was 4,864 and 50 per cent of the students were Kuwaiti citizens, and most students were female (61 per cent). At the beginning of the 1970s, graduate studies were introduced while medical education began in 1977.[125] In the early 1980s, a College of Sharia and Islamic Studies was established and a decree to create a Faculty of Social Sciences was issued in 1998.[126] The development continued and, for example, in 2013 Faculties of Public Health and Life Sciences were introduced. Today there are 1,565 faculty

---

123 Before the creation of the al-Mubarakiyya school in 1911, the sons of wealthy merchants were sent to India and Iraq for higher education; see Alebrahim 2019: 25.
124 In 1975–1976 one Kuwaiti female student was awarded a scholarship to England, but of the 255 available for studying in Egypt the same year 45 per cent went to women; *Kuwait Today: A Welfare State* 1963: 104 and Meleis, El-Sanabary and Beeson 1979: 119.
125 Meleis, El-Sanabary and Beeson 1979: 119f.
126 Kuwait has not yet perceived a development of universities defined as Islamic universities like many other Muslim communities and societies have in the last decades. For an example of a study discussing the influence of Islamic universities and their role in transmitting ideas on understandings of Islam, see Bano and Sakurai 2015.

members and 40,000 students.[127]

The Kuwaiti educational system suffered during the Iraqi invasion in 1990. Students who fled Kuwait at that time attended schools or universities abroad, and the Kuwaiti government in exile founded five schools in Egypt that followed the system of education in Kuwait. After the liberation, the school system was rebuilt and students of all levels were offered extended semesters and intensive programmes in order to catch up. To what extent this was successful is difficult to judge, but according to Safwat, the damage to the system was relatively light. In addition, transcripts, records and files in the system were not destroyed.[128]

As in many other Gulf countries, higher education and education in general has become a global business.[129] In higher education, private universities are relatively common in Kuwait. The first private university in the country was the Gulf University for Science and Technology (GUST) which received its first batch of students in the autumn of 2002. Today the list of universities accredited by the Council of Private Universities contains nine universities including GUST, and universities such as American University of Kuwait, Australian College of Kuwait and the Maastricht Business School.[130]

Other components of education such as literacy programmes and adult education as well as vocational training in Kuwait have contributed, alongside more formal types of education, to increasing the rate of literacy and vocational training among adult Kuwaitis since independence. In 2018, the literacy rate across the total population was 96.06 per cent (96.67 per cent for males and 94.91 per cent for females).[131] Official government records from 1957 indicate that 46 per cent of the male population and 74 per cent of females above 10 years of age were illiterate. This change has been achieved through an expansion of education and adult education since independence[132] and the expansion of vocational training and private

---

127 See http://kuweb.ku.edu.kw/ku/AboutUniversity/AboutKU/BriefHistory/index.htm Accessed February 6, 2022.

128 Safwat 1993: 18

129 For a general overview of higher education in Arabic-speaking countries, see Herrera 2007.

130 See http://www.puc.edu.kw/UnivTrust.aspx. Accessed February 24, 2019.

131 See http://uis.unesco.org/country/KW. Accessed March 15, 2019.

132 Meleis, El-Sanabary and Beeson 1979: 120

higher education in the 1990s. Although the development of vocational training was intended to open up possibilities for Kuwaitis to enter the job market, especially if they had not been able to go to university, and to promote the government's policy of young Kuwaitis replacing non-nationals in the workforce, this type of education is not especially popular as many Kuwaitis consider it less prestigious than attending university.[133]

Abd al-Aziz al-Babtain has lived throughout the formation of the Kuwaiti welfare state and has, like all other citizens of the country, benefited from the expansion of services since the advent of oil. In common with many famous entrepreneurs, Abu Sa'ud did not finish his formal education, a fact he has repeatedly stressed in interviews and conversations. Yet education is one of the areas he has chosen to engage in by serving on committees for the promotion of education and, more importantly, by creating a library and building a foundation that supports Arabic poetry, literature, and culture in Kuwait and in many other countries. These projects are informally linked to the broader educational goals of the country of developing an educated and trained workforce and of preserving the state and education as a tool to promote a Kuwaiti nationalism that supports the ruling family.

The activities of the al-Babtain Foundation – the creation of a poetry prize, publications and the initiative to promote dialogue between different cultures – all have an educational purpose. The ambition to educate is also central to its many investments in students, school-building programmes and training courses in the teaching of Arabic and poetry. Its support for students started in 1974 when Abd al-Aziz established a scholarship for disadvantaged students to go abroad and finish their education. In the first year the scholarship was in operation, five students were sent to the United States, United Kingdom and France. After the liberation of Kuwait the numbers increased, including students from countries defined by Abu Sa'ud as Islamic (for the most part countries with nominally Muslim majority populations that emerged after the break-up of the Soviet Union in December 1991). The number of students subsequently grew further, with the provision of support for 50 students from Palestine (male and female) and another 50 from African countries. According to Abd al-Aziz, the foundation has to date supported more than 10,000 students completing

133 See Bilboe 2011

their master's degrees and PhDs. The plan is to expand further; in one of our discussions in October 2016, Abu Saʻud stated that he had just signed off applications for students from Togo, Somalia and Chad to study abroad, and added that students from China, Niger, Togo and Russia were among those he had supported over the last 15 years. In addition, he also disclosed that, from 2016 on, the foundation would also fund the education of students from Australia, Russia and Brazil These activities are supplemented by the Foundation's funding for chairs in Arabic and Arab culture at universities throughout the world, as well as training programmes in Arabic.[134]

Poetry and the Arabic language have been at the heart of the al-Babtain Foundation since it began in Cairo in 1989 as the "Abdul Aziz Saud al-Babtain Prize for Poetic Creativity". The focus on poetry and Arabic has developed over the years to embrace a broader vision of promoting Arab culture through schools, centres and chairs for Arab culture.[135] According to the web page of the Foundation, al-Babtain chairs for Arab culture and support for programmes in Arabic studies are in place today in countries as diverse as Chad, China, France, Italy, Mauritania, Netherlands, Spain, Sudan, Togo and the United Kingdom,[136] and schools have been built in no fewer than 26 countries. Abu Saʻud also states that the foundation has actively worked to develop and deliver courses in Arabic for judges, teachers and ministers, as well as students in the Comoros. His rationale is that the Comoros is an Arab state where, over time, Swahili and French supplanted Arabic. Accordingly, Abu Saʻud claims, the Arabization effort has been received very positively by the people of the country and its president,[137] and the Comoros has become a model for similar work in Chad.

As Leichtman shows, Kuwait has been a generous provider of foreign aid, numbering among the top Arab donors. Leichtman gives many examples of how the state of Kuwait has assisted Syrians, Iraqis and Yemenis, and how

---

134 Atzori 2014: 37f and interviews with Abd al-Aziz October 17 and 18, 2016.
135 In article three of the Foundation's objectives it is stated that one aim is to contact "(...) Arabic language professors at Arab Universities, and in Oriental studies department at foreign universities, to explore means of cooperation in the field of Arabic poetry, regarding creativity, criticism and research." See *Years of Cultural Output 1989–2015* 2015: 10.
136 https://www.albabtaincf.org/chair-of-babtain. Accessed April 8, 2019.
137 Atzori 2014: 38. The Foundation's activities and part of an Arabization project in the Republic of the Comoros will be discussed further in chapter 6.

para-state organizations and Kuwaiti NGOs have engaged in development projects in many African states. Moreover, she demonstrates that Kuwait's humanitarianism is anchored in the public consciousness and constitutes a source of pride and an element of the identity politics of the state which promotes and showcases it, not only internationally but also domestically, to citizens of all ages to such an extent that the country's humanitarian engagement is featured in school textbooks. However, Leichtman also says that the humanitarianism of Kuwait is a strategic part of the foreign policy of the country and that the financial assistance provided by Kuwait is linked to the country's "effort to gain political support."[138] Many charitable and development organizations like the Kuwaiti Fund for Arab Economic Development (KFAED) are clearly associated with the Ministry of Finance, Ministry of Foreign Affairs and the Ministry of Social Affairs and Labour, while others are more international, such as the International Islamic Charitable Organization (IICO).[139] The aims can also be different in the sense that KFAED undertakes development projects and has the ambition to promote Kuwait, while the IICO combines activities which focus on the spread of Islam and development projects. The charitable and educational work of Abd al-Aziz and the al-Babtain Foundation is not formally linked to Kuwaiti ministries or policies concerning foreign assistance, but some of its activities broadly shadow the humanitarian assistance provided by Kuwaiti organizations.

The al-Babtain Foundation's choice of countries to support is linked to the intention to develop the areas in which Arabic is spoken and to promote a singular Arab identity in those areas. In the case of the al-Babtain Foundation, Islam appears as an embedded and self-evident value system that is closely aligned with its interpretation of Arab culture. In Abu Sa'ud's view, culture refines people's values. However, in his opinion, Arabs have lost touch with their culture and have been experiencing a cultural decline. He refers to the era of Harun al-Rashid, the caliph of the Abbasid caliphate who died in 809 C.E., and states that in those days the Arabs focused on culture and translated texts from the Persian, Roman and Indian civilizations. Arabs were respected and their language spread from southern France to China. As interest in Arab culture has declined over the last 500 years, he

---

138 Leichtman 2017: 5
139 Leichtman 2017:6f and 11, Benthall and Bellion-Jourdan 2009: 41 and 116 and Naser 2017.

has resolved to work towards revitalizing it. For him, culture is key to how Arabs should come closer to what he describes as the advanced nations. In conjunction with his ideas on culture, Abd al-Aziz takes a teleological view of religion – in other words, God created humans for a purpose. This purpose can only be effective if humans have high morals, contribute to society and achieve God's will by being good and productive individuals who observe the *zakat* (almsgiving, one of the Five Pillars of Islam) and seek blessings from other human beings. Seen in this light, the state has an obligation to promote a benevolent society. The relationship between the citizen and the state is founded on the state as a provider for the citizen in return for loyalty. For Abu Sa'ud, the true basis of this purpose in life – culture and morals – has been eroded in contemporary society, making it imperative that Arab citizens, especially the young generation, connect to their heritage in order to become part of the effort to create a good society.[140]

This overview of the development and the current state of healthcare, media and education in Kuwait illustrates how the state's rulers have engaged in and encouraged institution-building. Since independence, they have established strong institutions that make up Kuwait's comprehensive welfare system, education provision and the country's relatively free media. Their main objective in this drive, as stated at the beginning of the chapter, has been to preserve political stability and legitimize the right to dynastic rule. Through the creation of a bond between subjects and rulers in which it is the duty of the rulers to provide welfare and education in exchange for loyalty and stability, the state has managed to outmanoeuvre groups antagonistic to the new dynastic family-founded monarchism with power ambitions of their own.[141]

---

140 Interview with Abd al-Aziz October 17, 2016. On the role of *zakat* and charity, see Benthall and Bellion-Jourdan 2009: 7–28.
141 The idea of dynastic monarchism is from Herb 1999:67ff.

5

KUWAIT EXPERIENCING CHALLENGES: THE SUCCESS OF AL-BABTAIN

1960s boom and 1970s chaos: the desire to diversify and industrialize

Foreign powers have long intervened in the Gulf, drawn by the region's geographical importance and its position as a vital stopping-off point on multiple trade routes. The region's coastal areas were dominated by the Ottomans and then the British long before oil was discovered, and in the petrochemical era large multinational energy companies and the governments that own or back them have been closely involved in the pricing and exploitation of oil, by way of securing their own supply needs and furthering their geopolitical interests and designs. In the 1960s, however, a shift occurred in regional politics of the Gulf, which saw the region as a whole become more independent and the states there take greater control of their domestic oil reserves.[1]

In considering Kuwait's development thus far, this shift towards a more internal-looking mode in the 1960s followed the broader trend of development and the state's firmer control of the country's future – whether through its education system, media, new physical and economic infrastructure, broader welfare provision for citizens or organization of the state or culture. It was during this decade that Abd al-Aziz became the agent for many businesses, primarily in Kuwait and Saudi Arabia, but also in cities around the Mediterranean and in Afghanistan. His elder brother Abd al-Latif joined him in business in 1964, and his younger brothers, Abd al-Wahab and Abd al-Karim, who were at university until 1973, went to work for him after

---

1 For an introduction to the modern history of the Gulf, see Commins 2014. For a study on the ruling families including the al-Sabah, see Herb 1999.

gradutation.[2] Consumer goods has been a key business for the commercial enterprise of Abd al-Aziz al-Babtain. However, from the 1960s onwards, his portfolio expanded to include acquisitions and investments in several financial areas such as property, entertainment, education, banking, electronics, electrical appliances and fast-moving consumer goods, for example, packaged foods, beverages and other consumables. The development of Abu Sa'ud's business undertakings is an example of how merchants and trading families abandoned their former role of participating in the country's decision-making processes to focus on protecting their financial interests. Jill Crystal states, "[M]erchant claims have not been put forward because of a tacit deal between the rulers and the trading families, a trade of wealth for formal power."[3] In this context, as the state created a regulatory framework beneficial to Kuwaiti entrepreneurs, ties were established not only with old elites, but also with new and domestic entrepreneurs and businesspeople like Abd al-Aziz.[4] Crystal also states that the advent of oil income created changes in the coalition among the elite families and maintained continuity at the highest level of the political system.[5] Abu Sa'ud thus exemplifies a category of business people in Kuwait that has firmly given its backing to the rulers as they undertake to continuously provide a business environment promoting Kuwaiti entrepreneurs' interests to the extent that the latter become dependent on the state and the ruler.

An early attempt in the Middle East to challenge foreign interests over oil took place in the early 1950s. After a period of internal turmoil and involvement of foreign powers such as the United States, Britain and the Soviet Union, the Iranian prime minister Muhammad Mossadegh (1882–1967), who came to power in April 1951, attempted to nationalize Iran's petroleum industry to assert his country's independence from British and American oil

---

2 Atzori 2014: 37. Also note the Law of Commercial Companies from 1960 requiring that 51 per cent a copmpany should be owned by a Kuwaiti. Foreigners were also prohibited from owning property and could not do business in banking and finance. In addition, there were restrictions for import agencies and only Kuwaitis could start a company; see Crystal 1989: 431f.

3 Crystal 1989: 427, 430f

4 Abu Sa'ud represents a new type of self-made and pioneering entrepreneur and in this capacity he becomes a part of the balance of power in Kuwait discussed by Alebrahim 2019.

5 Crystal 1989: 427, 430f

monopolies.[6] His effort to nationalize the oil industry was not successful, and his government was toppled in a coup supported by the United States in August 1953. This was a difficult time to attempt to push back against the Great Powers. In the early 1960s, oil-exporting countries like Kuwait were in the process of discovering and consolidating their identity as nation-states and disengaging themselves from the last vestiges of colonial rule. Their economies faced uncertainty, subject as they were to overbearing European and North American influence and attempts to control global energy markets. The decision of major oil companies in the Gulf region in 1959 and again in 1960 to cut the price of oil without consultation with local governments and ruling bodies angered regional rulers, who saw such steps as arbitrary and profoundly threatening to their own states' sovereignty, since they undermined the Gulf rulers' ability to reach independent political decisions.[7]

After decades of growth, the so-called Golden Era, pressure began to mount on Kuwait and its neighbours in an area that they could hardly ignore: state finances. As the situation grew more critical, oil-exporting countries joined together to take on the global giants with a collective defence against foreign influence over oil politics.[8] This new collective approach to oil politics manifested itself in the formation of the Organization of the Petroleum Exporting Countries (OPEC) in Baghdad in September 1960. To begin with, OPEC comprised five oil-exporting countries working together to decide on key issues such as pricing and supply, and to act as a single independent body against foreign influences.[9] The intention was to assert the right of its member states to have enduring authority and control over their natural resources in the interest of their national development.[10] In its early days, OPEC was weak due to a high level of production of oil globally, but the June 1967 war between Israel and its Arab neighbours was a pivotal moment that signalled a fundamental shift in the balance of power in the politics of oil.

Following this assertion of independence, the 1970s were a turning point

---

6 Ayoob 1981: 119 and Commins 2014: 126f

7 Commins 2014: 168f

8 Ayoob 1981: 119

9 The first five member states were Iran, Iraq, Kuwait, Saudi Arabia and Venezuela.

10 For OPEC's self-presentation of the history of the organization, see https://www. opec.org/opec_web/en/about_us/24.htm. Accessed September 17, 2019.

for oil-producing countries in the Middle East. Direct foreign influence diminished, and outside control by non-regional forces over the politics and economies of oil production and exploitation decreased substantially. The establishment of OPEC and, later, of the Gulf Cooperation Council (GCC) in the early 1980s illustrated the need for collaboration between recently established states, but was also part of the process of moving from nominal to substantive independence. The regional collaboration in the context of the GCC was also impelled by the Iranian revolution of 1979 which deposed the Shah, civil unrest in Saudi Arabia that culminated in the seizure by militants of the Grand Mosque in Mecca in that same year and the war between Iran and Iraq from 1980 to 1988. The ambitious objectives of the GCC are outlined in the next chapter. In Article 4, it is stated that the collaboration between member states should concern several issues such as commerce, finance, customs, education, culture and legislation. The first Secretary General of GCC was Abd Allah Bishara, a Kuwaiti career diplomat.[11]

The Arab-Israeli War of 1973 (also known as the Ramadan, Yom Kippur, or October War) and the ensuing Arab oil embargo demonstrated the newly won independence and power of oil-exporting countries around the Gulf.[12] In 1973, a coalition of Arab countries led by Egypt and Syria joined forces to attack and invade Israel. The Gulf states, including Kuwait, which was one of the founding members of OPEC, pledged their support to the invading countries. Following the war, OPEC imposed an oil embargo on states that offered military or economic support to Israel. The embargo was absolute, and these countries – primarily the United States, South Africa, the Netherlands and Portugal – were unable to buy oil.[13] This significantly affected the economies of these countries but was also a turning point in the politics of oil. Global powers, states and/or transnational oil companies were no longer the masters of supply and pricing. Instead, OPEC had forced foreign powers to take its member states seriously. This was a new departure in the Gulf region. OPEC and its member states had shown that they could negotiate and impose their own agenda in global energy politics.[14]

---

11 Legrenzi 2015: 30–34
12 Ayoob 1981: 121
13 https://history.state.gov/milestones/1969-1976/oil-embargo. Accessed July 17, 2017.
14 For a brief overview of the actions taken by OPEC and its Arab member states in relation to the war in 1973, see Commins 2014: 200ff.

During the oil embargo of 1973, oil importers continued to purchase crude oil from the Middle East and North Africa. But with decreased supply from oil-exporting countries, the price of crude soared in the face of growing global demand. This was a very lucrative moment for the Gulf states and Kuwait in particular as they received huge amounts of foreign capital. New oil revenues poured into development projects, foreign investment and contributions to the welfare budget.[15] Funding was also now available for new projects such as the building of national armies and security forces.

However, this vast increase in oil revenues also brought to a head an issue that had been a point of concern for the rulers of Kuwait for some considerable time. Even in the early 1960s, the government of Kuwait had realized that its exclusive reliance on oil as a source of revenue was unsustainable for the future of the economy.[16] Fluctuating exchange rates, volatile oil prices and falling global demand had the capacity to inflict quick and lasting damage on the country's economy. There was only one solution, and that was to diversify the economy and counterbalance Kuwait's dependency on oil with other forms of industrial production. But familiar old problems reared their heads once more: the scarcity of skilled labour and the country's lack of non-carbon-based resources challenged efforts to diversify and further industrialize.[17]

The Kuwaiti government's response was to undertake central planning on a national scale, and direct all resources and efforts towards achieving nationwide objectives. Central planning began in 1962 when the first development plan for the late 1960s and early 1970s was put in place.[18] The dual aim of this plan was to reduce oil dependency and reliance on imported foreign labour. An additional purpose was to improve educational levels amongst Kuwaitis in order to boost the proportion of nationals in the workforce.[19] At the time, it was necessary for the government to act domestically in order to promote industrialization, since Kuwaitis lacked both the

---

15 Incomes from oil increased in Kuwait from US$1.4 billion in 1972 to US$6.5 billion in 1974, see Commins 2014: 202.

16 Salih 1991: 48

17 Salih 1991: 48

18 Owen & Pamuk 1999: 215

19 Owen & Pamuk 1999: 215

technical skills and resources to undertake any major industrial endeavours. But even with the support of a wealthy, powerful government, the road to industrialization was not easy. The will to diversify was hampered by rentierism; between 1970 and 1980, Kuwait's income from oil represented more than 90 per cent of governmental fiscal revenues. At the same time, the country reduced its oil production from about 3 to 1.6 million barrels a day.[20] Another obstacle was the need to embed a manufacturing industry in local society and to recognize the time it took to industrialize a society in a situation in which there is no historical relation to a mode of production. Industrialization in the Gulf was dependent to a large extent on external dynamics rather than internal ones.[21]

Industrialization in Kuwait succeeded in some regards but failed in others. Kuwait's economy stayed largely dependent on oil and there was, and still is, a strong link between oil revenues and government spending.[22] The capital gained from the 1973 oil embargo and in the years following was used to acquire a better infrastructure, construct more efficient oil operations and improve ports and tankers – all actions that helped increase productivity in the Kuwaiti oil sector.[23]

By the beginning of the 1970s, many Gulf countries had developed their own skilled workers and national expertise, enabling them to handle oil operations without foreign domination of the industry. Kuwait did the same, moving to nationalize the Kuwaiti Oil Company just after the 1973 war. By 1975, the nationalization process was complete, and the government was in full control of this commercial enterprise. The ability to run the oil industry nationally with less foreign assistance and the nationalization of the Kuwait Oil Company further strengthened Kuwait's position as a sovereign nation.[24]

In the development of the manufacturing sector in the mid-1970s, the expansion of larger businesses promoted the growth of professional Kuwaiti administrators and managers. Kuwaitis were less prevalent in the service

---

20 Kaboudan 1988: 45–47. Revenues from investments abroad is not included in the governmental fiscal budget.
21 Looney 1990: 533f
22 Kaboudan 1988: 47
23 Owen & Pamuk 1999: 205
24 Owen & Pamuk 1999: 206

sector and in mid-level positions, and were overwhelmingly outnumbered by non-Kuwaitis in the lower-level positions and in the ranks of manual workers, as well as in areas such as trade and construction.[25]

It was very difficult at the time to make domestic industries financially efficient and profitable. Two primary issues had to be dealt with: firstly there was a lack of skilled labour hindering efficiency and innovation, and secondly, there was the disincentive created by massive foreign investment, since much of the earnings was spent on speculation in property or stocks as well as on investments made abroad. At the time, foreign investments were mainly handled by the Kuwaiti Investment Office, which also established a fund with the purpose of allocating money to future generations in Kuwait.[26] A third issue concerned the vulnerability inherent in dependence on oil prices for government budgeting and how the government role was reduced to "(...) ensure income distribution rather than to plan its expenditures in a production-oriented manner that would enhance growth and development".[27] In other words, the focus of policymakers was to solve questions concerning deficits and their socio-economic effects, rather than diversify the industry and reduce dependence on oil. Although, from a financial perspective, it would have been theoretically possible to achieve diversification if the government had pressed for it, in practice it was difficult to accomplish.

The large amount of income received from foreign investments discouraged internal investment in domestic industries, as better returns on capital could be achieved by investing money outside of Kuwait. Even from the public sector and government, there was a dramatic reduction in domestic investment. In the 1970s and early 1980s, a growing proportion of government income came from overseas investments, and this was considerably larger in contrast to the revenue received from domestic investments.[28]

By the 1980s, foreign investment returns made up around 27 per cent of total government revenues.[29] Most of the money invested abroad was placed in highly effective economies in Western Europe and North

---

25 Lawson 1985: 17f
26 Owen & Pamuk 1999: 208
27 Kaboudan 1988: 48. See also Herb 2009: 382.
28 Lawson 1985: 18
29 Lawson 1985: 18

America. Foreign investments and financial speculation remained the chief monetary focus throughout the 1970s until the crash of the unofficial stock market, the Suq al-Manakh, in 1982, which forced the government to consolidate fiscal management. In 1975, the government of Kuwait made a final concerted effort to boost industrialization, with a plan for the period from 1975 to 1981. In the event, however, this plan was severely compromised by high inflation rates and the spectre of previous failures at state-sponsored industrial enterprise. Investment focus once again turned towards foreign investments, as revenues could be more easily obtained that way than from investing in more efficient economies.[30]

The government of Kuwait and many Kuwaitis deemed it unnecessary to invest in domestic industries when they simply could turn to other countries whose economies were more efficient and more developed. This new attitude of resentment on the part of the government and of many Kuwaitis, and lack of efficient and adequate investments into domestic industries, would have seriously negative consequences for both the business climate in Kuwait and the economy itself. The 1973 hike in the oil price and the enormous revenues that ensued enriched not only the government, but also trickled down into the pockets of many Kuwaitis, including Abd al-Aziz Sa'ud al-Babtain and his family businesses. At the same time, there was a lack of adequate financial instruments to handle the new-found wealth, and speculation and gambling would soon spin out of control. Kuwait made the same errors as many countries had before, by squandering its newly acquired wealth on financial speculation. Comparisons can be drawn with the Roaring Twenties in the United States when people became increasingly rich due to speculation until the Wall Street Crash of 1929 that led to the Great Depression in the 1930s.

Speculation and Kuwait's *nouveau riche*

With growing industrialization and the expansion of government institutions in Kuwait, a new class of professionals and administrators emerged. This new stratum of society would become the country's *nouveau riche* – a group that became firmly established over time.[31] As this new group of

---

30 Owen & Pamuk 1999: 215
31 Lawson 1985: 18

wealthy Kuwaitis was involved both in government administration and businesses as well as in large industrial projects, it was difficult for the government to regulate financial speculation within the country, resulting in an increase of speculative investments during the 1970s.

In the absence of an official Kuwaiti stock market, the search for investments that would ensure them financial security and maximize their profits led them to speculate heavily in either property or the unofficial Suq al-Manakh stock market.[32] Property speculation focused on land bought from the government during the era of urbanization in the 1970s. The land could later be sold back to the government or any other buyer at a higher price, yielding a healthy profit for the original investor. Another popular form of speculation at this time was in equities.

The Suq al-Manakh was an unofficial stock market where Kuwaitis could speculate on offshore stocks or so-called paper companies, as these stocks or companies could not be legally traded in Kuwait.[33] Speculative investments were high and a lot of Kuwaitis had a stake in the market. By the summer of 1982, investors had poured around 30 billion Kuwaiti dinars into the Suq al-Manakh.[34] Many Kuwaitis were making good profits, but this would soon come to an end as the market was not under any governmental regulation. Many Kuwaitis started to borrow money from the banks. The credit, however, was not regulated, and neither was there any deposit or safety net in the event that borrowers defaulted on their loans. By 1982, the market was facing a large bubble, meaning that many companies were overvalued and traded at a much higher price than they were actually worth. The situation further deteriorated when the so-called paper companies that had been created only for speculative purposes failed to show any signs of profits, growth or indications of a positive economic development. When it became evident to speculators that these companies were a sham, many withdrew their investments from the market. The inevitable crash of the Suq al-Manakh prompted comparisons with the 1929 Wall Street Crash or the bursting of the dot-com bubble in 2001, in the financial devastation

32 Lawson 1985: 18
33 According to al-Nakib (2016: 115), Suq al-Manakh was an illegal stock market, and the trading took place in companies that were banned on the official Kuwaiti stock exchange.
34 Lawson 1985: 18

that this collapse inflicted on the Kuwaiti financial and banking sectors. The resulting debts, numbering over 5,000, totalled US$92 billion. This huge sum was more than 17 times greater than Kuwait's foreign reserves. Subsequently, almost all commercial banks, except the National Bank of Kuwait, became insolvent, and Western European, North American and Japanese commercial interests were no longer eager to conduct business in the country. Furthermore from 1981 to 1983, oil exports fell by 50 per cent and the government ran its first ever deficit. Credit lenders were hit the hardest, as many speculators did not have the financial means to repay what they had borrowed. Neither had they used any security, making it doubtful that Kuwaitis were legally obliged to pay back their loans to the banks. In the end, the country faced a debt of 23 billion dinars.[35] Some of the Kuwaiti princes refused to settle their debts, and it took the Kuwaiti central bank until 1993 to clear the unstable banking structure of bad debts.[36]

Crash and aftermath

The fiscal mismanagement of the 1970s and early 1980s was devastating for Kuwait. The Golden Era was over, and Kuwait faced a crippling recession. The state had now proven itself incapable of handling financial investments, and unchecked speculation had severely shaken foreign investors' confidence in placing their money in Kuwait.[37]

There were also rumours that the government did nothing to stop the crash from happening because its chief priority was to regain political control. The increasing wealth of Kuwaitis meant that they had also gained a stronger foothold in both the administration of the state and the economy of the country. To prevent further power devolving to citizens, the government may have deemed the crash necessary to consolidate the power of the rulers further.[38] But despite the fact that Kuwait now faced severe financial difficulties, the crash failed to have a significant impact on

35 Owen & Pamuk 1999: 215
36 Henry and Springborg 2001: 189
37 Celine 1985: 11. Kuwait, Egypt, Israel and Turkey were among the first countries in the Middle East to open their stock market foreign investors; see Henry and Springborg 2001: 189.
38 Celine 1985: 11

the nation's overall wealth or standard of living. As one of the wealthiest oil producing countries in the world, Kuwait could rapidly amass the financial resources to turn the situation around.

After the crash of the Suq al-Manakh in 1982, the government shifted policy, as it recognized the pressing need to restructure the country's economy. The aim was to prevent such situations from happening again in the future. The ruling powers in Kuwait began to row back from the 1970s policy of foreign investments and speculation, focusing instead on domestic production to create a more sustainable and less volatile economy. In the 1980s, economic policies were geared towards strengthening the development of domestic industries, using funding in the form of welfare to consolidate relationships with parts of the population such as the Bedouins, sharing responsibility by re-establishing the National Assembly and setting up institutions that would administer and support the creation of domestic businesses.[39] By the beginning of the 1980s, oil prices had begun to fall. Kuwaiti oil companies received declining revenues, and consequently the government had fewer resources to distribute and invest. This further strengthened the conviction that the country needed to diversify its economy and create stronger domestic industries.[40]

The firm of Abd al-Aziz weathered and even prospered during this period of ups and downs. As noted above, the businesses that are today associated with the name Abd al-Aziz Sa'ud al-Babtain were established and developed in Kuwait from the 1950s onwards, and then expanded beyond the country.[41] And in conversation, Abu Sa'ud states that the turning point in his life came in 1959, when he was asked by a Lebanese businessman to become the local distributor for a certain brand of cigarettes.[42] This led to him securing the rights to be the sole representative of Marlboro in both Saudi Arabia and Kabul and marked the beginning of his business expansion abroad. Abu Sa'ud had married Zakia Abd al-Aziz al-Hamid in August 1960 and they had five sons. In due course, they would also join him in the firm.[43]

---

39 Lawson 1985: 19f
40 Celine 1985: 11
41 The following portrayal of Abu Sa'ud is from Qattan 2018.
42 Interview, October 17, 2016
43 During an evening meal at the *diwaniyya* of Abd al-Aziz on October 19, 2016,

Abd al-Aziz al-Babtain with his son (right), 1967.
Courtesy of the al-Babtain Foundation.

In 1964 and 1965 Abu Sa'ud expanded his network of commercial contacts, opening offices and stores in Iran, Pakistan, Iraq, Turkey and Italy, as well as in the free ports of Istanbul, Limassol, Cyprus and Alexandria in Egypt. He opened an office in Saudi Arabia in 1968 and set about forming a new company there with his two younger brothers Abd al-Karim and Abd al-Wahab after their graduation from university.[44]

Abu Sa'ud became involved with the developing electronics industry from 1970 onwards. He set up links with European, Chinese and North American companies in this new industry. In the early 1970s, he also started

---

he showed me a framed photograph of his father hanging on the wall. The photo, from the early years of the 20th century, showed his father, Sa'ud al-Babtain, in formal traditional dress (see portrait of his father in Chapter 2). Sa'ud al-Babtain died in 1961 at the age of 75, so never got to witness his son's great business success. Sa'ud al-Babtain had more than one wife and Abd al-Aziz had seven sisters and eight brothers; see Qattan 2013.

44 In different interviews, the years do not always tally. In Atzori (2014: 37) it is stated that the brothers came to work with him after university, but in 1973.

businesses in property, petrol-chemical and food products in Europe as well as the Americas. In common with most successful Kuwaiti companies, the different companies established by him focused mainly on retail and the distribution of consumer products from cars to telecommunications and phones, and to a lesser extent manufacturing products. Later, from the 1980s onwards, the al-Babtain Group diversified into a variety of investment projects, for example, entertainment, agriculture and education. In just two decades since embarking on his business career, Abu Sa'ud had forged a vast commercial empire, making him a very wealthy individual.

The trajectory of the businessman and poet Abd al-Aziz Sa'ud al-Babtain as a pioneer of Kuwaiti private business life accords closely with the timeline portrayed above of economic developments in Kuwait as a whole in the 1960s and the 1970s. Since the 1960s Abd al-Aziz and his companies had invested abroad. These investments expanded over the years and included assets and ventures into property, shares and investment funds to generate capital for investments within the group of companies.

The companies are also family-owned and controlled. Since the 1960s, Abd al-Aziz's brothers had been involved, and after them, Abd al-Aziz's sons became active in the various companies, especially from the 1980s onwards. Today they are responsible for running the businesses supported by Abu Sa'ud.[45] Over time, the wider family has been a source of recruitment for the businesses as well as for the different institutions set up in the name of Abu Sa'ud. One example of the overlap between business engagements and the activities of the Foundation is his nephew Abd al-Rahman al-Babtain, who is the General Secretary of the Abd al-Aziz Sa'ud al-Babtain Cultural Foundation, but who is also involved in many companies related to Abd al-Aziz. In addition, the positive relationship with the government and the ruling family of Kuwait is a source of great support for Abd al-Aziz in both his cultural activities and his business life.

In addition to the crucial turning point in his early business career, Abd al-Aziz also cites the 1970s as a period in which he felt he had attained such financial stability that he could return to poetry. In an interview, he pinpointed 1974 as the year of this particular turning point.[46] In the few accounts of his life so far, 1974 is not customarily identified with this event,

---

45 Interview, October 18, 2016
46 Interview, October 18, 2016

but rather as the year in which he inaugurated the first of his many ambitious projects to grant scholarships to students from Kuwait and other countries to complete their university education.

Abd al-Aziz's personal history finds distinct parallels in the lives of several other Kuwaitis of his generation. He belongs to a new group of wealthy individuals who, within a period of around 15 years, went from rags to riches and whose success in business has been complemented by involvement in various forms of philanthropy and the patronage of culture.[47]

War in the Gulf

In the aftermath of the Iran–Iraq War (1980–1988), Sheikh Jabir al-Ahmad al-Sabah sought to finally settle the border dispute with Iraq concerning the islands of Bubiyan and Warba. At the time, control over the islands secured access to the only navigable waterway to Gulf waters from Iraq, due to debris from the Iran–Iraq War blocking the Shatt al-Arab waterway. The Bubiyan and Warba islands were also part of a longer-running historical territorial dispute between Iraq and Kuwait. From an Iraqi perspective, they had been part of the Ottoman province of Basra and when the British ended the protectorate over Kuwait in 1961, the Iraqi prime minister, General Abd al-Karim Qasim, stated that the islands were an integral part of Iraq. This high-handed attitude towards Kuwait on the part of leading Iraqis is also evident in the substance and tone of the remarks made by the Iraqi minister and brother-in-law of Saddam Hussein, Adnan Khayr Allah al-Talfah, in the story recounted by Abd al-Aziz at the beginning of this book. In February 1989, the Kuwaiti crown prince, Sheikh Sa'd Abd Allah al-Salim al-Sabah, travelled to Baghdad to negotiate with Saddam Hussein. His hope was that Kuwait's wartime support for Iraq would persuade the Iraqi president to be more amendable on the territorial issue and to finally agree on a binding demarcation of the border. However, Saddam Hussein flatly turned down the request, thus signalling his country's continued territorial claims on the islands.[48] Iraq's longstanding territorial ambitions

---

47 Such a parallel example, although being from the ruling family, is Sheikha Suad al-Sabah, see http://www.arabtimesonline.com/news/grande-dame-kuwaiti-culture-drsuad-al-sabah/. Accessed June 10, 2019.

48 Freedman and Karsh 1993: 44

concerning Kuwait were only one point of contention as tension between the two countries mounted in 1989 and early 1990, during the lead-up to the Iraqi invasion.[49]

The war has usually been attributed to the dire economic situation Saddam Hussein's Iraq found itself in following the devastation and immense cost to the country of the war against Iran. During the war, Iraq had accumulated a debt of about US$80 billion, of which some US$10 to US$15 billion was owed to Kuwait. Furthermore, the damage to Iraq's cities and infrastructure left the country with an estimated US$230 billion reconstruction bill. Iraq's oil revenues at the time made up the most of the state's income but were insufficient to finance the budget, let alone the cost of reconstruction.[50] Although Kuwait supported Iraq in its war with Iran, it maintained diplomatic relations with Iran. From a Kuwaiti standpoint, the hope was to return to a form of neutrality after the war was over. Whereas during the war, the Iraqi leadership had tried to position itself as the saviour of the Arabs from the great enemy represented by the Islamic Republic of Iran, the Kuwaiti government had its own political interests and objectives and was more concerned with the possibility of a resurgence among the Shi'a community in their country.[51]

The crash of oil prices in 1985–1986 placed a severe strain on the oil-producing countries in the region and Iraq in particular. As a result, OPEC concluded an agreement to impose production quotas in an attempt to drive up oil prices. However, countries such as Saudi Arabia and Kuwait did not share the majority view of the OPEC membership as they saw more benefit in maintaining low oil prices and larger export volumes. This created a split within OPEC and among Arab oil-producing countries. Indeed, Kuwait's decision to exceed its production quotas[52] was specifically condemned by Saddam Hussein at the Arab Summit meeting held in

---

49 The many reasons for the Iraqi invasion have been studied thoroughly and ihere my intent is to give a brief overview. For detailed studies of the factors that led to the invasion and for somewhat different opinions among scholars on how to analyse the reasons for the Iraqis to occupy Kuwait, see Kostiner 2009: 78–140 and Khadduri and Ghareeb 1997.

50 The numbers are estimations, and they are not always exactly the same in all accounts; see Kostiner 2009: 78 and Freedman and Karsh 1993: 39–41.

51 Kostiner 2009: 83, 88

52 Renner and Aarts 1991: 26f and Kostiner 2009: 85

Baghdad in May 1990. He claimed that Kuwait's choice amounted to "economic warfare". He demanded that Kuwait not only adhere to the quotas but also that it write off Iraq's wartime debt and grant an additional US$10 billion to his country. Sheikh Jabir al-Sabah refused and, at a meeting in Kuwait later the following month, instead offered Iraq US$500 million to be paid over three years, but made it conditional on the border dispute being settled. However, in the face of continued Iraqi hostility and threats to settle differences by force, Kuwait finally agreed to abide by the quota restrictions on July 10, 1990.[53]

The Iraqi–Kuwaiti dispute also had an international dimension, since Iraq maintained that Israel and the United States were deliberately trying to weaken Iraq and the entire "Arab nation" by, for example, encouraging Kuwait to lower the price of oil. This statement was not surprising given the ongoing tense relations between the United States and Iraq in the years leading up to the invasion. From an Iraqi perspective, there was a lack of clarity concerning the US position on Iraq. Mixed messages on such topics as human rights, relations with Israel, sanctions, credit programmes and biological weapons from President George H. W. Bush, the US Congress, media and American representatives such as the delegation to Iraq in April 1990 headed by Senator Robert Dole, coupled with initiatives of collaboration and friendship towards Iraq, only served to confuse the Iraqi leader, but also made him critical of American policy. Saddam Hussein's meeting with April Glaspie, US Ambassador to Iraq, at the end of July has been the subject of much scrutiny by commentators, as this was emblematic of the broader ambiguity characterizing US–Iraqi relations. It is indeed possible to see this fundamental ambiguity as having misled Saddam into interpreting the ambassador's remarks as appeasement and construing what she said as a tacit approval on the part of the United States of an Iraqi invasion of Kuwait. With hindsight, of course, it was decidedly not the intention of Ambassador Glaspie to convey such a message.[54]

---

53 Freedman and Karsh 1993: 45–47, Khadduri and Ghareeb 1997: 105f and Kostiner 2009: 99f
54 Kostiner 2009: 81, Khadduri and Ghareeb 1997: 110–114 and Gause III 1994: 2
For extracts of the meeting between Glaspie and Saddam Hussein, see https://www.nytimes.com/1991/07/13/world/us-messages-on-july-1990-meeting-of-hussein-and-american-ambassador.html. Accessed June 14, 2019.

Another international and regional aspect of the discussions leading up to the Iraqi occupation of Kuwait relates to the state of inter-Arab relationships, at a time when the idea of pan-Arabism and the belief in mediation as the only acceptable solution in inter-Arab disputes had been steadily waning and when a space had opened for individual state sovereignty to be asserted even as lip service was still paid to pan-Arabism. State interests would still be promoted through regional organizations such as the Arab Cooperation Council (Iraq) and the Gulf Cooperation Council (Kuwait). As stated above, the Iraqi self-perception of being a leading Arab nation and a defender of Arab interests was not shared by Kuwait's rulers, who considered Iraq's demands as claims that could be negotiated and that the conflict between the countries could be solved in the spirit of Arab solidarity and trust. On the other hand, Kuwait's divergence from OPEC agreements and its reluctance to accept Iraq's claims for a debt reprieve were seen in Baghdad as acts that were incompatible with the concept of Arab solidarity. Consequently, the conflict between Iraq and Kuwait underscored the inherent tension between a generalized notion of Arab identity and one based on nationalism;[55] while lip service was paid rhetorically to the ideal of Arab unity, in practice individual countries pursued their own sovereign interests.

A mere five days after Kuwait agreed to adhere to the OPEC quotas, Iraq began mobilizing the Revolutionary Guard troops at its border with the Gulf emirate. The next day, Iraq sent a memorandum to the Arab League, accusing Kuwait and the United Arab Emirates inter alia of having conspired to lower the price of oil and of having stolen oil from the Rumayla oil field through slant drilling. Subsequently, Iraq widened its earlier demands to also include raising the oil price to US$25 per barrel, for Kuwait to compensate Iraq to the tune of US$2.4 billion for the allegedly stolen oil from the Rumayla oil field and for the Arab League to implement an economic plan to offset Iraq's war costs.[56] Notwithstanding the ongoing build-up of Iraqi forces and aggressive Iraqi rhetoric, Iraq's strategy appeared to be to intimidate Kuwait rather than actually to invade. Iraq continued to negotiate in the Saudi Arabian city of Jeddah, where talks to diffuse tension were

---

55 Kostiner 2009: 89, 91–94, 98, 100, 112 and Legrenzi 50f
56 Freedman and Karsh 1993: 47f and Kostiner 2009: 87

being held.[57] In Jeddah, the Kuwaiti delegation continued to believe that the Iraqi claims were a negotiating ploy, and given their history of mediating conflicts they made far-reaching promises of a US$9 billion grant, remitting wartime debt, and pledged to work towards raising the oil price and eventually to lease the island of Bubiyan to Iraq. The Kuwaitis' attempts to negotiate in the face of ever-increasing Iraqi demands failed to dispel Iraqi anger or avert military action. The Kuwaitis were thus caught by surprise when the invasion began in the early morning of August 2, 1990.[58]

The Kuwaiti armed forces of 16,000 soldiers were not mobilized and were vastly outnumbered by the 140,000 Iraqi troops who swiftly overwhelmed the country after crossing the border. Organized into two major offensives, the Iraqi troops, spearheaded by armoured divisions of the Republican Guard, sought to encircle Kuwait City and so prevent the escape of the Kuwaiti royal family.[59]

Concurrent with the main offensive, Iraqi special forces and helicopterborne infantry launched attacks on Kuwait City itself, with Iraqi commandos attacking the Dasman palace at around 4 a.m. By midday, the whole of Kuwait had been seized by Iraqi troops. Despite the speed of the assault, the invading forces failed to apprehend Sheikh Jabir al-Sabah and Crown Prince Sheikh Saʿd, who, along with many of their advisors, had already moved from the city to more secure "General Headquarters" at the start of the invasion.[60]

As pressure mounted, Sheikh Jabir and his closest family left the General Headquarters, drove in cars to Saudi Arabia and established a government in exile in the city of Taʾif. At the time of the Iraqi invasion, Abd al-Aziz was in his house in Geneva where he usually spends the period from mid-June to mid-September. Abu Saʿud recounted that his uncle offered the family's unconditional support to Sheikh Jabir in these unprecedented circumstances, and this was a confirmation of a relationship that was established earlier by another uncle. Abu Saʿud stressed the closeness of this bond by

---

57 For an alternative account of the prelude on both sides to the Jeddah meeting, the staunch positions held on both sides and the meeting itself, see Khadduri and Ghareeb 1997: 114ff. In this account the Kuwaiti delegation rejected the Iraqi proposals and did not present any counter proposals.

58 Freedman and Karsh 1993: 56f, 67 and Kostiner 89f, 90, 107

59 Freedman and Karsh 1993: 67 and Casey 2007: 88

60 Casey 2007: 89

noting that "His Highness attends our celebrations and funerals and has visited our *diwaniyya* in Ramadan". The already well-established relationship between the ruler and Abd al-Aziz's older relatives and its affirmation during the critical moments of the invasion and occupation of Kuwait helped him develop his personal relationship with the amir.[61]

Sheikh Jabir al-Sabah's successful decampment to Saudi Arabia was to have powerful repercussions on the course of the invasion.[62] Saddam Hussein's propaganda portrayed the invasion as a temporary intervention to support a liberal take-over of Kuwait. But with Iraq's failure to capture the royal family, the Sheikh's claim of legitimate power was not eclipsed as Hussein had intended. To further thwart the Iraqi plans to claim they were filling a vacuum of legitimacy, the Kuwaiti political opposition that had begun to call for democratic reforms in Kuwait before the war refused to collaborate with the Iraqis.[63] Instead, six low-ranking officers from the Kuwaiti navy were allegedly coerced to play this role.[64] As such the "liberal regime" was in practice non-existent and enjoyed no credibility among either the Kuwaiti people or internationally.[65] Instead, citing Iraq's territorial claims, which dated back to the period of Ottoman control, Iraq annexed Kuwait as the country's 19th province.[66]

A state on its knees, and an exodus

The Iraqi invasion took Arab mediators working to solve the disagreements between Iraq and Kuwait by surprise. For Saudi Arabia's King Fahd and Egypt's president Mubarak, it was evident that the time for mediation between Iraq and Kuwait had passed. Their efforts to negotiate and keep the disagreements between the two countries within an inter-Arab context had now failed and the dispute had escalated into a conflict of international dimensions, paving the way for the intervention of foreign powers. King Hussein of Jordan tried one last effort to get the Iraqi president to

---

61 Conversation October 17, 2016
62 Casey 2007: 89
63 Bulloch and Morris 1991: 119
64 Ghabra 1991a: 115
65 Freedman and Karsh 1993: 68
66 The Iraqi annexation of Kuwait was declared on August 9, 1990; see Khadduri and Ghareeb 1997: 140.

withdraw from Kuwait, but with no success.[67] Realizing that the invasion was a fact, King Fahd and President Mubarak worked to create an anti-Iraq coalition, since for King Fahd the prospect of having large portions of the Iraqi army near the oilfields in the northeast of his country was not an acceptable situation. For a couple of days, the Saudi king pondered the possibility of having US troops stationed in Saudi Arabia. On August 6, he made an unprecedented and highly controversial decision and gave the permission for a US-led multinational force to be deployed from Saudi Arabia.[68] The symbolic participation of other Arab countries in the multinational force was an important signal of Arab unity against armed aggression by one Arab country towards another.[69]

The invasion sparked a massive exodus of between 60,000 and 80,000 Kuwait's citizens, most seeking refuge in Saudi Arabia. A full third of Kuwaitis had been abroad at the time of the invasion, among them Abd al-Aziz and many of the al-Babtain family, so between the exodus and those already abroad, there were, according to Ghabra, some 380,000 Kuwaiti citizens in the country when Iraq invaded.[70] The initial days of the invasion saw the widespread looting of businesses, government buildings and private homes, mainly perpetrated by the Iraqi army, but in some cases by non-Kuwaiti residents.[71] Although looting by non-Kuwaitis mostly ceased by the second week of the occupation, the Iraqi Army continued to target, for example, government institutions, hospitals and factories, sending machines and equipment back to Iraq.

Far from welcoming the Iraqis as liberators, the Kuwaiti population,

---

67 For an account of the discussions between Jordan's King Hussein, Saudi Arabia's King Fahd, the Egyptian president Mubarak and the US president Bush, see Khadduri and Ghareeb 1997: 127ff.

68 Kostiner 2009: 107f. The response to the Invasion of Kuwait has been discussed in many sources. For overviews see Kostiner 2009 and Khadduri and Ghareeb 1997.

69 Ghabra 1991a: 120f

70 Ghabra 1991a: 116. According to Gause III (1994: 7), the population of Kuwait on August 2, 1990, was approximately 2 million. Less than half of the population were citizens. According to Gause III, an effect of the Iraqi occupation and its aftermath was that the population decreased by 25 per cent, but the citizens constituted still less than half of the population. Commins (2012: 248) states that a third of the Kuwaiti nationals were in exile during the Iraqi occupation.

71 Ghabra 1991a: 115

nationals and non-nationals alike, opposed the occupation, and a resistance movement developed.[72] Initially the resistance movement distributed leaflets against the occupation and hid foreigners who were under threat of arrest by the Iraqi army. Towards the end of August, they began to engage in small-scale attacks against Iraqi troops. Later the armed resistance also included car bombings and minor skirmishes with Iraqi forces.[73] Ali Hasan al-Majid, the head of Iraq's Special Security forces and notorious for his brutal suppression of Kurdish revolts against Saddam Hussein's regime in 1987 and 1988, was put in charge of the "province" of Kuwait. In addition to the armed resistance, peaceful demonstrations were also held: on the second day of every month, Kuwaitis would gather on rooftops and in unison protest against the occupation by waving Kuwaiti flags, shouting slogans and singing the Kuwaiti national anthem.[74]

However, the internal resistance was unable to significantly disrupt or ultimately dislodge the overwhelmingly superior occupation force, especially as al-Majid imposed a brutal repression of Kuwait's population. The methods of the Iraqi troops tasked with suppressing such activities included collective punishments, such as demolishing houses where weapons or even anti-Iraqi graffiti had been found or the entire city block if Iraqi casualties had been caused by an attack.[75] Extensive arrests were carried out, followed by interrogations which included the use of torture.[76] The repression became so severe that Sheikh Jabir, the ruler in exile, urged the resistance movement to cease operations in October 1990.[77]

The international community and an end to the war

Following the invasion, the international community was quick to respond to the Iraqi aggression. On the day of the invasion, the United Nations' Security Council (UNSC) passed Resolution 660, which condemned the invasion and allowed for economic and military action to be taken.

---

72 For a personal portrait of the invasion of Kuwait and the resistance of Kuwaitis, see Rajab 1993.

73 Casey 2007: 99 and al-Marashi 2003: 79f

74 Ghabra 1991a: 118

75 al-Marashi 2003: 83f

76 Ghabra 1991a: 118f

77 al-Marashi 2003: 86

This was the first time that the United Nations authorized a response to a crisis endorsing military force. More UNSC resolutions followed, which imposed full economic sanctions on Iraq, suspending all trade and transfer of funds to Iraq except for humanitarian shipments of food and medical supplies [78] especially as the administration of US president George H. W. Bush and Saudi Arabia feared a spillover of the crisis as Iraqi troops massed on the border with Saudi Arabia.

In response, an American-led coalition was assembled in the months after the invasion in 1990, including troops from several Arab countries. Coalition forces, mainly comprising troops from the United States, began their deployment to Saudi Arabia in early September, when 40,000 American military personnel arrived. The initial force was deployed for defensive purposes, but due to logistical constraints, was to be fully deployed by December 1, 1990. However, Saddam Hussein's continued refusal to adhere to resolutions promulgated by the United Nations to withdraw from Kuwait and the seeming ineffectiveness of the sanctions regime to compel him to do so prompted the Bush administration to adopt an offensive strategy.

The offensive approach required additional coalition troops, so President Bush decided on October 30 to double US troop deployments.[79] In the meantime, efforts continued to convince Saddam Hussein to withdraw his troops from Kuwait, including a last attempt to settle the Gulf crisis peacefully in Geneva, Switzerland. At this meeting, the foreign ministers of Iraq and the US, Tariq Aziz and James Baker, reiterated their respective standpoints, but no common ground was found from which to build an agreement.[80] With the deployment of additional troops, the coalition issued Iraqi president Saddam Hussein with an ultimatum to withdraw his troops by January 15, 1991.[81] Several last-minute diplomatic propositions were made in early January to Saddam Hussein's regime in an effort to compel him to withdraw.

---

78 Freedman & Karsh 1993: 81–84

79 Freedman & Karsh 1993: 201–206

80 For an account of the discussions in Geneva, see Khadduri and Ghareeb 1997: 154–156.

81 In the end of November 1990, the United Nations declared that if Iraq did not comply with all the prior resolutions by January 15, 1991, the United Nations authorized the international community to use all the force that was needed; see Kostiner 2009:116.

However, Saddam continued to refuse to withdraw from Kuwait, a decision that the Iraqi National Assembly supported on January 14, 1991. The coalition duly launched Operation Desert Storm on January 17, 1991, initiating a major air campaign against infrastructure, strategic and military targets in Iraq and Kuwait, under the command of US General H. Norman Schwarzkopf. In the first day alone, 1,300 attacks were carried out. Having met with little resistance, the air campaign was conducted practically unmolested, inflicting considerable damage on Iraqi troops and other targets. By February 23, the air campaign was deemed to have sufficiently paved the way for a ground assault. During this time, the Soviet Union had unsuccessfully attempted to broker a peace agreement to allow Iraq's withdrawal. However, as Saddam Hussein ordered the destruction and setting ablaze of the Kuwaiti oil infrastructure and wells on February 22, a last-ditch effort to obtain an Iraqi surrender was issued as an ultimatum for Saddam Hussein's forces to withdraw from Kuwait by February 25, but the Iraqi president refused.[82]

The coalition ground offensive began at 04.00 on February 24, 1991, with a two-pronged attack, whereby one main offensive was to push north towards Kuwait City as another group outflanked the Iraqi forces to the west. The objective was to cut off the main Iraqi force in Kuwait from Iraqi territory. The flanking forces, comprising 235,000 troops, had already begun their manoeuvre towards the west some twelve days before the launch of the offensive. The envelopment to the north of Kuwait succeeded as the scant Iraqi forces stationed in the northwest of Kuwait were taken by surprise. Meanwhile the northward offensive was able to overwhelm Iraqi defences with vastly superior firepower and the demoralized Iraqi troops surrendered *en masse*.[83]

On February 25, President Saddam Hussein ordered the withdrawal of Iraqi troops to their positions before the outbreak of the war. In practice, it signalled his compliance with the UN demands and his acceptance of a military *fait accompli*.[84] For the coalition, it became apparent that the ground offensive had been a complete success with only minimal coalition casualties, while the bulk of the Iraqi army in Kuwait had been rendered

---

82 Freedman & Karsh 1993: 301, 306, 372f, 384f, 385 and Kostiner 2009: 117–119
83 Freedman & Karsh 1993: 395–398
84 Freedman & Karsh 1993: 400–492

non-operational, suffering heavy losses and mass desertions. Fleeing Iraqi soldiers were heavily bombed as they attempted to retreat to Iraq. The allied assaults killed thousands of soldiers, and pictures of the annihilation of fleeing Iraqi forces shocked war correspondents, the US military and officials alike. Estimates of the number of Iraqi casualties range from 82,500 to 200,000, while the number of US fatalities was 376 dead in either combat or accidents.[85] By February 28, Kuwaiti forces had entered Kuwait City, which had been evacuated of Iraqi troops on February 25, and the regime could return from its exile. The Iraqi foreign minister agreed to abide by the remaining UN resolutions on February 26. With Kuwait liberated and the remaining Iraqi forces having escaped to safety in Iraq,[86] President Bush declared the war over the following day.[87]

In Iraq, popular uprisings took place in the months after the war. In Arabic they were referred to as *intifada al-sha'baniyya,* since they began in the month of Sha'ban 1411 (March 1991). Uncoordinated rebellions occurred with Kurds in the north and Shi'a Muslims in the south revolting against Saddam Hussein and his government. The protests arose as the result of a decade of war, repression and the attendant destruction of welfare provisions, all of which had left Iraqi society in a bad shape. Protests and uprisings were brutally repressed by the Iraqi authorities, though the international coalition established no-fly zones over northern and southern Iraq, which enabled forces opposing Saddam Hussein's rule in the north of Iraq to found the Kurdish Autonomous Republic. However, adequate support was not forthcoming to allow the establishment of a similar polity in the south of the country.

During the Iraqi occupation, Kuwaiti opposition leaders criticized the country's rulers for not warning citizens of the Iraqi threat and for having provoked the Iraqis. Talks between the opposition and the government continued throughout the occupation about how to reinstate the National Assembly.[88] At the end of the war, the Kuwaiti government estimated that

---

85 Khadduri and Ghareeb 1997: 178f. For a discussion about the consequences of the war for Iraq and Kuwait, see Khadduri and Ghareeb 1997: 180–224 and Commins 2012: 246–249.

86 Freedman & Karsh 1993: 399, 402 and Kostiner 2009: 119

87 Khadduri and Ghareeb 1997: 179

88 Commins 2012: 248

approximately 1,000 individuals had been murdered by Iraqi forces. Many more had been arrested and deported to Iraq.[89] Many Kuwaiti nationals and non-nationals had not only lost relatives or friends, but also property and other possessions.[90] Life under Iraqi rule had been harsh and communication with the outside world difficult. State support and economic benefits normally provided to Kuwaiti citizens had been discontinued. The earlier state-sponsored cooperatives that provided food at subsidized prices were still intact, but the food as well as public utilities such as water or electricity were no longer subsidized. On the other hand, during the seven-month long occupation, many utility bills went unpaid, and in April and May 1992 the Kuwaiti government wrote off such debts as had accumulated during that period. Government employees were paid their backdated salaries for the duration of the occupation and mortgages owed to state banks or agencies were exonerated. The government also provided families who had remained in Kuwait throughout the Iraqi occupation with a one-off payment equating to US$1,750.[91]

Abd al-Aziz rarely mentions the occupation of Kuwait in conversation. As previously noted, the photos adorning the walls of the al-Babtain *diwaniyya* are a reminder of the occupation and the ensuing war, but they also confirm the close relationship between the al-Babtain family and the country's rulers. In common with other Kuwaiti nationals, al-Babtain suffered considerable financial losses during the crisis, as his diverse business assets in Kuwait were confiscated.[92] However, his many projects and businesses outside Kuwait sustained his wealth, and after the liberation of Kuwait, Abd al-Aziz returned and his success in business continued. The end of the 1990s and the early 2000s is a period in which Abd al-Aziz al-Babtain and his family business network fared well financially, mirroring Kuwait's prosperity in general. Several of his companies were involved in rebuilding Kuwait, while the expansion of his business in the 1990s allowed him to recoup the losses incurred by the occupation.

In the course of rebuilding after the occupation, Abd al-Aziz Sa'ud al-Babtain launched a number of new philanthropic ventures. His previous

---

89 Freedman & Karsh 1993: 68 and Commins 2012: 248
90 For a personal portrayal of life under the Iraqi occupation, see Rajab 1993.
91 Gause III 1994: 61
92 Qattan 2013

endowments had included the al-Babtain scholarship for students to study at al-Azhar University in Cairo, founded in 1974, and the Abdulaziz Saud al-Babtain Prize for Poetic Creativity in 1989 – once again established in Cairo, which Abd al-Aziz regards as the capital of Arab culture, art and creativity. However, it was in the early 1990s, in the aftermath of the Iraqi occupation, that the foundation embarked upon a major expansion of its activities, setting up regional offices in Jordan, Kuwait and Tunisia and, later on, in Spain too. For Abd al-Aziz al-Babtain, returning to Kuwait after the occupation was not just about rebuilding his commercial portfolio in the country. His first poetry book entitled *Bawh al-Bawadi*, "Intimations of the Desert", was published in 1995. The same year, he was also awarded his first honorary doctorate, and the Foundation published the first of the al-Babtain Encyclopaedias documenting Arab poetry. The next year, he was also honoured with an award from the Tunisian president for his promotion of Arabic culture. These post-war developments can be seen as a decisive step that saw Abu Sa'ud devoting most of his energies to the field of Arabic language and culture, poetry and dialogue, and becoming more focused on his Foundation, poetry and philanthropy rather than his businesses. His five sons have long been centrally involved in the businesses, and Abu Sa'ud now performs more of an oversight role, confining his hands-on involvement to taking final decisions on major issues. This arrangement has allowed him to deepen his involvement with the Foundation in the second half of the 1990s and the early 2000s. From a financial perspective, the construction of the al-Babtain Central Library for Arabic Poetry in the heart of Kuwait City was a major investment by the Foundation. The library opened in 2006. Later, the building of the Abd al-Aziz al-Babtain Cultural Waqf was another major investment in Kuwait City. This is an almost 190-metre-high, 42-storey skyscraper in a central part of the city completed in 2010. Being a *waqf* (a charitable endowment), its proceeds go into a trust supporting charitable purposes.

These successes notwithstanding, the war was not without impact on Abd al-Aziz's attitude towards his cultural and philanthropic activities. The fraught relationship between Iraq and Kuwait, the war and the occupation of his country seems to have strengthened Abd al-Aziz's belief that Arab culture, identity, unity and solidarity were now in more danger than ever.[93]

---

93 *An Overview of Abdul Aziz al-Babtain* 2015: 27ff and conversation October 18,

The reborn metropolis, Kuwait City, 2011. © the author.

Throughout his life, he has been intent on counteracting the threat he sees to Arab culture and language, and when asked what cultural achievement makes him most proud or what his most important accomplishment has been, he points to the establishment of the Foundation and the al-Babtain dictionary for Arab contemporary poets. However, in response to a further question about his thoughts on the challenges facing contemporary Kuwaiti society today, he cites his hope that Kuwaiti society will recognize and become aware of the dangers of division. At the same time, he is concerned about Kuwaiti youth lacking spirit and application and hopes that his contribution through his cultural endeavours might encourage the younger generation to read more and inspire them to build a better future.

Of course, not all those living in Kuwait have been as fortunate as Abd al-Aziz al-Babtain. As a result of the Palestinian leadership's support for Saddam Hussein and Iraq, Palestinians living and working in Kuwait found themselves barred from returning or were expelled outright. The advocacy

2016.

by Yasser Arafat (1929–2004) of an "Arab" solution in place of the international coalition that ended the occupation of the country was particularly unwelcome in Kuwait. Others, from the Indian subcontinent or Southeast Asia, have not enjoyed the benefits of the safety net the government provided for Kuwaiti citizens, and the occupation and its aftermath saw their livelihoods destroyed or facing considerable and irretrievable loss of income, regardless of whether they had remained in Kuwait or had returned to their countries of origin.

Kuwaiti citizens have commemorated their country's liberation ever since 1991. Kuwait Liberation Day is celebrated on February 26 every year, but is also remembered on many other official occasions. It has become an important symbol for the creation of national unity and identity. However, it is also true to say that, in a country with such an overwhelmingly young population, most Kuwaiti citizens nowadays do not have any personal memories of the Iraqi invasion and occupation.

6

CONTEMPORARY KUWAIT AND
THE AL-BABTAIN FOUNDATION

Developments after the liberation of Kuwait

Perhaps it is an unfair comparison but, compared with the sprawling cities of Doha and Dubai, Kuwait City appears slightly tired and worn out. At least, this may be a visitor's initial impression when arriving in the country. Kuwait International Airport underwent renovation from 1999 to 2001 and a new terminal has recently been constructed, but the airport still feels small, sleepy and somewhat lacklustre. One gains a similar impression travelling from the airport to the heart of Kuwait City. Though the country's highways infrastructure is good and the importance of the car as the primary means of transportation is indisputable, the road system in Kuwait is still somewhat underdeveloped in comparison with Dubai or Doha.

Today Kuwait City stretches far along the seafront. Arriving at what can be described as the city centre, you find the usual high-rise buildings that dominate many capitals in the world, interspersed with lower-rise and sometimes older houses. Some of these are abandoned and pockmarked with bullet holes from the Iraqi invasion. Others which are regarded as outdated have been earmarked for demolition to make way for new developments. This arguably rather down-at-heel appearance of Kuwait City may well be a direct result of the 1900–1991 invasion. The war also ended a period that had seen Kuwait play a pivotal role in world affairs. Certainly the war and the associated reconstruction costs have forced the rulers in Kuwait to err on the side of caution when faced with the temptation to spend large sums of funding on a variety of spectacular prestige projects like their Gulf counterparts.[1] Another reason for financial restraint has perhaps also been a continuing fear and suspicion of Kuwait's Iraqi neighbours.[2] Before the occupation, Kuwait's diplomatic communication with Iraq had been very regular – the last official visit to Baghdad taking place just days before the invasion. After the occupation, it took until early 2011, almost two decades after the end of the war, for a Kuwaiti prime minister to visit Baghdad.[3] In an article in *The Guardian* from early 2011, Kuwaitis described the mood in the country at the time as one of apprehension, marked by a lack of confidence in society compared to the 1970s and the 1980s,[4] despite the country's enormous oil resources and Kuwait's postwar economic recovery and even spectacular development.

The invasion and the war of 1990 and 1991 was followed by the return of Sheikh Jabir al-Sabah from exile in Ta'if in Saudi Arabia[5] on March 15, fifteen days after the end of the war on February 28, 1991,[6] and his restora-

---

1 As an example of the costs linked to the occupation, the state of Kuwait is estimated to have spent more than US$5 billion to repair its oil-producing infrastructure damaged in the war.

2 Suspicion towards Iraq is not a new phenomenon in Kuwait. Sheikh Mubarak al-Sabah (r. 1896–1915) murdered his brothers Muhammad and Jarrah in order to become the ruler. He was encouraged to kill his two brothers by Kuwaitis who regarded him as a stronger leader than his brothers and as a person able to resist the threatened "Iraqization" of the country. Another example of the same character, also mentioned above, is the announcement, six days after the independence of Kuwait was declared in 1961, by the Iraqi leader Abd al-Karim Qasim that Iraq considered Kuwait a part of the *wilayat* of Basra and thereby a part of Iraq. Hence, in his opinion the British and the Kuwaitis did not have the right to make an agreement about the status of Kuwait, see Tétreault 1991.

3 In addition, the hundreds of Kuwaitis that were still missing several years after the war contributed to the Kuwaiti grievances; see http://news.bbc.co.uk/1/hi/world/middle_east/8048477.stm. Accessed August 12, 2018.

4 *The Guardian*, January 16, 2011. Accessed September 5, 2017.

5 It is tempting to speculate concerning the choice of Ta'if as the location for the exile. Apart from being the summer capital of Saudi Arabia, it has a connection to the history of the Prophet Muhammad. The link would be the status of the city of Ta'if in the confessional history of early Islam and the move to Ta'if as a reminder of how the Prophet had to move out of his hometown, failed in Ta'if, but later returned victorious.

6 In this war the casualty level was low, but regarding the number of individuals mobilized and the weaponry that was utilized it was the second greatest conflict since the Second World War, after the Korean War; see Halliday 1991: 223.

One of the bullet-strafed abandoned buildings that remained
after the Iraqi occupation, 2016. © the author.

tion as the amir of the state and the ruler of Kuwait. During the war, the government led by the amir worked effectively to provide services for Kuwaiti citizens such as healthcare abroad if required as well as support for the armed resistance by civilians and military personnel in the country during the Iraqi occupation. The access to national funds gleaned from oil revenues and deposited abroad was a vital resource for the government in exile.

Before the amir's return, a three-month period of martial law was declared to provide security for his arrival and to ensure the public's safety. Even though criticism has been expressed concerning the degree of power vested in the small constitutional monarchy, after the war, Kuwait established one of the more independent legislatures among Arab countries.[7]

---

7 The elected parliament in Kuwait that was dissolved in 1986 had not, according to Halliday, been shown much respect by the amir and after the war the ruler was not particularly interested in a democratic development in Kuwait or to subject finances and the work to reconstruct the country to a transparent process open to the

Indeed, the Iraqi invasion of Kuwait and the perceived external threat have helped rather than hindered the steps taken by the rulers to democratize the decision-making process in the country.[8] Popular participation was seen as a way of consolidating the legitimacy of the political system of the Gulf emirate and fending off outsiders' territorial ambitions.

The relationship between the ruling al-Sabah family and the idea concerning nationhood of Kuwait is founded on their historic role as governors. This legitimacy was also supported by references to Islamic theology concerning the kind of trusteeship that should ideally exist between humans and God. Another point often cited to reinforce the bond between rulers and citizenry was the centrality of the rulers in the construction of a Kuwaiti national identity. In the aftermath of the liberation from the Iraqi occupation, the concern expressed by citizens on the general mismanagement of the country in the years before also had to be addressed.[9] In the rebuilding of the country, the accumulated wealth of the oil economy became a form of insurance guaranteeing the government's capability to restore infrastructure.

The funds enabled the rulers to make investments that retained the loyalty of the citizens, thereby securing their power. Thus, the oil revenues continue to be the foundation for a social contract in which the citizens are dependent on the state. The development and character of the public sector were fashioned in support of this system of dependency – also described above as clientelism. A challenge to the al-Sabah family in the 1970s and the 1980s was the development of associations and allegiances that channelled the ambitions of various interest groups. Many of these groups opposed the rulers and strived to form a democratic system of governance in Kuwait.

---

public. Halliday states, "Given the serious incidence of corrupt administration and incompetence shown by the royal family in the 1980s, there was considerable concern among Kuwaitis about the pattern of the post war system in the country." See Halliday 1991: 228f.

8 For an article devoted to this statement, see Yetiv 2002.

9 After the al-Sabah family fled to Saudi Arabia, and nine days after the invasion, the rulers signed a contract to launch a £6 million campaign in the US under the name of "Free Kuwait". The rulers also established an Arabic daily newspaper, *Sawt al-Kuwait*, and an English language magazine by the name of *New Arabia* to support their message, see https://www.telegraph.co.uk/news/obituaries/1956367/Sheikh-Saad-al-Sabah.html. Accessed August 26, 2018.

Ghabra states that before the Iraqi invasion, a new political consciousness had evolved, characterized by a belief in pluralism and the rights and coexistence of multiple groups in society.[10]

The political forces in Kuwait and in exile during the Iraqi occupation supported al-Sabah as the rulers of Kuwait, but during this period, they also worked for democratization in the country after the liberation. The government in exile reassured its critics and interlocutors that it was intending to base postwar governmental institutions on the 1962 constitution, which had been suspended in 1986. However, the authorities did not manage to allay the opposition's suspicion about their commitment to a democratization in post-occupation Kuwait.[11] Therefore, taking these concerns about what the postwar conditions may entail into consideration, it was, from the ruler's point of view, a matter of legitimacy of the leadership of the ruling al-Sabah family to rapidly rebuild Kuwait after the war.[12] In addition to rebuilding the country, the revenues from the oil industry made it possible for the rulers to acquire a degree of support from the domestic opposition through the maintenance of a system of financial security that surrounded citizens, in combination with promises about democratic reform. However, the income from the oil exports was also the foundation for a foreign policy in which countries become dependent on aid programmes from Kuwait.[13]

Economic recovery after the Gulf wars

The system of governance that developed in Kuwait as early as the 1940s effectively turned the emirate's merchants, who used to derive their power from their wealth, into clients of the state. The wealth of the state after the discovery of oil eclipsed their economic power and diminished their

---

10 Ghabra 1991b: 213

11 Ghabra 1991b: 214. For reports in media on the discussions between opposition and the rulers, see https://www.nytimes.com/1991/02/28/world/war-in-the-gulf-the-royal-family-kuwait-s-joy-tempered-by-rift-over-absolutism.html. Accessed September 17, 2018.

12 Even if the population were divided, the resistance and opposition to the Iraqi occupation was very strong among Kuwaitis. However, no consensus existed about politics after the war; see Barakat and Skelton 2014.

13 In the spring of 1988 the minister of state, Sa'ud al-Usaymi, claimed that Kuwait was giving aid to 64 developing countries; see Kostiner 2009: 88.

political influence considerably. According to Ghanim al-Najjar, they faced the choice of being incorporated to the new political and economic reality or being left aside. The result was a new breed of merchants linked to the ruling family and acting as part of the government bureaucracy. In al-Najjar's words, "they all came in".[14] The incomes of the oil industry were used to buy off domestic as well as external adversaries and also to create dependencies and generate support in the country and abroad. But to reduce the politics of the emirate to the fluctuations in the balance of power between the rulers and the merchants would not do justice to Kuwait's social and political complexity: it is important to recognize that the history of Kuwait has been shaped through the interactions of a number of economic, political, religious and social forces beyond the state, the rulers and the merchants. Abdulrahman Alebrahim has attempted to map this complexity, by differentiating between religious scholars, the emirate's labour force, the Bedouins, the villagers, the country's Shiʻa communities and the intelligentsia. Alebrahim points out that these different groups have been representing and pursuing a diversity of interests. He argues that these groups have been acting as balancing powers between the ruling family and the merchants, and states that they have been playing a role in political debates from the early 20th century by throwing their support behind either the merchants or the ruling family.[15]

Prior to the Gulf War, Kuwait's financial history was not particularly characterized by its resilience. The Suq al-Manakh unofficial stock market collapsed in 1982, as we have seen. The resulting debts, numbering over 5,000, totalled US$92 billion, and the subsequent financial crisis was not really resolved until some ten years later. Kuwait's vulnerability to fluctuations in oil prices and its fragile financial system demonstrated the need for

---

14 This statement is from an interview with professor Ghanim al-Najjar, Department of Political Science, Kuwait University carried out by Mary Ann Tétreault in 1990; see Tétreault 1991: 578.

15 For example, representatives of what Alebrahim call the balancing powers constituted a majority among the candidates in the 1961 Constitution Assembly elections. As a result of the elections, a majority among the elected members of the Assembly also belonged to the balancing powers and they voted for the 1962 constitution; see Alebrahim 2019: 3. Beaugrand discusses how alliances and belonging to ethnic or religious groups in Kuwait are utilized, and she describes fluid and interest-based relationships that primarily serve the rulers; see Beaugrand 2016: 235.

a private sector and a modern financial district that could generate multiple sources of income, encourage direct foreign investment and provide elasticity to the economy.[16]

At the heart of the Kuwaiti economy is the reliance on "petrodollars" – the revenue generated by lucrative oil and gas reserves. These still typically account for some 90 per cent of the government's overall revenue.[17] This income has guaranteed Kuwaiti citizens' social security, social aid and medical care, while also providing generous subsidies for electricity, housing and healthcare. Furthermore, by the 1990s, over 90 per cent of working citizens enjoyed comfortable and well-paid "white-collar" jobs subsidized by the state.[18] Therefore, both economically and socially, Kuwait is almost entirely dependent on the state subsidies from oil and gas revenues that in turn allow the ruling Kuwaiti dynasty to preserve its authority. Thus, the Gulf emirate continues to meet the criteria of Hossein Mahdavy's "rentier state" typology.[19] Still, notwithstanding Kuwait's dependency on oil and gas, this classification of an autocratic and lethargic political system is not entirely applicable to the recent transformations of the modern Kuwaiti state.

Unlike other autocratic societies in the Gulf region, Kuwait's society and politics have, according to al-Khouri, modernized in line with the developments of international liberal norms by diversifying its economy, society and labour force, while at the same time extending political rights and granting electoral enfranchisement to women.[20] Other commentators see political turmoil and instability, the closing of the National Assembly, the suppression of civil rights and the failure of the rulers to address

---

16 Moore 2001: 136. Concerning the value of the debts, Moore quotes Darwiche 1986: 50.

17 al-Khouri 2008. The increased price on oil and gas in the years 2018 and 2019 made oil revenues grow. At the same time, in the fiscal year ending in March 2019, non-oil revenues continued to grow by 24 per cent compared to the earlier fiscal year, see https://www.kuna.net.kw/ArticleDetails.aspx?id=2811446&Language=en. Accessed November 5, 2019.

18 Sadowski 1997: 7

19 al-Khouri 2008. The idea of rentier states is discussed by many scholars, and a prominent reference developing the idea is Beblawi and Luciani 1990. See also Yamada and Hertog 2020.

20 al-Khouri 2008

socio-economic challenges as well as divisions in society between ethnic and religious groups, nationals and expatriates that characterized the country before the war as important elements of the postwar discussions concerning reconstruction. The discussion on the authority and legitimacy of the al-Sabah ruling family and its government had major impact on the process of economic recovery and the choices that were made regarding the physical, financia, and societal reconstruction of Kuwait.[21]

However, the postwar period was a moment when, as Barakat and Skelton claim, "the government failed to capitalize on the window of opportunity represented by the brief moment of post-liberation national unity."[22] The postwar government's ambition to reinstate the pre-war society, establishing the same form of social contract in which the government and the ruler provided citizens with welfare, meant delaying elections and entailed denying women the right to vote. In depriving women of the ability to stand in elections, Kuwait's leaders squandered an opportunity to engage half of the population in the great project of national unity in the aftermath of the Iraqi occupation. Instead, to compensate citizens, consumer loans outstanding at the time of the Iraqi invasion were cancelled by the government, salaries were boosted by 25 per cent and subsidies were increased.[23]

Following the US-led and UN-backed military intervention in Kuwait, Iraqi forces fled the country and dynamited between 60 to 85 per cent of Kuwaiti oil wells. The apocalyptic scenes of blazing wells blackening the skies over Kuwait were a powerful symbol of the economic catastrophe visited upon Kuwait by the invasion. The decimation of Kuwait's oil infrastructure – coupled with the slump in oil prices that had taken place in 1986 – resulted in almost two years without any oil exports or banking and no Gross National Product (GDP). Subsequently, an investment package of US$65 billion was created to restart the economy. Some US$20 billion were allocated to rebuild the oil sector, US$20 billion to stabilize the financial sector, US$16 billion to cover the military costs of "Operation Desert Storm" and US$11.7 billion in arms imports mostly from the United States.

---

21 See Barakat and Skelton 2014 for a discussion on various aspects concerning the reconstruction of postwar Kuwait.
22 Barakat and Skelton 2014: 16
23 Barakat and Skelton 2014: 17

Without any revenue over this period, Kuwait was forced to liquidate US$90 billion of foreign assets and loans.[24]

In the years after the occupation, the Iraqi state was forced to channel considerable sums in US dollars into Kuwait. Eight years after the war, the Iraqi government had handed over US$30 billion in reparations and 5 per cent of the country's oil incomes were utilized to further compensate Kuwait and pay the outstanding US$22 billion. The repayment of the US$15 billion that Kuwait lent Iraq prior to the invasion still remains unaddressed, and questions concerning looting under the occupation have not been settled either. These payments from the Iraqi state supported the rebuilding of Kuwaiti society but did not resolve many questions that were important to Kuwaitis concerning loved ones who had gone missing or who were taken as prisoners of war during the occupation.[25]

Despite the extensive disruption caused during the Gulf War, the petroleum industry re-established its dominant position within the Kuwaiti economy and once more became the main driving force behind the country's economic recovery in the 1990s and early 2000s.[26] As a result of the successful postwar reconstruction programme and the resetting of international borders 1,800 feet north into the lucrative Rumayla oil field,[27] by the first quarter of 2002, Kuwait was extracting around 2 million barrels a day.[28] And, with the price of a barrel increasing from US$30 in 2003 to US$100 in 2008, the petroleum industry's contribution increased from 88.7 per cent to 93.2 per cent of the total government revenue during this period.[29] Furthermore, the 25-year plan and government-backed "Project Kuwait", directed US$7 billion towards improving the output and production capacity of the Abdali, Bahra, Ratqa, Rawdhatayn and Sabriya oilfields to above three million barrels a day.[30]

---

24 Sadowski 1991: 7

25 https://www.theguardian.com/world/2011/jan/16/gulf-war-anniversary-kuwait. Accessed October 7, 2018.

26 By the end of 1993 the production of crude oil was at the same level as before the Iraqi occupation and the capacities of the country's refineries were completely restored in 1994; see Barakat and Skelton 2014: 17.

27 Pfeifer 2002: 10

28 Pfeifer 2002: 12

29 al-Khouri 2008

30 Pfeifer 2002: 12

Although Kuwait's oil production prospered and exceeded the quotas set by OPEC, the Kuwaiti economy continued to be too petroleum-dependent.[31] For instance, in the early 2000s, Kuwait had the lowest Foreign Direct Investment (FDI) in the Gulf region, with a negligible tourist industry, as indicated by the fact that the number of passengers using its airports was 6.5 times fewer than the UAE.[32] Indeed, as the private sector expressed frustration over the slow pace of innovation and the extent of corruption within the National Assembly, Kuwaiti politicians have been under pressure to shake off the country's un-entrepreneurial reputation and develop policies that would give Kuwait a more international outlook.[33]

Perhaps the greatest barrier to the Kuwaiti private sector was the difficulty in accessing property, 90 per cent of which is owned by the government. Indeed, the government is unwilling to sell this land because it is profitable. An added complication is the interpretation of landownership in Islamic law, which stipulates that the rulers of the state are responsible for protecting the land.[34] Therefore, while not actually selling the land, the state allocates land for development through a "Build-Operate-Transfer (BOT) mechanism" whereby the private sector "finances, builds and operates the facility" without owning it.[35] These projects, which are comparable to public-private partnerships, include the development of Faylaka and Bubiyan into tourist islands, the construction of a new "City of Silk", expansion and modernization of the airport and seaport, as well as the development of a subway system.[36] Furthermore, as a result of the

---

31 Pfeifer 2002: 12

32 Herb 2009: 377. In 2014, there were 208 companies listed on the Kuwait Stock Exchange, and 11 of them were non-Kuwaiti companies. At the same time Kuwait opened to foreign banks, but very few non-Kuwaiti banks have taken advantage of this. The Free Trade Zone has not been a success. The legislative amendments and the various initiatives appear not to have served the purpose of developing the business sector; see Nosova 2018.

33 Herb 2009: 381. Businesspeople in the private sector also saw foreign investors as a threat and contributed to the government not knowing how to develop private business sector; see Nosova 2018.

34 See the discussion above on the interpretations of Islamic law and landownership in Kuwait as a foundation for the legitimacy of the ruler and as part of a strategy to create a notion of the nation of Kuwait ruled by the al-Sabah family.

35 Herb 2009: 386

36 Herb 2009: 386. Most of these projects seem to be in the state of planning and

long-term funding of the education sector, the service sector and bureau-cracy were no longer entirely reliant on foreign workers. Nevertheless, the incentive for local enterprise has remained low because public sector jobs continued to be accessible and highly subsidized, accounting for about 90 per cent of Kuwaiti working citizens.[37]

With economic data showing an increased dependence on oil revenues throughout the early 2000s, and public sector and state subsidized jobs con-tinuing to employ around 90 per cent of Kuwaiti citizens, the policy meas-ures meant to diversify the Kuwaiti economy were not transformational during the early 2000s.[38] In part, this could be attributed to the absence of sophisticated economic governance structures within the Kuwait policy community, such as influential market-orientated think tanks or a highly technocratic and autonomous central bank. More significantly, the expec-tation of generous public hand-outs was engrained within Kuwait's system of dependency as a rentier state. For example, in a 2006 survey in which Kuwaiti voters listed their political preferences, the most popular policy was for the government to pay off consumer debts, ahead of both health-care and housing. With privatization polling in 16th place, stock-market reform at 18th and a desire to increase FDI in the last place, this survey illustrated that the economic rationale to diversify was not matched by a public willingness to accept policies associated with a free-market under-standing of economics.[39] Furthermore, Kuwaiti economic policy faced serious challenges in the 2010s: a period of parliamentary upheaval during the Arab Spring uprising, major public protests in 2011, mass resignation of the government, and the constitutional court's ruling that the elections of February 2012 were illegal.

Other challenges faced by Kuwait are domestic energy insecurity and environmental degradation. Between 2009 and 2010, energy capacity for the hot summer months was not sufficient in the emirate and the popula-tion faced power cuts. This was also a sign that energy consumption had

---

have been moved forward in time from the moment they were introduced, especially the subway system, the development of tourist infrastructures and the City of Silk. A new airport terminal opened in 2018 and seaports have been modernized.

37 Herb 2009: 382

38 al-Khouri 2008

39 Herb 2009: 383

grown considerably during the past three decades, outpacing upgrades in energy infrastructure. Similar problems occurred in neighbouring Gulf states and led to increased collaboration in the GCC and the connection of the power grids of Bahrain, Kuwait and Saudi Arabia. The GCC's low prioritization of energy diversification policy was reversed in the 2000s as new projects were introduced in all GCC countries. Environmental problems linked to the petroleum industry and consumption such as air and water pollution have also posed significant challenges to Kuwait as well as its GCC neighbours, although Kuwait faces significant problems related to the military confrontations of the two Gulf Wars and Iraq's scorched-earth policy during its occupation of Kuwait. Finally, global warming and climate change are also putting stress on Kuwaiti society and the country's already fragile biodiversity,[40] bringing to the fore the need to come up with innovative and sustainable solutions that the rentier-state logic cannot provide. The rulers used their financial strength to support economic benefits to Kuwaiti citizens and businesses through subsidies [41] but were reluctant to champion ideas on environmental, economic, political and social change.

Striving to become a major financial centre

Alongside the increased production of oil between 1990 and 2001, Kuwait's postwar economic strategy sought to increase international investment in line with the recommendations of the International Monetary Fund (IMF) and the World Bank. In 1995, following high government investment, Kuwait reopened its stock market to foreign capital. And in 1997, Kuwait began to accept international investors into the petrochemicals industry. The top rate of corporation tax was cut from 55 per cent to 25 per cent, and firms were able to be 100 per cent foreign owned.[42] Similarly, the Kuwaiti economy became increasingly aligned with the United States. For instance, the US become the second largest purchaser of Kuwaiti exports

---

40 See Luomi 2012 and Alahmad et al. 2020
41 On the economic benefits to Kuwaiti businesses creating an advantage for local businesspeople and protecting them from international competitors, see Nosova 2018.
42 Pfeifer 2002: 12. For foreign business, a 15 per cent flat rate tax was introduced in 2008. And tax could be further reduced or the company even be totally exempted from it entirely; see Nosova 2018.

and the top supplier of its imports, and Kuwaiti interest rates and wider monetary policy was also aligned with the US. Significantly, despite historically having a conflicted relationship with Iran, the Kuwaiti government established economic ties and allowed Iranian traders to access the port of Shuwaykh.[43]

One idea to strengthen the economies of the GCC-member countries was the introduction of a unified GCC or Gulf currency and a monetary union. With the exception of Kuwait, Gulf currencies are pegged to the US dollar. The volatile financial situation for the US dollar and the Euro in the years around 2009 prompted the discussion about a *Khaliji* currency and a monetary union. The main reasons for introducing a union were the empowerment of the GCC to launch its own monetary policies, control regional inflation, improve financial stability in the region and meet challenges such as global financial turmoil. In general, a monetary union would also, it was argued, strengthen the role of the GCC locally and internationally. The new currency was supposed to be introduced in early 2010, but the plan never materialized. One factor that derailed it was the lack of organization and of an adequate decision-making process. Another hurdle was that there was no instrument to establish reliable data on the different national budgets, nor any agreement on periodical audits of official figures. Other problems concerned the creation of a reliable and comparable consumer price index that would enable a better understanding and monitoring the various levels of inflation. There was also widespread scepticism among the public and business communities concerning a monetary union and a unified Gulf currency.[44]

More recently, Kuwaiti governments have become determined to develop an international financial community in an endeavour to increase private sector growth and become less reliant on oil revenue. In a speech in 2013, the amir Sheikh Sabah al-Ahmad al-Jabir al-Sabah stated, "It is time to launch a new decisive phase and a major qualitative move aimed at achieving comprehensive reforms and complete development. It has become necessary to rectify old concepts. It is time to adopt a new work methodology".[45] The ruler's statement underlined the urgency to reduce

---

43 Pfeifer 2002: 13
44 *The Middle East*, February 2009, issue 397
45 https://www.gfmag.com/magazine/january-2014/

dependency on oil and the need to implement a four-year programme to promote the private sector.

Likewise, the prime minister, Sheikh Jabir al-Mubarak al-Hamad al-Sabah, suggested that the generosity of the existing welfare state should be reassessed to keep government spending below oil revenues, including a review of US$16 billion worth of spending on goods and services which account for 22 per cent of the annual budget.[46] The government proposed a four-year reform programme in 2013 to reduce public subsidies for utilities and commercialize the region. Initially put forward in 2010, the US$110 billion development programme attempted to modernize the city to increase Foreign Direct Investment (FDI), with one measure allowing locals and foreign companies to develop on 4,000 acres of land. Furthermore, a "Capital Market Authority" was established to encourage FDI and private sector enterprise.[47] A reason from a financial and government point of view to develop the private sector is that while the majority of Kuwaitis work in the public sector and their salaries have doubled since the financial crisis in 2008, foreign workers occupy most private sector professions.

Kuwait's financialization was strongly influenced by executive officials who recognized the dysfunctional nature of the rentier regime, the instability of global oil prices and the necessity to prepare for the eventual exhaustion of oil wells over the next 90 years.[48] Nonetheless, this paradigm shift has also been shaped by the international policy community. In particular, the International Monetary Fund (IMF) drafted the Article IV consultation with Kuwait in 2013.[49] Several of the structural reforms carried out by the government to boost non-oil revenues and reduce public-sector subsidies have followed on from the recommendations made by the IMF, a case

---

kuwait-reshaping-the-welfare-state. Accessed October 10, 2019.

46 Azoulay and Wells 2014: 43

47 https://www.gfmag.com/magazine/january-2014/kuwait-reshaping-the-welfare-state. Accessed October 10, 2019. Despite all their efforts, Kuwait is also judged to lag behind other Gulf countries concerning the development of the non-oil sector; see the discussion on economic diversification in Kuwait in Nosova 2018.

48 Azoulay and Wells 2014. Another form of preparation for the future is the way Kuwait and other GCC-countries have acquired farmland in Africa and Asia to ensure long-term food security; see *The Middle East*, February 9, Issue 397, and Shepherd 2013.

49 https://www.gfmag.com/magazine/january-2014/kuwait-reshaping-the-welfare-state. Accessed October 11, 2019.

in point being the reduction of corporation tax.

The attempts to internationalize the Kuwaiti economy have also been constrained by the scrutiny of the National Assembly. For example, when Gaz de France Suez won a contract in 2012 to develop the al-Zour North power and desalination plant, a public-private partnership, it was opposed by the Assembly because it failed to establish a shareholding company. The disagreements resulted in a three-year delay to the plans.[50] The plant eventually opened in early December 2015. In the short term, these structural reforms resulted in a modest 3 per cent GDP increase of non-oil-based industries in 2013. Arguably, the financial and infrastructure programmes have provided a foundation to encourage greater FDI and facilitate economic diversification.[51]

The diversification of the economy is a discussion that has been taking place in all Gulf countries for decades.[52] These discussions always acquire a new urgency whenever there is a drop in oil prices, and become less pressing in times when the price of oil and gas is high. Nevertheless, the GCC countries are reliant on hydrocarbon revenues and state expenditure is dependent on the price hydrocarbons – their predominant, if not sole, source of revenue. For example, in 2015–2016 Kuwait recorded a 45.2 per cent decrease in government revenues in the first eight months of the fiscal year and a 46.1 per cent drop in oil revenues over the same period.[53] Kuwait has not developed and diversified its non-oil sector of the economy in comparison to other GCC-states. The country has large hydrocarbon resources and a small population of nationals. The situation is quite different in Saudi Arabia, Oman and Bahrain, countries which either have fewer resources or larger populations of nationals. The Foreign Direct Investment (FDI) is low compared with other Gulf economies. Changes and restructuring of the financial sector can be described as slow, and a reluctance to change is often attributed to the rulers seeing subsidies as a vehicle for ensuring

---

50 https://www.gfmag.com/magazine/january-2014/kuwait-reshaping-the-welfare-state. Accessed October 11, 2019. Gaz de France Suez changed the company name in 2015 to Engie.

51 https://www.gfmag.com/magazine/january-2014/kuwait-reshaping-the-welfare-state. Accessed October 10, 2019.

52 For an account of the discussions in the Gulf and in Kuwait, see Coates Ulrichsen 2017.

53 Coates Ulrichsen 2017: 3

regime security, but also the defensive position adopted by the parliament concerning changes in public benefits.[54]

One example of initiatives to change the dependency on oil products is the introduction of value-added tax (VAT). Although the Gulf Cooperation Council agreed to impose VAT by the end of 2018, Kuwait's National Assembly delayed its implementation. Plans to introduce it in April 2021[55] did not materialize and at the time of writing the expectation is to bring in VAT by 2022, according to a March 2020 report by the International Monetary Fund (IMF) – thus making it possibly the last of the GCC states to do so.[56] Likewise, the Kuwaiti government was unable to introduce austerity measures with a view to reducing its public spending, with the National Assembly instead negotiating for these reforms to apply solely to foreign workers and non-citizens. During 2015, the government legislated subsidy reforms at a significantly slow pace, and electricity and water price hikes were implemented to businesses and foreigners.[57] Healthcare fees were increased for foreign workers, alongside limits on hospital usage, public service availability and even usage of public roads.[58]

Transformation initiatives have been launched in all GCC countries, often as an integral part of national renewal programmes. In the case of Kuwait, the Kuwait Vision 2035 was presented in 2010. like many other such programmes in the Gulf, this initiative was devised by a foreign consultancy company. In Kuwait, the former British prime minister Tony Blair's firm was chiefly responsible. However, the programme was not well received and gained no support among policymakers. Moreover, when the costs of the plan became public, the prime minister who commissioned it, Sheikh Nasir Muhammad al-Sabah, was forced to step down and the plan was abandoned.[59] Five years later, in 2017, Kuwaiti policymakers

---

54 Nosova 2018

55 See https://www2.deloitte.com/sa/en/pages/tax/articles/e.html# and http://www.kna.kw/clt-html5/news-details.asp?id=30070. Accessed July 30, 2020.

56 https://www.imf.org/en/Publications/CR/Issues/2020/03/27/Kuwait-2020-Article-IV-Consultation-Press-Release-Staff-Report-and-Staff-Supplement-49294

57 In addition, in 2015 banks in Kuwait were not doing well and trade surpluses were very low. However, banks were recovering financially in autumn 2016; see *Kuwait Times* March 27, October 18 and 19, 2016.

58 Smith Diwan 2018: 7

59 Olver-Ellis 2020: 6

drafted a new plan entitled "New Vision 2035". A common objective of all these programmes, including those for Kuwait, is to develop an economic sector with a decreased dependence on hydrocarbon products, to expand the private sector and to transform the Gulf states into knowledge-based economies.[60] A general goal is also to reduce government spending by scaling down subsidies and services, and to also restructure employment patterns by spending less on public-sector employment for nationals.[61] Yet these grand schemes fail in large part to take the current political context of economic change into consideration. They are products of a top-down perspective, and do not take into account the political realities and networks of the Gulf countries.[62] Another problem is that the private sector is also dependent on subsidies. However, the higher corporation taxes that have been imposed, and the introduction of VAT and a levy on personal income, in conjunction with a drive towards the privatization of government bodies, do perhaps represent the first signs of a gradual shift that is taking place in Gulf economies.[63]

My intention here is neither to discuss the rentier state or the relationship between the Assembly and the rentier state nor to go into the "no representation without taxation" question in any great detail.[64] Rather, my aim is to link the discussions on proposed changes of income tax in the country to the discussions on identity and citizenship. Today Kuwait has a flat-rate corporate tax of 15 per cent, levied exclusively on companies with foreign ownership. Companies owned by Kuwaitis or other GCC nationals are not liable to the corporation tax. Companies in Kuwait are also obliged to

---

60 In order to change Kuwait into a knowledge-based society, a reform of the educational system is needed, preferably in conjunction with shifts in regard to the legal contexts as well as the social ethos concerning, citizenship, democracy and gender; see al-Nakib 2015.

61 Azoulay (2020: 160) sees the rulers as trapped by the welfare spending and the expectation from citizens to "have a stake in the state's assets". Combined with the unequal distribution of wealth, the idea of a social contract is impossible to uphold.

62 Coates Ulrichsen 2017: 6ff, Nosova 2018: 27ff and Hertog 2020

63 For ideas on reform of wealth sharing and social safety in Kuwait, see Hertog 2020.

64 In the case of Kuwait and elsewhere in the Gulf, there are good reasons to continue and develop the discussions on the rentier state and relations to parliament, taxation and the public. Perhaps it is time, as Michael Herb suggested already in 1999, to give the idea of no representation without taxation a "decent burial"; see Herb 1999: 259.

contribute to various levies such as *zakat* (obligatory charitable donations), National Labour Support Tax and a compulsory and annual support to the Kuwait Foundation for the Advancement of Sciences (KFAS) to a rate of 1 per cent of their net profits respectively.[65] Individuals do not currently pay personal tax on income or wealth regardless of nationality.[66] Discussions on taxation in Kuwait are linked to debates in the Assembly and elsewhere about increasing the current number of people granted citizenship. Today it is capped at not more than 4,000 per year. The current debate surrounding the increase of this number is connected to the discussion about the nationalization of the workforce and the reduction of the dependency on expatriates. Members of the Kuwaiti Assembly have proposed the naturalization and granting of citizenship to *biduns* and to children of Kuwaiti women married to non-Kuwaitis.[67]

The need to diversify the private and public economy of Kuwait has been the subject of scholarly debate for decades. It has also been an ambition that has been declared in all the Kuwaiti budgets in recent times. The changes that have been suggested in terms of policies and large infrastructural projects have often been delayed and slowly introduced. The thinking about various forms of taxation has also been a slow process from concept to implementation. The link between taxation and representation is an intriguing one, and it may be the case that the introduction of personal tax in Kuwait will be accompanied by new legislation concerning naturalization and citizenship. If so, one possible solution may be a diversified system of taxation connected to a form of naturalization in Kuwait in which people are granted varying degrees of citizenship. Governments in the Gulf have begun outlining a system in which citizenship is graded and linked to

---

65 For more details on corporate tax in Kuwait see https://taxsummaries.pwc.com/ kuwait/corporate/taxes-on-corporate-income or https://home.kpmg/xx/en/home/ insights/2015/07/kuwait-thinking-beyond- borders.html. Accessed September 15, 2020.

66 For a detailed summary of tax in Kuwait, see https://www2.deloitte.com/content/ dam/Deloitte/xe/Documents/tax/me_tax_business-kuwait-guide.pdf. Accessed September 2021. All laws and information concerning tax are available on the Kuwait Government Online Page, see https://e.gov.kw/sites/kgoEnglish/Pages/eServices/ LegalPortal/Legal.aspx#. Accessed October 12, 2020.

67 See http://www.arabtimesonline.com/news/assembly-oks-bill-on-number-of- people-to-be-granted-kuwaiti-citizenship-in-18/. Accessed November 18, 2019.

economic and political benefits and entitlements such as the right to vote and women's right to pass citizenship on to their children.[68] In devising a more inclusive approach to citizenship, the benefits and subsidies directly associated with citizenship will probably have to be scaled down. However, the problem with such a solution is the potential change in the role that the country's rulers have assigned to themselves – namely that of distributors of wealth, an activity which, as we have seen, provides much of the rationale for their legitimacy.

Consequently, subventions may still be provided in form of no-strings cash grants and other subsidies to citizens, but may be offset in future by higher tariffs for water and electricity, and a reform of the generous pension system.[69] This proposal is also linked to developments in foreign policy and aid programmes.

The al-Babtain Foundation: aid programmes and foreign policy

> Kuwait lives under the protection of Islam as its religion, Arabism as its homeland, cooperation as its strategic path, tolerance as its motto, fraternity as its guidance, constitution as its modus operandi, justice as its rule, progress as its responsibility and peace as its goal.[70]

The statement above by the amir Jabir al-Ahmad al-Jabir al-Sabah outlines Kuwait's position regarding foreign diplomacy. Since the 1960s and according to the rulers, Kuwait's foreign policy has been based on neutrality and mediation.

Kuwait has positioned itself as a central player within Middle Eastern and international affairs, acting as a mediator in conflicts and tensions. During the 1960s, Kuwait mediated between Saudi Arabia, Yemen and Egypt. Furthermore, to reduce regional tensions arising from Iran's claim to Bahrain, Kuwaiti diplomats presented a case to the UN and organized diplomatic meetings in Geneva. Similarly, in the 1970s Kuwait sent

---

68 Kinninmont 2013: 47f
69 For a discussion on policies on sharing wealth, its context and consequences of financial reforms regarding subsidies in Kuwait, see Hertog 2020.
70 Naser 2017: 105

a delegation to resolve the conflict between East and West Pakistan, and established broad discussions across the GCC during the Omani–Yemeni crisis. During the Lebanese civil war of 1975–1990, Kuwaiti officials called an emergency meeting with Arab foreign ministers, and also played a central role in establishing the United Arab Emirates. As an elected member of the UN Security Council, Kuwait has also used this global platform to condemn Israel's policies regarding the Palestinians and its claims on Jerusalem, while pledging investment in international donor organizations to remedy the humanitarian crisis in Iraq and Syria.

In the early days of its independence, Kuwaiti aid programmes were directed towards Arab countries. After criticism of Kuwait and the organization of Petroleum Exporting Countries (OPEC) following the oil embargo of 1973, Kuwait extended its aid programmes to non-Arab and non-Islamic countries. The Kuwaiti government also became more active in channelling funding through existing organizations like OPEC, the United Nations and the International Monetary fund (IMF), and in encouraging its national oil company to take part in international discussions concerning industrial development. At the same time, the investments made by the government of Kuwait in financial markets like the City of London are considerable. Kuwait also supported the Palestinian Liberation organization (PLO) and backed Iraq in its war against Iran between 1980 and 1988. Between 1961 and 2011, the Kuwait Fund for Arab Economic Development (KFAED) also granted loans and foreign aid to a total amount of US$16 billion to approximately 100 countries.[71] During the Syrian conflict that began in 2011, Kuwait is reported to have been one of the main funders of both Shi'a and Sunni opposition groups in Syria through *diwaniyyat*, local charities and online funding platforms. Although the government has not provided direct support to the Syrian opposition, funding of various extremist groups is evident in lower levels of government, with some MPs admitting to financing Syrian rebel groups.[72] The support given to various parties in conflicts, to countries and foreign aid programmes, or through foreign investments were all part of a coordinated strategy to strengthen the legitimacy and independence of the government in Kuwait, but also in the eyes of other Arab countries and in

---

71 Naser 2017: 105
72 Buscemi 2017: 266

the world in general.[73]

The many facets of the work of the al-Babtain Foundation mirror the official Kuwaiti government policy of providing development assistance to foreign countries.[74] The businessman and poet Abd al-Aziz is adamant that he has no financial support from the government. Perhaps any links should be understood as more symbolic, a manifestation of his and the foundation's support for the state and the ruling family as well as part of formal civic sector.[75] The Foundation at large has given assistance to more than 60,000 students for training courses in Arabic, and graduate and postgraduate education. The students are primarily from Africa and Asia, but also from Kuwait. They include more than 8,000 who have studied at al-Azhar University in Cairo.[76] According to officials of the Foundation, there are no restrictions regarding the disciplines studied by the students. Abu Sa'ud is very proud of the careers the students have made. He has maintained contact with many of them and has been delighted to witness the success they have enjoyed in their chosen careers as government ministers, ambassadors, university professors and governors.[77]

The inauguration in Cairo of the Abdulaziz Saud al-Babtain Prize for Poetic Creativity in 1989 was specifically designed to honour poets and literature.[78] The idea was also to "(...) reinstitute the role of poetry in the

---

73 Tétreault 1991: 583f, Leichtman 2017 and Naser 2017
74 Today the initiative named the Saud al-Babtain Kuwaiti Scholarship for Postgraduate Studies offers 400 scholarships annually to students from Africa, Arab countries, Central Asia, Balkan countries and Europe; see *Abdelaziz Saud al-Babtain: Biography & Cultural Achievements* 2017: 50
75 al-Babtain Foundation is active in several countries. It started in Cairo, but today the undertakings are mainly conducted from Kuwait. In general, the Law of Association in the country prohibits foundations and associations to engage in what the state defines as politics. Consequently, most associations and NGOs are registered as public benefit societies; see Hafidh 2017: 99ff.
76 For changes and discussions about of al-Azhar's move towards an educational institution, including disciplines like engineering and business administration and the role of its graduates, see Skovgaard-Petersen 2010 and Zeghal 1999.
77 The information in the paragraph is from a discussion on email with Haidy Abdel Latif at the al-Babtain Foundation, September 12, 2017, and interview with Abd al-Aziz, October 17, 2016.
78 The first two sessions were held in Cairo in May 1990 and in October 1991. The occupation of Kuwait is not mentioned in the various documentations of the

life of our nation". In this context, the term "nation" denotes not only the broader Arab nation, including Kuwait, but also countries which in the view of the al-Babtain Foundation have lost their Arab heritage, such as the Union of the Comoros. A third aim that has been more strongly emphasized in recent years is the Foundation's belief in intercultural dialogue, a rapprochement between cultures and religions leading to tolerance and non-violence. In the bylaws of the Foundation, it is stated that the objectives should mainly be to enrich "(...) the Arabic poetry movement, poetry criticism, encouraging communication between poets and those interested in Arabic poetry and enhancing links among them (...)".[79] This task is enacted through seminars, sessions, forums, the establishment of a library and a number of publications.

Branches of the Foundation were later established in Tunisia, Jordan, and Kuwait. Since its establishment, the Foundation has held many conferences and forums, and has issued more than 400 publications about poetry and poets. Major conferences are usually held bi-annually, with the opening ceremonies attended by diplomats, ministers, representatives of royal families and other dignitaries. In addition to the three first sessions held in Cairo in 1990, 1991 and 1992, conferences have been held in Fez in 1994, Abu Dhabi in 1996, Beirut in 1998, Algiers in 2000, Manama in 2002, Córdoba in 2004, Paris in 2006, Kuwait City in 2008, Sarajevo in 2010, Brussels in 2013 and Marrakesh in 2014. These sessions comprise different panels on the various aspects of poetry. During the sessions in Europe, several panels discussed multiculturalism and the theme of a dialogue among civilizations. In the most recent conferences, organized by the Foundation from 2017, this concept of "dialogue among civilizations" has been further elaborated.

Currently, the Foundation strives to foster a broader idea termed "culture for peace". The first step in this endeavour was taken as early as 2001, when Abd al-Aziz launched an initiative for "(...) dialogue and convergence between civilizations and religions, as he thought of a new purpose for the Foundation in the intercultural and inter-civilizational dialogue together

---

foundation. The only reference to the occupation is that the prize for the best poem in the second session in 1991 was shared by the Egyptian poet Rabeh Lotfi Juma for his poem "Kuwait's Liberation", see *Years of Cultural Output 1989–2015* 2015: 17.

79 *Years of Cultural Output 1989–2015* 2015: 9

with its literary role."[80] Accordingly, the Abdulaziz Saud al-Babtain Center for Intercultural Dialogue was founded in Spain to fulfil the mission of promoting cultural and religious dialogue and values such as tolerance, coexistence and open-mindedness. One key task was to "(...) explain the real Islam (...)" and "(...) to communicate that Muslims are advocates of peace and love (...)". The ambition to present what the Foundation understands as authentic Islam is in addition to its focus on language and literature, but the content of this form of Islam is not explained. Under the umbrella of the Center for Intercultural Dialogue a number of chairs in Arabic language and culture have been established or existing chairs supported at several universities, for example, Córdoba, Granada, Malaga, Seville, Nice, Roma Tre, Beijing, Barcelona, Oxford, Mogadishu, Palermo, N'Djema, Djibouti and the Comoros.[81] Linked to the chairs in the south of Spain and the University of Córdoba is also a global prize for historical and cultural research bringing new perspectives to the understanding of history or culture of "Islamic civilization in Andalusia".[82] From the perspective of the Foundation, the historic Andalusia is regarded as an "Islamic civilization".[83] The shift towards a focus on "dialogue among civilizations" was further corroborated by a decision by the Board of Trustees of the Foundation in 2013.[84]

---

80 *Abdulaziz Saud al-Babtain: Biography & Cultural Achievements* 2017: 52

81 *Abdulaziz Saud al-Babtain: Biography & Cultural Achievements* 2017: 52

82 The chair at the University of Córdoba was the first one established in 2004, see *Abdulaziz Saud al-Babtain: Biography & Cultural Achievements* 2017: 54f. and https:// www.ugr.es/~al_babtain/index.php. Accessed July 28, 2020. The al-Babtain Foundation also has a representative in Spain. Adjunct or Associate Professor Nader al-Jallad, University of Córdoba, was the representative in 2012 and 2013; see https://www.kuna. net.kw/ArticleDetails.aspx?id=2250169&language=en. Accessed December 4, 2019.

83 However, the prize and one of the recipients, Professor José Ramírez del Río, University of Córdoba, has been discussed in the media since he is a representative for Córdoba of the right-wing and Islamophobic party VOX. See http://www.congreso. es/portal/page/portal/Congreso/Congreso/Diputados/BusqForm?_piref73_133315 5_73_1333154_1333154.next_page=/wc/fichaDiputado?idDiputado=304&idLegisla tura=13. Accessed July 28, 2020, and https://foreignpolicy.com/2019/04/27/spains-vox-party-hates-muslims-except-the- ones-who-fund-it-mek-ncri-maryam-rajavi-pmoi-vidal-quadras-abascal/. Accessed July 28, 2020.

84 *Years of Cultural Output 1989–2015* 2015: 9 and *Abdulaziz Saud al-Babtain: Biography & Cultural Achievements* 2017: 52ff.

The Foundation's forums are literary events focused on various topics related to poetry and are primarily attended by poets, writers and academics. Notable forums include those organized in Tehran and Shiraz in Iran in 2000 and the one on Arabic poetry held in Iraq in 2005. Like the sessions, the forums have taken a topical direction in recent years towards discussions on peaceful coexistence and a dialogue among civilizations, and more recently a culture of peace. This shift related to a broader restructuring of the Foundation aimed at making Arabic culture and Cultural Studies the main focus of interest and poetry a subdivision of the Foundation.[85] To accentuate the changes, the Foundation was renamed in 2015. Its new name is the Abdulaziz Saud al-Babtain Cultural Foundation and, in addition to earlier collaborations with academic institutions in Rome, a branch of the Foundation was established in the Italian capital in 2016.[86]

The international aspect of the al-Babtain Foundation is also clearly in evidence in the many schools that it has established. By 2017, a total of 25 schools, colleges and institutes had been founded. Many are in Arab countries like Algeria, Egypt, Iraq and Morocco, but others are in Azerbaijan, India, Kazakhstan, Kyrgyzstan, Mali, Mongolia and Pakistan. According to the Foundation, they are created as charitable institutions on behalf of Kuwait, and they are therefore linked to Kuwaiti charity in general. Some of the schools have been established in the name of Abd al-Aziz, but others are named after members of the ruling family in Kuwait or the country itself. A third option is a combined name linking Kuwait and the specific country where the school is located as a brotherhood or friendship project. In a similar spirit, Abu Sa'ud has instituted a number of humanitarian projects outside Kuwait, ranging from a medical centre in Iran, a wedding ballroom for persons with low income in Saudi Arabia, a Kuwaiti Cultural Hall in Palestine and the renovation of mosques in Arab countries and Muslim nations such as Mali.[87]

A prime example of how the al-Babtain Foundation's and official Kuwaiti foreign and foreign assistance policies work closely in concert

---

85 This was stated by Dr Tuhami Abdouli, member of the Board of Trustees of the Foundation of Abdulaziz Saud al-Babtain's Prize for Poetic Creativity, October 16, 2016.

86 See *Abdulaziz Saud al-Babtain: Biography & Cultural Achievements* 2017: 43ff

87 *Abdulaziz Saud al-Babtain: Biography & Cultural Achievements* 2017: 60ff

with one another is their engagement with the Union of the Comoros. The island nation of the Union of the Comoros is situated in the Indian Ocean between the coast of Tanzania and the northern tip of Madagascar. The population numbers around one million and is mostly of African and Arab origin, but other groups are present in the form of people identifying as Indian, Chinese and French. Estimates vary, but there are also at least 200,000 Comorians in France. The Comoros is a member of the Arab League, and the country has three official languages: Comorian, Arabic and French. Sunni Islam is the dominant religion, while Ismailis and Roman Catholics are among the religious minorities.

In 2014, the governments of Kuwait and the Comoros signed an agreement to give *biduns* in Kuwait citizenship in the African archipelago state. The government of Kuwait is buying citizenships for *biduns* and giving them an opportunity, through their new status, to apply for residency and work permits in Kuwait as third-party nationals.[88] Although this provided much-needed funding for the Comoros, in Kuwait activists and parliamentarians were critical of the procedure.[89] Later the citizenship programme was investigated in the Comoros and former presidents were accused of embezzling public funds.[90]

To provide free courses in Arabic language, training in Arabic for media and prosody, poetry and poetic diction, the al-Babtain Foundation embarked upon a 15-year programme in the Comoros in May 2009 to "(...) revive and disseminate the Arabic Language in the Comoros and to

---

88 Beaugrand (2016: 243) sees the Central System to Resolve Illegal Resident's Status announced in November 2014 "(...) the granting of the Comoros 'economic nationality' to Kuwaiti *biduns* as a compulsory way to regularize their presence on Kuwaiti territory." The opportunity to buy Comoros citizenship appears to have been available before 2014; see https://www.aljazeera.com/news/2018/3/24/comoros-passports-abused-by-mafia-networks. Accessed April 4, 2019.

89 The question of whether *biduns* were to be naturalized through Comorian citizenship was still an issue in March 2016 when a delegation of Kuwaiti parliamentarians visited the Comoros; see *Kuwait Times*, March 29, 2016.

90 See https://www.bbc.co.uk/news/world-middle-east-29982964, and http://country.eiu.com/article.aspx?articleid=1684237152&Country=Comoros&topic=Politics&subtopic=Forecast&subsubtopic=International+relations, and https://www.reuters.com/article/us-comoros-passports-exclusive/exclusive-comoros-passport-scheme-was-unlawful-abused-by-mafia-networks-report-percent20idUSKBN1GZ37H. Accessed June 15, 2019.

Arabicize the signs of the streets and the governmental buildings."[91] Since French is the administrative language of the Comoros, this effort included Arabic language training for officials such as judges and ministers, as well as sessions for school teachers.

In its first year, 2009, the programme expanded to include the creation of a department for the training of Arabic teachers at the University of the Comoros. A language laboratory for Arabic was created and the Foundation took a decision to build a Kuwait Center for Islamic and Arabic Studies in the capital Moroni. In 2011, around 1,300 students were involved in training courses to teach Arabic to non-speakers, organized by the Foundation. The Cabinet of the Comoros also took a decision on the significance of training ministers in Arabic through language classes provided by the Foundation. Notably, the Foundation provided the president of the Comoros of the time, Ilkiliou Dhoinine, with a private instructor in Arabic.

Other projects initiated by the Foundation to support the Arabization programme and to bridge the geographical distance to the Comoros was to Arabize street names in the capital, sponsor Comorians' pilgrimage to Mecca and Medina (*hajj* and *umra*) and raise the salaries of teachers in the country. In recognition of his efforts, Abd al-Aziz was awarded citizenship of the Comoros and the honorary Commando Badge from the Presidents of the Comoros in 2010 and in 2011 respectively.[92]

The initiatives taken by the Foundation in the Comoros are paralleled by similar initiatives (albeit not always of the same scope) in other countries, with training courses in Arabic being organized in Afghanistan, Chad, India, Iran, Kazakhstan and Kyrgyzstan. These projects were targeted at countries with large Muslim populations and those with historic and contemporary connections with the Arab world.

Abd al-Aziz's achievements have been honoured in many countries. Since 1995, he has received no fewer than 14 honorary doctorates as well as numerous prizes and awards, along with other tributes recognizing his and the Foundation's contributions in supporting poetry, literature, culture and intercultural communications. Many of the awards are from countries in which not only the al-Babtain Foundation is active, but where Kuwait's

---

91 *Abdulaziz Saud al-Babtain: Biography & Cultural Achievements* 2017: 52 and *Years of Cultural Output 1989–2015* 2015: 135f
92 *Abdulaziz Saud al-Babtain: Biography & Cultural Achievements* 2017: 21, 32

various state agencies for charity are also involved. The largest national development fund, the Kuwait Fund for Arab Economic Development (KFAED), was established in 1961, the year the country gained its independence. According to Law 25 of 1974, KFAED's mandate is to assist and develop the economies of Arab countries as well as those of other nations.[93] The work should be in line with the directives issued by the prime minister, who declared that it should "serve the national interests of the State of Kuwait and support its regional and International foreign policy."[94]

One can perhaps regard the al-Babtain Foundation and Abd al-Aziz as part of a broader foreign policy and security strategy of the Kuwait state that maintains relations with a number of countries through charity and other links such as supporting young individuals to study abroad.[95] Abd al-Aziz is one part in a client relationship with the rulers of Kuwait, who have the capacity to reward individuals.[96] The loyalty such a relationship implies, and the material benefits and opportunity structures it provides, create a bond between wealthy individuals and the rulers, not only in Kuwait but also in several of the Gulf states. Abd al-Aziz belongs to a network of similarly very prosperous individuals running family-owned and family-controlled companies. Having stepped down from a daily involvement in business life and decision-making, they have dedicated themselves to philanthropy and projects in the broader sphere of culture.

Among his cultural achievements, Abu Saʿud also cites the Monday meetings, *al-Ithnaniyya*, in Saudi Arabia in his honour, which were held in the *diwaniyya* of Sheikh Abd al-Maqsud Khuja (in February 2000) and in the *diwaniyya* of Sheikh Muhammad bin Salih al-Naʿim (in December 2003).[97] Sheikh Abd al-Maqsud Khuja is a Saudi businessman who heads the Khuja Group. His family, which originates in Turkestan, settled in Saudi Arabia

---

93 For an overview of the legal aspects of philanthropy in Kuwait, see Khallaf 2008: 139ff. Khallaf also gives a brief introduction to the philanthropy of Abd al-Aziz al-Babtain; see Khallaf 2008: 139.

94 https://www.loc.gov/law/help/foreign-aid/kuwait.php. Accessed September 10, 2019

95 Naser 2017

96 This is following the statements on cliency made in Tétreault 1991.

97 For the various activities of the *al-Ithnaniyya*, see its Facebook page, https://www.facebook.com/alithnainya and its YouTube channel, https://www.youtube.com/user/Alithnainya/featured. Accessed July 28, 2020.

in the first half of 20th century.[98] Sheikh Abd al-Maqsud and Abd al-Aziz are both members of the Board of Trustees for the Arab Thought Foundation – a Saudi-based organization founded in 2000 and committed to "(...) instilling pride in the traditions, principles and values of the nation by promoting responsible freedom, reinforcing Arab solidarity and strengthening and unifying Arab identity, while preserving the diversity and plurality."[99] In a manner similar to Abu Sa'ud, aside from his role in business, Sheikh Abd al-Maqsud also undertakes a number of activities relating to photography, literature, arts and antiquities, and he is also involved in various boards on science and technology.[100] Such networks provide Abd al-Aziz and his family with business opportunities for his companies and valuable contacts for his Foundation and they can also function as channels of communication between states through prominent business leaders also active in the cultural life of a country.[101] It is also a network that can support governments as a back channel for negotiations. Abd al-Aziz has stated in several conversations that he has been involved in negotiations and in conveying messages to the governments of Iran, Algeria and Libya. At the same time, he is at pains to stress that he receives no support, either financial or political, from the government and that his network consists of contacts he has personally built. Abd al-Aziz has personal contacts with most leaders in the Gulf. He always invites politicians to his events, but, as he says, this is not in any way linked to the Ministry of Foreign Affairs in Kuwait.

The life of Abd al-Aziz as a businessman and philanthropist is not unique and is comparable to that of many North American and European industrialists and businesspeople. The foundations and religious organizations funded by such prominent individuals have long promoted the development of educational institutions in Africa and Asia during the colonial and post-colonial era. More contemporary examples are the many foundations

---

98 For the programme in honour of Abd al-Aziz, see http://
alithnainya.com/tocs/default.asp?toc_id=20297&toc_brother=-
1&path=0;2;19480;19487;20070;20088;20297. Accessed July 28, 2020.
99 https://www.arabthought.org/en/whoweare/overview. Accessed September 16, 2019.
100 https://www.arabthought.org/en/member/43/sheikh-abdul-maqsoud-khojah. Accessed September 16, 2019.
101 An example is also the way the Iraqi leader channelled a message to Kuwaiti rulers in the story that was recounted at the beginning of this book.

created in family names supporting projects in primarily Africa and Asia. Likewise, Abu Saʿud's role as a conveyor of political messages between states stands in a long tradition of private individuals and organizations acting as conduits of information. Abd al-Aziz's mirroring of the foreign policy of autonomy and non-alignment of the state of Kuwait is also evident in his and the Foundation's ambition to establish good relations with countries and institutions which from a Gulf perspective could be perceived as sensitive. In recognition of his cultural efforts, Abu Saʿud received an honorary doctorate from Tehran University in the Islamic Republic of Iran 2014.

According to the Foundation, he is the first Arab to receive a doctorate from Tehran University. Abd al-Aziz has also been recognized by the University of Yazd in Iran for his role in establishing courses enhancing the knowledge of Arabic at Iranian universities.[102] He was also honoured at the current House of Wisdom in Iraq in 2013 for his services to Arab culture and the Arabic language. The engagement with countries that are often characterized as hostile to the Gulf states parallels the Kuwaiti aspiration to build relations with countries and institutions that strengthen the autonomy and the non-alignment policy of Kuwait.[103]

Kuwait is a country in which charity is a source of pride. Kuwaitis are, according to Leichtman, "socialized in a spirit of humanitarianism and charitable giving at a very young age."[104] The charity initiatives and educational projects developed by Abd al-Aziz and his Foundation are part of such a spirit and the small-state strategy developed by the rulers of Kuwait to avoid conflicts and achieve security for the country.[105] Another feature of the strategy is to brand Kuwait as a country driven by a humanitarian commitment and the love of peace, playing a geopolitical role in mediating and solving conflicts.[106]

---

102 *Abdulaziz Saud al-Babtain: Biography & Cultural Achievements* 2017: 11, 31

103 For a study on the role of development assistance in Kuwaiti foreign policy towards issues in the Middle East from 2003 to 2014, see Naser 2017.

104 Leichtman 2017: 3f

105 Among the early institutions established in Kuwait was the Charitable Society, al-Jamʿiyya al-Khayriyya. It was founded in 1913 as a collaboration between merchants and religious scholars inspired by the reform-oriented thinking of the Egyptian religious scholar Rashid Rida and his journal *al-Manar*; see Alebrahim 2019: 26f and for the influence of Rida, see Halevi 2019.

106 See the statement concerning the Kuwaiti candidacy to the United Nation's

The projects launched by Abu Saʻud and his Foundation focus on Arab culture and the Arabic language. It is not part of an Islamic *daʻwa* oriented charity and aid that is also launched from Kuwait.[107] The al-Babtain Foundation sends students to the classic Sunni institution of learning in Cairo, al-Azhar University. However, this is more of a general recognition concerning the status of al-Azhar as an institution of learning, rather than seeing education at al-Azhar as a training in Islamic teachings. The foundation also sends young people on the *hajj* and *umra* pilgrimages. Abd al-Aziz can certainly be described as a pious and devout Muslim, but for him and the Foundation, Islam is primarily an element of Arab culture and an integral part of his aim to increase knowledge of and awareness about Arab culture. It is perceived as a positive outcome if a student sent to al-Azhar or on the *hajj* strengthens his or her religious knowledge and sentiments on a personal level. Study at al-Azhar also gives students, as well as the Foundation, expanded networks due to the international reach of the institution.

Those sent on pilgrimage are selected from poorer backgrounds and given the opportunity to undertake a journey they could never otherwise have made without financial assistance from the Foundation. This enables the individual to fulfil a task that is generally perceived as a religious duty within Islam, something that every Muslim is expected to do in their lifetime, but which is financially out of reach for most.

The endeavours of the al-Babtain Foundation in Europe and North America cannot perhaps be seen as charity or aid, but there are still certain features of its role there which overlap with its activities in Africa, Asia and Europe. The support of academic chairs and programmes at universities and educational institutions in Europe is designed to maintain and encourage the study of Arab culture and the Arabic language, as well as the study of Islam. From the point of view of the Foundation, these efforts are exercises in bridge building. Their starting point is that the study of the Arabic language and Arab culture is inherently positive and will produce constructive

security council, http://www.kuwaitmissionun.org/kuwait-s-candidacy-to-the-united-nations-security-council-2018-2019.html. Accessed September 19, 2019. Another example is deputy foreign minister Khalid al-Jarallah's statement in 2016 that the humanitarian aid is part of the state foreign policy; see *Arab Times*, March 29, 2016.

107 I am here referring to the Muslim charities claiming to carry out Islamic aid portrayed in Benthall and Bellion-Jourdan 2009.

results and foster relations and understanding between different civilizations. This aim of supporting higher education also chimes in with Kuwaiti foreign policy, in that it sees the country as a bridge-builder between cultures. The Foundation's promotion of international dialogue is the reflection of the need of a small state to engage on many levels in its international relations. The relationship of trust between Kuwait's ruler and Abd al-Aziz ensures that there is complete symmetry between the foreign policy of the state and the actions of the al-Babtain Foundation.

Kuwaiti politics and uprisings in the Middle East

The protests, demonstrations, uprisings and wars that took place in the Middle East from the Jasmine Revolution in Tunisia in 2010 to the outbreak of civil war in Syria the following year did not leave the Gulf states unaffected. The extent to which demonstrations and unrest were linked to similar developments in other countries is difficult to judge.[108] On the Arabian Peninsula, early protests arose in four countries: Bahrain, Kuwait, the Sultanate of Oman, and Saudi Arabia. Later on, a full-scale war erupted in Yemen.

In the Gulf states, the strong link between the economy and political decision-making is at variance with the situation in Syria and Egypt. In particular, the ability of the rulers of the wealthy GCC states to hand out cash, create job opportunities in the public sector and increase workers' wages is a powerful mechanism for curbing any desire among citizens for political freedoms. It effectively deprives political protest of any potential social or economic underpinning.[109]

The demonstrations that were staged in Kuwait in 2011–2012 followed a pattern similar to protests in Egypt or Syria[110] and used similar rhetoric, although each country had its own individual history of opposition. Middle Eastern or Gulf countries are not uniform, and the calls made by

---

108 Buscemi states that the series of protests that started in Kuwait in 2011 were related to the corruption allegations against members of the National Assembly, and persons in the cabinet were inspired by the protests and demonstrations taking place in Egypt and Tunisia; see Buscemi 2017: 263.

109 Coates Ulrichsen 2013: 35–37

110 Terms like *irhal*, "leave" and expressions like *karamat watan*, "a nation's dignity" were utilized in the organization of protests; see Buscemi 2017, 263.

many Kuwaitis for economic, political, religious and social change were coloured by specific recent developments in the country's history.[111] For example, decades of discussions in Kuwait on the role of tribal groups within the state, the role and function of the rulers, questions concerning a Kuwaiti identity and discussions about the political status of women all featured in the domestic protest movement in Kuwait. And the events of 2011 and 2012 brought to an end a period of relative political stability within the country.[112]

The uncharacteristic period of civil unrest and protest was fuelled primarily by young people and by Islamists making known their opposition to the status quo. As noted above, these protests occurred against the backdrop of a wave of mass movements throughout the Gulf and Arabia, commonly referred to as the "Arab Spring". While other demonstrations across the region were revolutionary and often violent, it has been asserted that Kuwait's relatively peaceful protests reflected the country's intricate balance of power, between the elected legislative National Assembly and the ruling al-Sabah family and its appointed executive. The civil unrest thus gave vent to the opposition's desire to strengthen their influence without directly challenging the regime or the authority of the amir.[113] This assertion may be somewhat contentious, since the opposition did after all call for the prime minister, Sheikh Nasir al-Muhammad al-Sabah, to step down and appealed for the establishment of a constitutional monarchy. The long-standing lack of power of the Kuwaiti Assembly to block legislation and force ministerial resignations also exacerbated the period of instability in the National Assembly from 2011 to 2014. The resignation of the prime minister in November 2011 led parliamentarians to conclude that dissent was their most effective way of achieving change and gaining

---

111 The study of the local roots of the protests and civil unrest in Kuwait's constitutional history is the starting point for Abdulrahman Alebrahim's study on politics in Kuwait before the independence; see Alebrahim 2019: 1. More generally Nonneman says that the series of political reforms that appeared in the first years of the 21st century indicate that the Gulf states are not "(...) quite so uniformly and unchangeably 'autocratic' as commonly perceived (...); see Nonneman 2011: 3.
112 Smith Diwan 2018: 6. Azoulay's study on the tribal politics discusses the limitations to a political patronage and the relationship between the rulers and tribal opposition in the period 2011 to 2014; see Azoulay 2020: 177–195.
113 Mohamed 2019: 9f

influence, a factor which in itself contributed to the waves of protests that soon followed.[114]

In parallel to discussions and protests in the Assembly, youth-led activists took to the streets of Kuwait in 2011 to demand political reform and to condemn corruption. It is estimated that up to 20,000 demonstrators took part. On November 16, young protesters and opposition MPs stormed one of the halls of the parliament building demanding the resignation of the prime minister. The prime minister Nasir al-Muhammad al-Sabah had allegedly transferred approximately US$350 million of public funds to bribe the votes of sixteen MPs, nearly a third of the National Assembly. Following increased public outrage, the amir accepted the prime minister's resignation in December 2011 and dissolved the National Assembly.[115]

During protests in 2011, opposition groups, primarily tribal and Islamist, were united under the "A Nation's Dignity" campaign, and Twitter and other social media outlets became a venue to increase publicity of the campaign through bilingual content and sharing foreign media and posts from human rights activists. Protests ranged from peaceful night-time sit-ins in front of the National Assembly to desecration of national symbols. In order to gain maximum media coverage, these attacks were often directed against iconic Kuwaiti landmarks that evoked sentimental ideas of national unity. During the storming of the National Assembly, the protestors claimed it as "a house of the people" and began a hunger strike after being allegedly imprisoned without trial. Those imprisoned released a political declaration, which was disseminated on the internet in both Arabic and English.[116] Nine MPs, almost all representing different tribes, were also incarcerated, but later released after being found innocent by a court.[117]

In 2012, Islamist and tribal opposition candidates gained a majority in the February elections.[118] The MPs that had participated in the protest and stormed the parliament were re-elected. This parliament ran until June 2012 and criticized the power balance between the appointed executive and the elected legislature. The new parliament proposed a law safeguarding

---

114 Smith Diwan 2018: 5f
115 Azoulay 2020: 179f and Coates Ulrichsen: 2014: 214.
116 Buscemi 2017: 263f
117 For more on the tribal context of the protests, see Azoulay 2020.
118 See Azoulay 2020: 181f

the independence of the courts. It also sought to open up the private sector and increase the transparency concerning tenders. But the legislature also attempted, but failed, to introduce radical measures such as the death penalty for blasphemy and a "morality police" to monitor women in public spaces. This was not entirely unprecedented. The role of *shari'a* law, its interpretation, practice and position within the legal system, has been discussed in Kuwait ever since the state's first constitution was promulgated in November 1962.

Article 2 in the first constitution states that *shari'a* is an essential source of legislation. Some members of the constitutional assembly favoured an understanding of *shari'a* as *the* source. In the discussion during the early 1960s, the impossibility of interpreting and applying Islamic law in a modern society was the notion behind the idea to comprehend it as *an essential* source. In the current discussion in the National Assembly, representatives supporting an Islamization of the state seem to approach the question of the relationship between *shari'a* and the state in a piecemeal fashion. Theirs is a strategy that would gradually Islamize everyday life, rather than promote an Islamic Kuwait through a change of the constitution.[119]

Amidst fears of a regional wave of violent unrest during the Arab Spring, Kuwait's foreign policy shifted from a softer position of mediation and diplomacy towards a united Arab-Gulf security approach. In 2012, the interior ministers of all Gulf Cooperation Council states agreed the Internal Security Pact (ISP). This treaty called for cross-border cooperation, sharing of citizens' biometric data and coordination of anti-terror laws and security practices. It also advocated mutual policing and military operations, intelligence sharing and the extradition of wanted individuals. Despite being signed by all six GCC leaders at the Bahrain Summit, the ISP was not ratified by the Kuwaiti National Assembly, as the Kuwaiti Foreign Affairs Committee rejected it.

The collective opposition feared that it would enable the government to impose considerable suppression of protest. For example, Article 16 of the Pact enforces mandatory deportation across the GCC for any, loosely defined, "crimes". Therefore, it would be illegal to criticize any regime across

---

119 For the discussion about the first constitution, see *Dustur. A Survey of the Constitutions of the Arab and Muslim States* 1966: 101f. On the legal status of Kuwait at the time of independence, see Pillai and Kumar 1962.

the GCC, significantly infringing upon freedom of expression and potentially resulting in large-scale censorship.[120] The Foreign Affairs Committee of Kuwait rejected the ISP in April 2012 though it had been approved by the foreign minister and prime minister as a necessary security measure within a period of regional instability. In May 2012, the amir further blocked proposals to make all Kuwaiti legislation comply with Islamic law. Amidst this parliamentary crisis, the amir controversially suspended the National Assembly in June 2012 for a month, which was shortly followed by a decision from the Constitutional Court that annulled the result of the election and reinstated the 2009 Assembly. The subsequent National Assembly failed to reconvene twice under the prime minister, as MPs boycotted parliamentary sessions.[121] In October 2012, the amir dissolved the Assembly for a second time, and issued a decree to amend the electoral law by reducing the number of votes cast by an individual in one district from four to one. And he redrew constituency boundaries before the election of a new Assembly in December. Despite a concerted propaganda effort by the monarchy, opposition forces campaigned against the decree and on October 21, 5,000 people rallied a "March of Dignity" that was forcibly put down by riot police.

Subsequently, the December elections were largely boycotted by major opposition groups such as the conservatives and Islamists. The result was that smaller tribes and Shi'a groups gained a disproportionate influence.[122]

As a result of increasing protests in 2012, the government passed new cyber-security legislation to effectively control and monitor social media and online news outlets. Likewise, most parliamentary immunity was revoked as 70 parliamentarians and activists had been put on trial in 2011 for criticizing the regime. In 2016, an electoral law was passed to prevent those convicted of insulting religion or defaming the amir from running for office. Inevitably, this significantly reduced the public platform of opposition politicians.[123]

---

120 Yom 2019

121 Coates Ulrichsen 2014: 214 and 224

122 Coates Ulrichsen 2014: 226

123 Smith Diwan 2018: 6f. The allegations concerned the storming of the Assembly and corruption. The nine former parliamentarians and activists were acquitted in December 2013; see https://www.bbc.co.uk/news/world-middle-east-25297907. Accessed November 19, 2019.

In 2013, following two years of opposition protest, the prominent Popular Action Bloc *member* and former MP, Musallam al-Barak, was sentenced to five years in prison. The former parliamentarian criticized the amir's proposed amendments to the country's constituency boundaries and electoral law. Coining a phrase at a public rally that became a slogan for the movement, "We will not allow you" (*lan nasmah lak*), Musallam al-Barak was accused of undermining the authority of the amir and the ruling family.[124] The conviction of Musallam al-Barak symbolized the Kuwaiti government's and royal family's intractable position on freedom of expression. While they sanctioned the existence of a controlled plurality within Kuwaiti institutions and media outlets, they would not countenance any questioning of the authority or wisdom of the amir.[125]

Throughout 2014, as political turmoil and insecurity spread throughout the Arab and Gulf region, the Kuwaiti government demonstrated its sense of insecurity by significantly constraining freedom of speech. Provisions in the constitution, such as Law 24, were used extensively to allow the government discretion in approving or denying prospective or existing Civil Society organizations. Despite Article 36 of the Kuwaiti constitution outlining a complete freedom of expression,[126] these laws were also coupled with other security measures such as Article 25 of Kuwait's 1970 penal code, which allows authorities to imprison protestors who undermine the authority of the amir. For example, blogger Sara Al Driss was sentenced by the Kuwaiti Criminal Court for four Tweets that challenged the rule of the amir. Likewise, the Ministry of Commerce and Industry was given the authority to ban media outlets at the request of the government, while the Press and Publications Law criminalized any journalism that criticized the amir. Although these laws were radical in nature, they did not fundamentally amend the constitution or the existing Kuwaiti political system.

According to one human rights organization, the crackdown on freedom of expression within Kuwait demonstrates that its political plurality is more

---

124 This type of statement by opposition leaders makes problematic the claim that criticism was stated without challenging the rulers and the authority of the amir.
125 https://www.nytimes.com/2013/04/16/world/middleeast/kuwait-gives-5-year-term-to-dissenter.html. Accessed November 13, 2019. See also Azoulay 2020: 182–184.
126 The article on freedom of opinion and expression has been part of the constitution since it was first published in November 1962; see *Dustur. A Survey of the Constitutions of the Arab and Muslim States* 1966: 102.

informal than a defining feature, since it is dependent on the discretion of the amir and the executive.[127]

The Arab uprisings had two key regional and geopolitical ramifications in the Gulf. Firstly, an increased presence of Iran; and secondly, the demise of a joint Gulf strategy. Following the invasion by Iraq and with approximately 30 per cent of Kuwait's population identifying as Shiʻa, Kuwait has a sense of geopolitical insecurity. Kuwait has subsequently developed several cultural and trade links with Tehran, with many wealthy Iranian business-people residing in Kuwait. But in some respects, Kuwait has also hardened its stance towards Iran. Nonetheless, it operates within a constrained environment of being intimidated by Iran while concurrently recognizing its economic and cultural ties. Therefore, Kuwaiti diplomats used a double-edged approach to defend Gulf interests while simultaneously trying to mediate with Iran. Despite joining the Saudi led air-strikes in Yemen in 2015, it hosted talks between the Yemeni government and Iranian-backed Houthi rebel leaders in 2016. Furthermore, in 2017, the Kuwaiti foreign minister Sabah al-Khalid al-Hamad al-Sabah travelled to Iran to deliver a letter that stated that the GCC would endeavour to reduce its geopolitical tensions with Iran. Similarly, Kuwait opposed the US president Donald Trump's withdrawal from the "Joint Comprehensive Plan of Action" (i.e. the Iran Nuclear deal), by announcing that the agreement promoted security and stability in the region.[128]

The practical results of the protests, demonstrations and civil unrest that took place in the GCC states from 2011 to 2014 were meagre in terms of increased political participation, political freedom and a desire for more dignified societies. However, many of the ideas motivating the protests still remain and are part of formal or informal public discussions. During a visit to Kuwait in the second half of October 2016, I found the upcoming elections in November to be a recurrent topic in the media. The discussion revolved around the amir dissolving the Assembly (the seventh dissolution since 2006) and the debates among leading political personalities on whether they should take part in polls. Growing corruption and public spending, taxes, fuel subsidies, economic reform and the performance of

---

127 https://www.civicus.org/images/Joint_CIVICUS_GCHR_UPR_Submission_Kuwait.pdf. Accessed October 31, 2019.
128 Smith Diwan 2018: 12f

public administration in general were other matters that were aired in the media. These issues are not new, and these discussions indicate that many of the questions raised during the civil unrest in 2011 and 2012 are still to be addressed. In the *Kuwait Times* it was noted that the dissolution of the Assembly also coincided with the filing of three requests to question the ministers of finance and justice on rising petrol prices.[129]

Questions concerning succession form one of the topics of concern. In the Kuwaiti context, succession is restricted to the descendants of Sheikh Mubarak al-Sabah and to the branches of the al-Sabah family known as the al-Ahmad and the al-Salim. A rivalry exists between these two branches, and ambitious sheikhs vie for influence and try to position themselves favourably for future opportunities. Linked to this is also the discussion about the role and function of the rulers, and this concerns identity in the broad sense. The status of expatriates, questions on citizenship and the *bidun*, the different Sunni and Shi'a communities and their relationship to the ruler and the government, and the status of tribal populations are all interwoven with economic, political, social and religious discussions in Kuwait.

In my conversations with Abd al-Aziz and the staff at the Foundation, the civil unrest of 2011–2012 was not a topic of discussion, even though we did touch upon other turbulent events in recent history.[130] Yet one of the core questions underlying the events in 2011 and 2012 concerned the construction of a Kuwaiti national identity. This question relates to the activities supporting the conceptualization of Arab culture that have occupied Abd al-Aziz and the al-Babtain Foundation for years. The so-called Arab Spring did not result in the rise of a pan-Arab movement, but in the Kuwaiti context, to be Arab is often utilized as a national identity linked to a broader transnational shared identity between Arabs of different nationality. Even if Abu Sa'ud likes to avoid talking about national politics and is

---

129 The dissolution of the National Assembly was recommended to the amir by the Cabinet and was justified by reference to security challenges due to regional conflicts and the need for a new government in times in which Kuwait faces many problems; see *Kuwait Times* October 17 and October 19, 2016.

130 Some of the persons affiliated to al-Babtain Foundation know about my earlier fieldwork and publications on Syria. They have guided me and arranged meetings for me with Syrians working for al-Babtain. In these conversations, the unforgiving repressiveness of the Syrian regime has been a common topic. However, we have never discussed the situation in Kuwait.

not directly involved in protests, the work of the al-Babtain Foundation plays a role within the state supporting the creation of a national and transnational constructed Arab kinship.

The relationship between Abd al-Aziz and the ruling family can be characterized as an example of a client-patron relationship. The opportunities given to Abu Sa'ud, but also taken by him as an entrepreneur, lessen his desire to be directly part of the political life of the country. However, in this relationship he also expects that through his support, the rulers must deliver. He becomes part of a successful financial elite that is not characterized by its involvement in local politics, but rather by being part of a system that upholds the current power. In a sense, the statement reiterated above that Abd al-Aziz dislikes politics is not entirely true. What he dislikes is a society in disorder and in turmoil. To claim to have an aversion to politics or to be uninterested in politics is itself an intrinsically political statement since it, under certain conditions, and certainly in the case of Abu Sa'ud, is premised upon an acceptance of the ruler. In practice, the hiring of a former politician, Touhami Abdouli, as the general director of the al-Babtain Foundation would seem to counter the "official" line that the Foundation is completely apolitical. For the Foundation, Touhami is important precisely as a result of his political contacts in countries around the Mediterranean, and the development of the new initiative of the Foundation to initiate dialogues of peace. Hence, on an international level the al-Babtain Foundation is clearly political, and Touhami is a key to international contacts needed to promote a discussion among political leaders about initiatives concerning peace.

The work of the al-Babtain Foundation and Kuwaiti history, be it recent or otherwise, underlines how identities are fluid and not monolithic and sometimes have only a weak relationship with kinship, or possibly even no connection whatsoever. Identities are conceptualized for various purposes and practices. Rather than being owned and static, the term "identity" is conceptualized on individual and collective levels, often supporting ambitions that can be broadly defined as political and a matter of recognition.[131]

This understanding of the term "identity" also connects to how Islam has an increasing presence in the activities of the al-Babtain Foundation

---

131 This statement builds on ideas in Fukuyama 2019 and Butler 2011.

since I first visited it over 10 years ago. Abd al-Aziz al-Babtain and many of the officials at the Foundation, are devout Muslims. This means that they follow the general teachings and practices of Sunni-Islam. These include performing the daily prayers, fasting during the month of Ramadan, not drinking alcohol and understanding Islam as a source for their construction of a personal moral code. Abd al-Aziz also states that he is against mixing Islam, Christianity and Judaism with politics. In his opinion, politics has its own methods and characteristics, while religion is between people and God and concerns ethics and beliefs.[132] However, the shift at the Foundation from the organization of conferences celebrating poetry to also include conferences on the dialogue among civilizations has made Islam and politics more visible. This change also alters the ambiance of the conferences and addresses a new audience. The majority of the participants are now politicians, journalists, academics and educators rather than poets and writers.

In the more recent conferences, topics such as Islamophobia in Europe have been tabled as well as the idea of a clash between civilizations. At the Abdelaziz Saud al-Babtain Center for Intercultural Dialogue in Spain, one key aim is to explain "real" Islam to non-Muslims. A prize was also created in the name of the famous *hadith*-scholar Muhammad al-Bukhari (810–870) to strengthen cultural and intellectual ties between states in Central Asia and Kuwait. The support for people from the Comoros to go on pilgrimage is also an example of how Islam is a part of the work of the Foundation as part of a broader Arab culture. The role of Islam and identity will be further discussed in the final chapter.

Politics, Islamists and the quest for democratization

On November 11, 1962, the amir of Kuwait, Abd Allah al-Salim al-Sabah presented the first constitution of the independent nation.[133] It had been subjected to a vote by a Constituent Assembly. This assembly spent two months before the vote examining a draft prepared by legal specialists. Many of the articles were comprehensively discussed and it took time before

---

132 Interview with Abd al-Aziz, October 17, 2016.
133 Abu Sa'ud's views on this will be discussed in the next chapter devoted to him and the Foundation.

they were generally accepted in the Assembly. One of the more thoroughly reviewed was Article 2, which states that the religion of the state is Islam and Islamic law is a main source of legislation. Some of the members of the Assembly were adamant that Islamic law should be *the* definitive source of legislation, while their opponents regarded such an approach to the application of Islamic law as unworkable.[134] In the discussion, the opponents to the idea of making Islamic law the source for legislation pointed out that in the modern state to chop off the hand of a thief is not appropriate and that Islamic law is incompatible with a functioning modern economic system, involving as it does banks, insurance and other financial institutions that, of necessity, violate the *shari'a* proscription of *riba*, or usury.[135]

Because of the executive power of the Kuwaiti monarchy, several scholars, such as Schultziner and Tétreault, state that Kuwait cannot be considered as a democracy by comparative standards.[136] Furthermore, the reigning al-Sabah family has formal control over the selection and appointment of executive ministers and government positions, and the amir is responsible for calling elections and dissolving the Assembly.[137] Nonetheless, in comparison to the wider Gulf region and for the citizens, Kuwait demonstrates

---

134 The discussion of the role of Islamic law in the constitution and in relation to the legislation has been recurrent in many Muslim majority countries since their independence from any form of foreign governance. One example is the amendment to Article 2 of the 1980 Egyptian constitution in which a change was made from making the principles of Islamic law *a* source of legislation to the declaration that Islamic law is *the* source of legislation. For different aspects of discussions about Islamic law and legislation, see Brown and Revkin 2018, Parolin 2009 and Toll and Skovgaard-Petersen 1995.

135 This paragraph on the first Kuwaiti constitution paraphrase's the presentation in *Dustur: A Survey of the Constitutions of the Arab and Muslim States* 1966: 101f.

136 Schultziner and Tétreault 2011: 1. In *Political Change in the Arab Gulf States* (2011) Tétreault, Okruhlik and Kapiszewski state that economic and political reforms have taken place in Kuwait and the GCC states. Liberal and civil rights have increased in the last decade and people have more of a voice in national discussions. The countries in GCC cannot be described as they are in a transition to democracy, but the developments of rights and democratization are also a process and the end point is still unclear; see Tétreault, Kapiszewski and Okruhlik 2011: 2f.

137 Azoulay and Wells 2014: 44. Article 107 of the constitution states that the amir has the right to dissolve the Assembly by a decree that demonstrates the reasons for the closure. Moreover, if dissolved, elections for a new Assembly should be held within a two-month period from the date of the dissolution.

a relatively open, semi-democratic parliamentary system.[138] Established in 1963, the "oldest and most powerful parliament in the region" exercises its power through its ability to veto legislation and pass votes of no confidence in its ministers.[139] The veto powers of the wholly elected Assembly provide scrutiny of the appointed executive and increase overall accountability of the executive. But, as Assembly members have insignificant influence over policy formulation, they exercise their power by blocking bills, which often simply results in deadlock. One upshot of this is the persistent delaying of large-scale projects.[140]

Furthermore, the National Assembly is an arena for discussions, debates, and conflicts in search of Kuwaiti identity and the articulation of the rights and responsibilities of those who share that identity. One point is that: "(...) throughout the debates a tacit understanding remains that these disagreements will not be allowed to threaten the basic consensus on the Kuwaiti national identity. The result has been a strong national identity with workable national institutions but an identity that has involved a constant process of maintenance and reconstruction."[141] Hence, the National Assembly and the state institutions are spaces in which a Kuwaiti political identity has emerged.

In the context of the quotation above, Crystal argues that Kuwait differs in regard to many of its neighbours since it has a more established national identity deriving from its longer identity as a nation (going back to the 18th century). A point concerning identity is also the legal and social exclusion of certain groups in society such as the *bidun*, expatriates and women. The discussions about the role of women and the tribes in the political life of Kuwait as well as the debates of what norms and values a Kuwaiti identity entails expose the fluidity and differences in the understanding of the

---

138 Kapiszewski (2006: 98ff) describes the developments in the Assembly of Kuwait and how it differs from most national assemblies in the Gulf.

139 Azoulay and Wells 2014: 44

140 Herb 2009: 380. The National Assembly has also known long periods of closure. When elections to the Assembly were held in 1981, they followed a period in which it had been closed for five years by the government; see Tétreault, Kapiszewski and Okruhlik 2011: 3. The day after the parliament was dissolved in October 16, 2016, the *Kuwait Times* (October 17) published a chronology of significant events in the history of the parliament.

141 Crystal 1992: 4. Questions concerning identity in Kuwait will be further discussed in chapter 7.

identity. The idea of a Kuwaiti identity is a source of contention, especially when the term "identity" is to be conceptualized.[142]

The significant degree of stability and control maintained by the al-Sabah dynasty is exemplified by the fact that, even taking into account the 2011–2012 protests, there have never been any significant political or military attempts from within the country to overthrow the regime.[143] Furthermore, the principal factor that has contributed towards Kuwaiti political stability has been Kuwait's rapid industrialization by the oil industry, enriching the country and overseen by the ruling dynasty. Subsequently, the rulers and the governments have created a system of patronage and dependence, typical of a rentier economy, where citizens are dependent on a generous welfare state and public sector funded by oil and gas revenues.[144] To maintain a strong grip on power, the rulers shift support between interest groups in order to undermine any possibility of coherent alliances forming among the opposition, and also to control the image of Kuwait, the Kuwaiti and the right to Kuwaiti citizenship.[145] For example, the tribal communities have become less loyal to the government and seen by the rulers as a threat, and Shi'a groups have moved from being oppositional into the government establishment.[146]

Another explanation for the stability of the Kuwaiti ruling family is the ability of the rulers, the government and the political elite to pragmatically react to international events. Kuwait's proactive foreign policy, building relations with many countries and the ambition to mediate in conflicts

---

142 See Beaugrand 2016 and 2018 and Azoulay 2020 for discussions of how the government and the rulers in Kuwait have supported various interest groups over others in order to forestall the possibility of a united opposition forming, and to maintain their power.

143 Herb 1999: 158. Herb's statement was made before the protests in 2011 and 2012. However, it is doubtful if the protests in these years can be assessed as a political movement threatening to overthrow the government. Also, see Azoulay 2020 and Beaugrand 2016 for protests and politics between 2006 and 2014 in the parliament and in relation to elections in Kuwait.

144 Azoulay and Wells 2014: 44

145 The opposition is, following Longva, in the context of Kuwait not referring to a political party, group or movement. It refers to individuals who aim to introduce changes in a system in which the power is defined and belongs to the ruling family; see Longva 2013: 115f.

146 Beaugrand 2016: 240–244 and Azoulay 2020

have been assiduously promoted by the country's rulers to avoid being unduly affected by external constraints.[147] When the threat of Iraqi invasion first loomed in the early 1960s, the amir and the government believed that a constitutional and parliamentary system would be able to unite a diverse society under the banner of Kuwaiti national identity. Rather than letting interest groups (such as the old class of wealthy merchants) and new reformist organizations (such as the Arab nationalists of the Cultural Nationalist Club) flourish outside the state, those who advocated parliamentary democracy believed that pluralism would contain their growth and prevent national dissent.[148]

Part of the dynasty's impetus to create a parliamentary system was to maintain its legitimacy and to build coalitions within a diverse internal society after losing international support from the British Empire.[149] Without ignoring Kuwait's unique political experience and culture, alongside the ruling dynasty's liberal tendencies, recent political transformations in Kuwait must be considered within a wider international framework of democratization.[150] Scholars recognize that the process of democratization is usually a global phenomenon that manifests across large regions in "waves". During the early 1960s in what is described as "the second wave" of democratization, the African continent witnessed the growth of a number of independence movements, and 1960 was the "year of Africa". Similarly, the process towards female enfranchisement in Kuwait during the 1990s and early 2000s coincided with the "third wave of democratization" and the collapse of the USSR.[151]

On a global level, the third phase of democratization demonstrated a transformation of international political norms in a post-Cold War political paradigm, and democracy movements and reformist political elites emerged across the African continent and Eastern Europe.[152] Regionally, the al-Sabah dynasty experienced pressure from Saudi Arabia, as many Saudi princes were against a process of liberalization while preferring a

---

147 For a discussion on foreign policy of small states, see Elman 1995.
148 Ghabra 1991b: 201f
149 Herb 2016: 8, Herb, 2009: 339
150 Herb 2016: 8
151 Bratton and Van de Walle 1997
152 Wiseman 1995: 3

restoration of strong monarchical control within Kuwait. Yet neither in Saudi Arabia nor in Kuwait are the ruling families of one mind, and, as in other countries, the difficulties of promoting democracy cannot be attributed merely to the self-interest of the rulers.[153] In the 2000s, liberal and electoral democracies faced a crisis, with the years following the economic recession of 2008 being described as "democracy in retreat". Certainly, the number of democratic states decreased during this period.[154] This global trend is in favour of the rulers and of a status quo policy in regard to taking further steps towards democracy.

The erosion of the political-economic division of labour among the Kuwaiti elites coincided with increasing economic and social problems in Kuwait. Domestic dissatisfaction with the regime grew rapidly as autocratic regimes collapsed throughout Eastern Europe with the dismantling of the USSR in the early 1990s and Kuwaitis focused their own efforts on the restoration of democratic rights at home. For more than a year preceding the Iraqi invasion, members of virtually every social group in Kuwait – including women, who at the time were denied the right to vote or run for political office – participated in demonstrations and other political activities aimed at restoring the constitution. Although the opposition worked well within the bounds of reformist rather than revolutionary politics throughout this period, the internal turmoil in the country was a strong indication of the limits to which oil revenues could be used as instruments of domestic political appeasement.[155]

Kuwait also displays some political features of a rentier system beyond its financial reliance on oil and gas revenues. Throughout Kuwait's recent history, despite large parts of the population being disenfranchised, there have been relatively few demands by both men and women for a fuller democracy.[156] Part of this is due to rentierism, which has allowed Kuwaitis to be relaxed about political rights, as the "absence of taxation coupled with huge social benefits" has encouraged citizens to accept the prosperous status quo.[157] The political class is therefore dominated by the interests of

153 Halliday 1991: 229
154 Fukuyama 2019: 3ff
155 Tétreault 1991: 581
156 Schultziner and Tétreault 2011: 6
157 Schultziner and Tétreault, 2011: 7

state bureaucracy, and state employees enjoy large state-funded salaries and pensions regardless of their productivity or qualifications. Moreover, the "high level of political participation encourages its dependence on oil", as the parliament represents the interests of the public sector.[158]

Political participation and public consciousness have manifested themselves in other ways, and Kuwait has a nuanced relationship with the rentier state classification. For instance, during the late 1970s and early 1980s, the "Social Reform Society" arose as one of "the most important Islamic associations in the entire Gulf region", setting up committees on cultural, theological and social issues.[159] Similarly, the Shiʿa-led "Cultural and Social Society", was also successful as a pan-Islamic force, spreading its influence through trade unions and cooperatives.[160] Although the Kuwaiti system experienced prolonged periods of political censorship during the 1980s, alongside the frequent dissolution of Parliament, political participation has remained relatively consistent.[161]

Turnout in the May 2008 elections was around 70 per cent, much greater than many European democracies who often criticize regimes such as Kuwait's. As long as the sovereignty of the royal family is not undermined, relatively open political discussion occurs across social spaces, such as in the *diwaniyyat*.[162] More recently, since the expansion of social media, Twitter and other online platforms have become a modern outlet for political discourse, with Kuwait being one of "the most Twitter-connected countries per capita".[163] For example, during recent discussions over housing shortages – which have been one of the most pressing political issues of recent years – one profile, "@na6er_bait", meaning *natir bayt* or "waiting for a house", was followed by "about two thirds of all Kuwaiti Twitter users".[164]

One interesting aspect of the Kuwaiti political system is the moderate Islamism of the Muslim Brotherhood and the Salafi strands.[165] The Kuwaiti

---

158 Herb 2009: 375
159 Ghabra 1991b: 207
160 Ghabra 1991b: 208
161 Ghabra 1991b: 211
162 Riad al Khouri 2008: 2
163 Azoulay and Wells 2014: 45
164 Azoulay and Wells 2014: 45. In 2013 roughly one-third of all Kuwaiti citizens were on a waiting list for homes provided by the government; see Azoulay 2020: 159.
165 In Ostovar's analysis of images from *jihadi* online forums, one figure from about

Muslim Brotherhood, founded in 1951, and the Islamic Constitutional Movement (ICM), created in 1991, have supported the idea of accountable governance from the very outset. Despite the spread of Islamist movements and ideology since the founding of the Muslim Brotherhood in Egypt at the end of the 1920s, and the more recent developments since the war in Afghanistan and the founding of the Islamic Republic in Iran, the Kuwaiti Muslim Brotherhood and the Islamic Constitutional Movement have been comparatively pragmatic and peaceful in recent history. They ended their relationship with the international Brotherhood, which did not support the liberation of Kuwait through the involvement of non-Muslim troops. Members of the Egyptian Muslim Brotherhood were also arrested by Kuwaiti security services in 2014. The Kuwaiti Brotherhood was not considered a security threat and was allowed to continue to promote its aim of Islamizing Kuwaiti society. The ambition of the Kuwaiti Brotherhood, at least on the part of the ICM, is shaped by local realities more than a desire to overthrow the government, and it has regularly proclaimed its loyalty to the ruling family. The Kuwaiti Muslim Brotherhood and the Salafis have operated as "insider" interest groups that are fairly loyal to the regime while simultaneously focusing on specific political and regional issues, rather than operating as an "outsider" opposition to the government.[166]

Partly due to the prosperous welfare state and a context of political stability and plurality, the Kuwaiti Islamist groupings have exercised compromise and have not sought to radically Islamize society while instead promoting gradual reform. Also, the Islamic Constitutional Movement, which combines these groupings, advocates several liberal policies regarding the National Assembly and has declared its loyalty to the ruling family. The Kuwaiti Muslim Brotherhood is more focused on Kuwaiti politics rather than the separate national and international Muslim Brotherhoods, which have a regional or international agenda. For example, the Kuwaiti Muslim Brotherhood supported the deployment of US-led troops in the liberation

---

2005 depicting Kuwait conveys the hope that jihadist movements should be more rooted as well as active in the country; see Ostovar 2017: 94.

166 Freer 2015 and Freer 2018. Since the state of Kuwait's establishment, its rulers have supported religious movements and individuals as well as their opponents. The point would be to keep religious interests as well as other oppositional groups divided; see Tétreault 1993: 281.

of Kuwait. On the one hand, the ICM has argued for an "Islamic identity and true Arab loyalty", alongside policies that reject female suffrage and would restrict female working hours while penalizing "religiously sensitive commentary". On the other hand, it has simultaneously worked with other political groupings in the Assembly to create a middle ground, and has not campaigned to enshrine *shari'a* law within the constitution.[167]

Kuwait's moderate form of Islamism was popular amongst voters in 2012, who elected the Brotherhood and Salafis to 34 of the 50 Assembly seats.[168] The Muslim Brotherhood and the Salafi movement continued to lobby for peaceful change, and had support in important institutions such as the Assembly, charities, academic institutions and mosques.[169] Furthermore, when the amir dissolved the Assembly and issued a decree that would reform the voting system, the ICM and Salafis boycotted the elections, resulting in a turnout of 39 per cent, demonstrating its widespread support and loyalty.

Subsequently, the ICM have produced a document which promoted a liberal "Civil Democratic Movement", which ensures a "full parliamentary system, with a stronger legislature, independent judiciary and revised criminal code".[170]

The Kuwaiti Muslim Brotherhood experienced a significant decline in political influence during its boycott of the Assembly from 2012 to 2016. Sunni and Salafi groups were affected by the change in electoral law and their number of Assembly seats decreased from 23 members to four. Additionally, the Islamic Bloc was unable to prevent unpopular austerity measures that were passed during this period and feared that the government would enable other liberal transformations of Kuwaiti society. This unsatisfactory state of affairs spurred opposition forces to return to the Assembly with the self-proclaimed Umma Party. This decision united opposition parliamentarians and rebranded the Muslim Brotherhood's identity as one that was focused on Kuwaiti political issues, rather than on the agenda of the controversial and international Muslim Brotherhood across the region. Hence, while other opposition forces boycotted the 2016 elections or were

---

167 Freer 2015
168 Freer 2015: 12
169 Buscemi 2017: 265
170 Freer 2015: 13

debarred from running, the Muslim Brotherhood and the Islamic Constitutional Movement demonstrated considerable pragmatism by standing at the 2016 election and cooperating with the amir and the elected government.[171]

Ultimately, there appears to be a realization within the Muslim Brotherhood that it is far more influential and effective as an insider parliamentary group rather than as an extra parliamentary protest group. The nature of being an "insider group" also makes it unsurprising that the Muslim Brotherhood decided to stand in 2016 considering how uninfluential they were outside the Assembly in comparison to when they were inside it.

The quest for democracy has been inextricably linked with Kuwaiti society since independence. The rulers of the country navigate their way through various domestic challenges and external pressures. The crown prince, who also acts as prime minister, is responsible for appointing ministers. According to Longva, the role of the National Assembly to many Kuwaitis, especially those in opposition to the rulers, is to control the government and "(...) prevent it from abusing its power."[172] The rulers appear to pragmatically steer the country forward permitting a certain degree of opposition in Kuwait and staying out of trouble in the Gulf region and in the wider Middle East. The death of the amir Sabah al-Ahmad al-Jabir al-Sabah on September 29, 2020, does not appear to have changed the way the country's rulers do politics. At the age of 83, the new amir, Sheikh Nawaf al-Ahmad al-Sabah, was sworn in on the day his predecessor, his half-brother, died. Sheikh Nawaf had already served in several high positions. He was the defence minister during the Iraqi invasion in 1990 and he has been the crown prince since 2006. He appears popular within the larger al-Sabah family and is known for his unassuming nature and low profile.

Consequently, the new amir is likely to continue on the same path as his predecessors and uphold the privileges and responsibilities of the monarchy – in continuation of what Michael Herb has described as a dynastic monarchy in which the rulers control the significant ministries.[173] In the longer term, questions of labour migration, democracy, minorities, human rights and women's rights are matters that must be addressed.

---

171 Freer 2018 and Smith Diwan 2018
172 Longva 2013: 115
173 Herb 1999: 265f

Demography and Kuwait's migrant workers

The six countries on the Arabian Peninsula which form the Gulf Coop-eration Council (GCC), Kuwait among them, are the largest receivers of impermanent migrants in the world. Since the advent of oil, the numbers of non-nationals has increased rapidly. According to a Gulf Research Center (GRC) review of national statistics from 2010 to 2016, non-nationals con-stitute 49 per cent of the total population of 51.5 million in the GCC. In Qatar and the United Arab Emirates, almost 90 per cent of the population are non-nationals.[174] Today these countries have a relatively long history of workforces which, in a strictly legal sense, are temporary, but which, in practice, are there to stay. In the case of Kuwait, citizens are a clear minority in their own country. Kuwaitis are aware that an even larger proportion of nationals in the workforce would be desirable, but are disinclined to see any growth in the population through naturalization.[175]

In 1945, the proportion of migrant workers in the Kuwaiti workforce was 5 per cent. The rapid development of the oil industry changed this. As early as 1949, the number of migrants in the workforce had mushroomed to 68 per cent. However, until the 1970s, the migrant workforce came pre-dominantly from other Arab countries.[176] Oil or petrochemical products as the main driving force in the economic system of Kuwait has created a system that AlShehabi (2015) calls a "petro-modernist state" referring to an economic order founded on capitalism, yet supported by the income from basically one single product. Throughout the years since oil was discovered, renegotiations took place and the financial revenue allocated to the state and the ruler of Kuwait increased, and made it possible for the government to create the "petro-modernist state" in the sense that the public sector became the prime mover in the development of, for example, infrastruc-ture, administration of the state and healthcare services for citizens. AlShe-habi's petro-modernist state parallels the discussions on rentier states above and also the discussion about Islam and landownership and how the rulers took the role as God's trustees in respect of the state of Kuwait.

---

174 See http://gulfmigration.eu/gcc-total-population-percentage-nationals-foreign-nationals-gcc-countries-national-statistics-2010-2016-numbers/. Accessed October 12, 2017.

175 Longva 2013: 122

176 AlShehabi 2015: 7f

By 2010, the number of foreign workers in the Kuwaiti labour force was 83.2 per cent of the total workforce.[177] As for the total population in the same year, the nationals were close to 32 per cent while the non-nationals constituted just over 68 per cent.[178] According to the Public Authority for Civil Information in Kuwait, the nationals constituted 30.47 per cent and the non-nationals were 69.53 per cent. These numbers date from June 2017 and translated into individuals the total population at the time was a little more than 4.4 million, of whom 1.35 million were Kuwaiti and just over 3 million were non-Kuwaiti.[179]

The report shows nationality in the country as encompassing Kuwaitis, other Arabs, Asians, Africans, Europeans, North Americans and South Americans. Of the 1.35 million Kuwaiti nationals, almost all of them are listed as Muslims. In the statistics, there are 267 nationals listed as Christians and 8 as "other/not-stated". The Arab nationals total some 1.21 million people, of whom 65,610 are Christians and 5,889 belong to the undefined category. The rest are Muslims. In the Asian category, the total number of people is 1.78 million. This is therefore the single largest population group in Kuwait. In this group, a little more than 772,000 are Muslims while around 713,000 are Christians and the remaining, almost 300,000, are defined as "other/not-stated". Another detail to emerge from these statistics is that within the European group of almost 17,000 persons, more than 6,300 are Muslims. As regards North Americans, the number of Muslims is higher and constitutes more than half of the population holding a North American citizenship living in Kuwait (more than 11,600 out of a total of more than 20,200 persons).[180] Christians and Muslims are not broken down in different denominations or traditions, and thus there is no information on the proportions of Sunni or Shi'a Muslims.

Another point is the question about how to locate the group of *bidun*, those stateless and disenfranchised residents living in Kuwait and seen as illegal immigrants by the state, and their religious affiliation and affinities[181]

---

177 Shah 2012: 142
178 Shah 2012: 139
179 See http://stat.paci.gov.kw/englishreports/#DataTabPlace:PieChartNat. Accessed October 1, 2017.
180 See http://stat.paci.gov.kw/englishreports/#DataTabPlace:ColumnChartEdu Age. Accessed October 8, 2017.
181 For the politics concerning the numbers of *biduns*, see Beaugrand 2018: 33ff. The

given their size as a minority in the country and their presumably "Muslim" faith. In addition, the statistics shows that in the categories of Arabian and Asian, the number of women is only one-third of that of men. However, there is no significant shift in belonging to a particular religious tradition. Among Europeans and North Americans, the statistics are somewhat different. Among European citizens, females comprise close to 50 per cent (7,628) and about 40 per cent of them are Muslims. Among the North Americans, women are a little more than a third of the total number (7,873), but almost 70 per cent of them are Muslims (5,227).[182]

Another aspect of demography concerns the age structure of the population. Kuwait, like so many other countries in Africa and Asia, has a very young population. It was estimated, for example, that in 2010 more than 38 per cent of the population was under the age of 15.[183] In June 2017, Kuwaiti statistics show that of the population of Kuwaiti nationals, just over 55 per cent are under the age of 25.[184] The demographic structure of expatriates does not mirror the Kuwaiti numbers. Among non-nationals, a little over 31 per cent are under the age of 25.[185] Although I have used the official Kuwaiti sources here, there are some discrepancies about the absolute numbers if one compares different sources. The conditions of working-class migrants and their lack of security and their vulnerability are not limited to Kuwait or the Gulf countries. It is a global problem today, but in Kuwait, and more generally in the Gulf, the disproportionately large number of migrant workers compared to citizens is the foundation for a host of social disparities and inequalities that also have political implications and form the basis for all kinds of discrimination, inequality and legislation that sustains inequality.[186]

---

situation of the *biduns* in Kuwait and those who fled during the Iraqi occupation has been long discussed by organizations like Human Rights Watch; see https://www.hrw. org/legacy/reports/1995/Kuwait.htm. Accessed April 4, 2019.

182 See http://stat.paci.gov.kw/englishreports/#DataTabPlace:ColumnChartEdu Age. Accessed October 8, 2017.

183 Shah 2012: 141

184 http://stat.paci.gov.kw/englishreports/#DataTabPlace:ColumnChartGendrGov. Accessed October 9, 2017.

185 http://stat.paci.gov.kw/englishreports/#DataTabPlace:ColumnChartGendrGov. Accessed October 9, 2017.

186 Longva 2013: 117f

Like other Gulf countries, Kuwait's international economic reputation has, over the last decade, also been compromised by reports of human trafficking and poor conditions for foreign workers. In 2014, the United States classified Kuwait as a Tier-3 human trafficker – "among the most problematic countries" for the eighth consecutive year, while other US sources have presented evidence showing the vulnerability of abused foreign workers in Kuwait who have been unable to report mistreatment.[187] Likewise, in 2018, following a string of stories of abusive Kuwaiti employers and the incidence of suicide among foreign workers, the Philippines suspended sending workers to Kuwait, thus damaging Kuwait's credibility as a provider of safe and fair employment for foreign workers. One report concerned the murder of Joanna Demafelis, a 29-year-old maid whose body was discovered inside the freezer of her employer, causing public outrage, especially as this was just one of seven similar such cases. Eventually, Kuwait and the Philippines brokered an agreement which allowed workers to keep their passports and mobile phones, while being guaranteed basic amenities including housing, food and health insurance. Furthermore, the agreement stipulated that employment contracts were to be renewed with the approval of Philippine officials.[188]

In 2015, standard contracts for migrant workers were improved and in 2016, migrant workers were given right to change employer after three years of work, without requiring the consent of the former employer. These changes did not include domestic workers, however, and in 2016 the Assembly passed a law improving the conditions of domestic workers . This included a weekly day off, a 12-hour working day including rest and a 30-day annual paid leave, and benefits after the termination of their employment, such as one month's salary for each year of work. In 2016 and 2017, a minimum wage of 60 Kuwaiti Dinars (US\$200) per month was introduced, as well as payment of overtime compensation. While these changes have undoubtedly improved standards, the existing control and inspection regime monitoring the working and living conditions of domestic workers remains weak, and no instruments exist for enforcing change. As a result,

---

187 See https://www.hrw.org/world-report/2015/country-chapters/kuwait. Accessed September 3, 2020.
188 See https://www.bbc.co.uk/news/world-asia-44088011 and https://www.hrw.org/world-report/2019/country-chapters/kuwait. Accessed September 20, 2020.

domestic and other workers under the *kafala* system are still very vulnerable and dependent on their employers and risk maltreatment.[189] The *kafala* system of sponsorship to regulate labour migration emerged in the 1950s and has been heavily criticized ever since, with ongoing discussion about how to make it more equitable and also possibly to replace it with an alternative that is fit for purpose. Indeed, the announcement in 2016 of the Ministry of the Interior that it was offering partial amnesty to illegal residents in Kuwait indicates that the *kafala* system has forced too many migrant workers underground.[190] In 2011, the Kuwaiti government declared its intention to introduce policies reducing the dependency on foreign labour and promote increases in the Kuwaiti labour force, especially in the private sector in order to address the problems caused by Kuwait's dependence on foreign labour and the abuses of the current labour recruitment and management arrangements. Nevertheless, this is not the first time that such mission statements have been made only to be subsequently disregarded. Indeed, the ambition to increase the number of Kuwaiti workers through various nationalization policies in the past has not been realized.

Yet regardless of the status of migrants, it remains beyond question that migration has changed Kuwait. The demographic composition of the country today is radically different to that of the era prior to the discovery of oil. According to GCC statistics, the largest group of foreign workers in Kuwait since 2012 come from India (nearly 700,000), followed by Egypt (almost 500,000), Bangladesh (about 190,000) and the Philippines (about 161,000). Migration, especially on this scale, affects such things as the infrastructure of the country, education, trade and economic relations, international relationships and the practice of religion. It also affects daily life in a variety of ways – the goods on offer in shops, the languages spoken as well as the media landscape. Such major changes have created a Kuwait which has increasingly come to challenge the image of Kuwaiti and Arab identity promulgated by the country's rulers and formerly enshrined in the national consciousness.

---

189 See https://www.hrw.org/world-report/2019/country-chapters/kuwait. Accessed November 14, 2020.

190 *Kuwait Times*, January 29, 2016

Women in Kuwaiti society: political participation

The worldwide struggle for women's rights has intensified since the 1960s, and Kuwait is no exception.[191] The position of women in Kuwaiti society has throughout history been conditioned by several circumstances. Among them are various traditions, interpretations and practices of religion, tribal customs, differences between the rural and urban environments and the experience of being ruled successively by the Ottomans and British. In the 20th and 21st centuries, as the modern world began to impinge upon Kuwait, the question of women's rights became bound up with the establishment of an independent state. The creation of the state of Kuwait had legal implications for the position of the women who were citizens. Oil income also played a part, raising the living standards in the country and opening up opportunities for the education of women and for participation in the labour market. The oil economy and the wealth it has generated was also the driving force behind the entry of female migrant domestic workers into Kuwaiti households. As outlined above, their position in society is quite different to that of women who are Kuwaiti citizens. Even so, Kuwaiti female nationals do not share the same citizenship rights as their male counterparts. Even though Kuwaiti women were granted full political rights in 2005, legal differences exist in, for example, the personal status code concerning divorce and inheritance. Also, important for the status of women are their social and economic opportunities such as education in Kuwait or abroad, as well as their prospects of becoming part of the work force.[192]

The first visible mobilizations in pursuit of equality and ending the social segregation of women were inspired by the *an-nahda* movement, which from the late 19th century sought to promote social progress and claimed that the traditional frameworks regulating social practices should be interpreted in ways that took on board social change. Although initiated by young upper-class men who had studied in Egypt, this movement inspired the aspiration of inclusion and equity among Kuwaiti women and gave rise to a tradition of women's activism.[193] The first demonstrations

---

191 For a brief overview linking the global struggle to Kuwait, see Rizzo, Meyer and Ali 2002 and Alzuabi 2016: 689.

192 Tétreault 1993

193 al-Mughni 1996: 33

that can be characterized as feminist were held in the mid-1950s when women marched to the market square and set fire to black cloaks (*abayas*) in protest against their exclusion from Kuwait's newly established foreign study programme.[194]

One year after the 1962 constitution, the creation of two rival women's societies, the Arab Women Development Society (AWDS) and the Women's Cultural and Social Society (WCSS) – both part of an umbrella organization called the Kuwaiti Women's Union – marked the emergence of the organized Kuwaiti women's rights movement. WCSS, an organization with modest, yet not insignificant ambitions, worked to enable women's presence in the public domain while also taking part in conferences organized by the United Nations on women's rights and in pan-Arab conferences since the 1970s.[195] The AWDS put forward an agenda – quite radical for its time – which advocated equality in the labour market, a redrafting of family law with input from female legal experts with a view to increasing rights and safeguards for women, the restriction of polygamy and the extension to women of the right to vote and be elected to public office.[196] In 1973, the organization's campaign for the introduction of a draft equal rights bill in the Assembly stirred up unprecedented controversy and prompted a backlash from conservative circles and led to government intervention. Amid fears that traditional social values were being eroded, the state ordered the dissolution of the WCSS in 1977, while, less than a year later, the AWDS leadership was charged with fraud (although these claims were never investigated), its founder and president Nouria al-Sabani went into exile and a female government official was appointed president of AWDS, which was eventually disbanded in 1980. With the dissolution of the AWDS, the WCSS, led by Nadi al-Fatat, became the primary actor in the 1980s women's rights movement.[197]

Before the 1990s, the role of women within Kuwaiti society was relatively progressive in comparison to the wider Gulf region, as women were permitted to work and drive. In a Gulf context, Kuwait and Bahrain are often held up as being somewhat better in comparison to other states of the

---

194 Tétreault 1993: 282. Also see Buscemi 2016: 190.
195 Krause 2009: 16 and Olimat 2009: 201f
196 al-Mughni 1996: 33–4
197 Schultziner and Tétreault 2011: 2, Olimat 2009: 201f and Tétreault 1993: 288f

region where women's freedoms are concerned.[198] Nonetheless, the 1980s also saw the emergence in Kuwait of a significant anti-women's movement led by "Islamists, tribalists and social conservatives".[199] Indeed, in that same period, many Sunnis were influenced by the establishment of a theocracy in Shi'a Iran and sought to present women's rights as fundamentally inimical to Islam. At the same time, however, Kuwaiti Shi'a who supported Islamic movements abroad also supported the rights of Kuwaiti women to participate in elections.[200] Although the Kuwaiti parliament was relatively liberal in its ability to veto government legislation, paradoxically it was at the same time highly illiberal in its fierce opposition to the extension of political and social rights for women.[201] Subsequently, though women won the right to vote and stand for office in 2005, Assembly members continued to argue for discriminatory policies towards women, such as gender segregation at universities and labour laws that encouraged women to retire earlier than men.[202] The Kuwaiti legislation pertaining to education and labour stipulates a gender equality, but these laws have not informed actual state policies[203] or are not adequately effective given societal resistance.

Notwithstanding the agenda-setting influence of the women rights' movements between the 1960s and 1980s, the most significant factor promoting female suffrage in Kuwait was the active and militant role played by women in the underground armed resistance movement during the Iraqi occupation. The participation of women in the actions against the Iraqi invaders and in support of the Kuwaiti rulers increased female consciousness and activism, and also won recognition from political elites and

---

198 Krause 2009: 14

199 Schultziner and Tétreault 2011: 9

200 Schultziner and Tétreault 2011: 3–9 and Rizzo, Meyer and Ali 2002: 654

201 Regan Wills regarded the discussion on female suffrage in Kuwait as an example of a democratic paradox. It was an occasion in which the principles of inclusiveness and liberalization as foundations for democracy were in competition. According to her, the amir's will to pass a controversial decision without the consultation of the Assembly or the wider public "constituted a strong blow to liberalization." See Regan Wills 2013: 175.

202 Schultziner and Tétreault 2012: 282. The suffrage of women in 2005 was approved in the parliament by 35 votes in favour and 23 against. At the time, the number of voters increased from 195.000 to 350.000, and women constituted 57 per cent of the electorate; see Olimat 2009: 203.

203 al-Mugni 2001: 63

the executive. In consequence, the rights of women became a key part of the public debate about how best to rebuild Kuwait after the liberation. The Gulf War thus significantly changed attitudes within Kuwaiti society, prompting serious discussions about female political participation and "ideological orientations towards women's rights".[204] It became common-place for men, Shi'a and Sunni, to argue that women's rights and suffrage are fully compatible with the Quran and *shari'a*.[205]

Subsequently, the amir and Kuwaiti executive made efforts to promote gender-related changes during the 1990s and early 2000s, in the face of par-liamentary opposition. Moreover, when the amir dissolved the Assembly in 1999, he issued 63 decrees, including one that granted female suffrage. Despite the amir asking the Assembly to allow female suffrage as a mark of respect to him, almost all the decrees, except those of a budgetary nature, were rejected. These included a subsequent "women's rights bill", which was voted down. An identical bill was introduced by members of parlia-ment opposed to the ruler. This one also lost by a margin of two votes.[206] Opponents of the bill argued that these rights undermined Islamic culture and were driven by a government attempting to appease its European and North American allies.

Following a series of embarrassing defeats in the Assembly in the early 2000s, the Kuwaiti Government "acted with uncharacteristic resolution" to ensure that a women's rights bill would pass.[207] Prior to the vote, the govern-ment openly promoted female suffrage across the national media, a cam-paign that by chance coincided with female-led suffrage movements, street demonstrations and activism in the media. Most significantly, the govern-ment provided "material incentives" to Assembly members, by agreeing to legislation that would raise government employee salaries and pensions. In total, some predicted that the government paid a total of US$50 million in concessions to gain enough parliamentary support for the bill.[208] And so, more than 40 years after the 1962 constitution that promised equality under the law, Kuwait women achieved full political rights in May 2005

204 Schultziner and Tétreault 2011: 8 and Olimat 2009: 202
205 Schultziner and Tétreault 2011: 8, 12
206 Regan Wills 2013: 173
207 Schultziner and Tétreault 2011: 3
208 Schultziner and Tétreault 2011: 4

with the approval of parliament.

In 2005, the amir also appointed the first woman to a cabinet position, with Massouma al-Mubarak being named as the minister of planning and minister of state for administrative development; two years later, she became minister of health. Nuriya al-Subaih was appointed minister of education in 2007. However, both ministers received a great deal of scrutiny from the Assembly, and al-Subaih was threatened with dismissal if she failed to maintain educational segregation. al-Mubarak was forced to resign after criticism in the Assembly in 2007 and al-Subaih stepped down after the elections in 2009.[209] In the election of 2006, 28 female candidates stood at the hustings, and in 2009 four were elected to the assembly.[210]

The years leading up to the 2009 election were also coloured by activism by youth and women to promote reform and the establishment of five electoral districts in the country. There were also protests against vote-buying and corruption. In the demonstrations and rallies in 2006, women and young men were active participants as well as organizers and leaders. These protests were greatly facilitated by social media and the opportunity to organize rallies with the help of text messages, email and blogs. In a similar manner, women and young people played a significant role in an informal activism during the protests of 2009 against corruption and the prime minister. This broke with the idea of gender-based social interactions since participants, male and female, were unrelated.[211]

The Arab Spring did not politically mobilize Kuwaiti women to the same extent as it did other regional, more revolutionary movements. Across Tunisia, Libya, Egypt, Morocco, Yemen, Jordan and Syria, Arab Spring movements were fundamental in shaping a demand for improved civil liberties. Women were central to these movements in two regards. Firstly, they provided a narrative for greater women's rights; secondly, they were essential in a grassroots organizational capacity. During the protests in Kuwait, women's rights were less prevalent in the uprisings.[212] In 2011

---

209 Shultziner and Tétreault 2012: 282f

210 For a study of the development of women's political participation from 1999 to 2012, see Regan Wills 2013.

211 This paragraph builds on Buscemi 2016: 194.

212 Youth and women participated in the street rallies in 2012, and even if they primarily protested corruption and in favour of the "dignity of the nation", *karamat watan*, women were a visible part of the public protests; see Buscemi 2016: 195f.

and 2012, the political discourse in Kuwait transformed in such a way as to play down the issue of women's rights. The debates surrounding the 2009 election had focused on salient questions concerning women, including more inclusive social services, family laws, employment opportunities for women, childcare support and citizenship rights for children of Kuwaiti women wedded to non-Kuwaiti nationals. By contrast, during the protests that swept Kuwait City in 2011–2012, the political focus shifted towards tackling corruption and developing democracy.[213]

In the elections of 2012, all Kuwaiti female MPs lost their seats and the Assembly convened without any female representatives. During this period, prominent female parliamentary candidates, such as Massouma al-Mubarak, experienced a considerable decline in their vote share. For instance, the number of votes cast for al-Mubarak fell from 14,247 at the 2009 election to just 7,563 in 2012, reducing her ranking in District 1 from first to eleventh place. The first ten in the ranking got a seat in the parliament.[214] In scholarly discussions about female suffrage and developments from the 1990s to 2012, one can observe the complexity of the discourse on politics and the participation of women, and how the question of women's suffrage has been part of strategies and political manoeuvring among various interest groups in Kuwait. The support of the ruler may be more to do with a political strategy to undermine certain positions in local politics and at the same time to appease international opinion. Labels such as "Islamist", "Sunni", "Shi'a", "liberal" and "tribal" represents a variety of interests and do not represent any fixed and definite positions on female suffrage or other political questions.

Groups and individuals have also shifted their opinions depending on strategies and alliances. Olimat also describes how unprepared women's rights movements were after 2005 and how they failed to build alliances with other interest groups and individuals in the Kuwaiti political environment. He and others also point to the fact that women were not voting for women in the elections and that a feeling of uncertainty surrounds female

---

213 The result of the election in 2012 and the Arab spring is discussed in detail in Olimat 2012.
214 Shah 2012: 142 and Olimat 2012: 182. In the 2008 election, the parliament was elected in accordance with the new five constituency-system (the 50 officials are elected from five constituencies).

political leadership in Kuwaiti society in general.[215] This discussion also identifies a gap between an elite of women striving for women's rights based in Kuwait City and women living very different, less privileged circumstances. There are also clear ties between many of the prominent women in women's organizations and the ruling family, leading to the suspicion that those organizations may be less about promoting women's concerns and more about supporting the ruler and representing the interests of those in power. In addition, the discussions and activities concerning women's rights are taking place in a society that is not democratic and in which the role of parliament has been very volatile since independence.[216]

Much of Kuwaiti private life is still shaped by a patriarchal, custom-based and hierarchical understanding of domestic and family responsibility. In national discourse, family metaphors abound. The ruler is portrayed as the "father" of the nation leading his "children" towards prosperity and serving their needs. The metaphors also conflate the terms "family" and *watan*, "nation". In this context, women become "mothers of the nation" and their principal responsibility is to maintain the values and stability embedded in the conceptualizations of the terms "nation", "mother" and "family".[217] However, Kuwaiti societal norms have experienced a significant degree of change. For example, car ownership and usage has resulted in far fewer women being confined to the home.[218] Additionally, Kuwaiti women have been moderately integrated into social, political and economic spheres, with educational attainment now higher with women, and more women than men graduating from university in 2009.[219] Family metaphors and the education of women are also linked to the question of national security.

Education and women's rights are part of a national programme aimed

215 See the discussion in Olimat 2012.

216 Olimat 2012 and 2009, and Krause 2009. See al-Mughni 2001 for a detailed discussion about the ties between women's organizations and the ruling family. In their connection to the ruling family and the power, women's organizations are controlled by the state and are, according to Krause, not string vehicles pressuring for reform; see Krause 2009: 32–35.

217 The family metaphors have been commented upon by many scholars studying the Kuwaiti society. For a summary, see Krause 2009: 25f.

218 Schultziner and Tétreault 2011: 5

219 Herb 2009: 382

at creating a stable society and a Kuwaiti identity.[220] Almost half of the national labour force in Kuwait consisted of women in 2008, which was higher than most other Gulf countries such as Qatar (36 per cent), the United Arab Emirates (22 per cent) and Saudi Arabia (16 per cent). Indeed, the female national labour force in Kuwait also increased from 2 per cent in 1965 to 46 per cent in 2008.[221]

In the al-Babtain Foundation, gender equality is not discussed in any of the material they have published in print or online. Women are not part of the decision-making bodies of the Foundation in Kuwait. Women work in the library and at the Foundation, but mostly in clerical roles. However, among invited guests at events concerning poetry and in international discussions organized to discuss future events, women are present. It is evident that the al-Babtain Foundation has no specific strategy regarding gender issues, but within the organization there is a willingness to include women as participants in planning meetings and events.

A measure of social progress for Kuwaiti woman is the recent and more frequent participation of women in *diwaniyyat*. As outlined above, the *diwaniyya* is central to Kuwaiti culture and civil society as an informal social meeting place and facilitates discussions on matters concerning politics and society. Because the *diwaniyya* is a traditionally masculine concept, the mixed or women's meetings are sometimes referred to as *jalsa* or *jama'a*, "gatherings". The participation of women in the *diwaniyyat* demonstrates the incremental social transformation taking place in Kuwait and the fluidity of gender conceptualizations.[222] Furthermore, it has strengthened female civil society networks while facilitating the discussion of politics.

Another example of this transformation is the significant progress that Kuwaiti women have made in the judiciary despite the opposition of the Assembly. In March 2014, the Kuwaiti Ministry prevented women from applying for legal research positions before a two-year evaluation of the 2013 cohort. Allowing women to apply for the post of legal investigator is a landmark development for Kuwaiti women, as in theory, women could go on from there to apply to become prosecutors or even judges. A court

---

220 Krause 2009: 26

221 Shah 2012: 142. In 2014 the female workforce participation had increased to 43 per cent; see Alzuabi 2016: 689.

222 On women and *diwaniyyat*, see Stephenson 2011.

decision in 2014 rejected the Justice Ministry's order and 21 women were admitted onto the programme.

The opening of *diwaniyyat* to women and the legal decision to admit women to investigator positions show that the progress made by Kuwaiti women goes beyond merely the number of female MPs in parliament. This advancement of women within society and the judiciary is an important development from a long-term perspective. At the same time, the overall picture of women's advancement in Kuwaiti society is far less positive. There has been little in the way of affirmative action to raise gender awareness or strengthen the position of women, and only limited participation of women in civil society.[223] Other obstacles to the raising of the status of women in society are the increasing rate of divorce, the persistence of domestic violence and a lack of economic empowerment for women.[224]

Ultimately, questions of women's suffrage and rights are part of a wider public discourse in contemporary Kuwait. The application of gender in the Kuwaiti constitution and female participation in politics and administrative positions have been debated since the country's independence. Underlying actions from the rulers is their primary ambition to stay in power. Hence, the promotion of female suffrage from the amir is part of a political, economic and social strategy that also includes the aspiration to make women a public part of the society. The point here is that the development of an increased number of women in education, the workforce or in the Assembly is not driven solely by aspirations of equality or human rights. Rather, the advancement of women's opportunities in Kuwait is linked to wrangling and positioning in the country's power politics.

Opposition or support of women's participation in public roles, including being a member of the Assembly, is found in all social groups of Kuwaiti society. Among the individual and collective interests found under the umbrella of tribal formations, Islamists and liberals there is support for and opposition to women's rights. The complex politics surrounding women's

---

223 After liberation, voluntary organizations created during the Iraqi occupation were important. Volunteers worked in hospitals, bakeries and collected rubbish. These voluntary associations were discussed as a foundation for building a democratic Kuwait including an emancipation of women; see Ghabra 1991b.

224 For a discussion on the various constraints in Kuwait to the enhancement of women's positions in society and recommendations of the future, see Alzuabi 2016: 698–701.

rights cannot be simplistically characterized as "negative Islamists" versus "positive liberals" against a background of a unitary view of "Islam".

Since Kuwait's independence, organizations promoting women's rights have been led by elite women often connected with the ruling family. This is a form of co-opted and state-sponsored organizational framework, eventually complemented by state-sponsored social media activity. Having said that, in more recent years, movements promoting female participation in all walks of public life have been developing outside the framework of the state-sponsored organization, and this is also the case for social media supporting women's rights in Kuwait.

At the end of the day, change and development in everyday cultural practices, and a greater awareness of life in other contexts through old and new media have influenced the life of women. Also, Kuwaiti women themselves have been key players in the advancement of social change and emancipation. Their agency is a key component in the changes that have occurred for female Kuwaiti citizens over the last few decades. Currently, the subtler changes mentioned above concerning women's access to education, their role in the judiciary and the entry of women into certain leadership positions that were formerly the preserve of men are all signs of an ongoing and more profound change in Kuwaiti society. Unfortunately, these changes may prove to be fragile if women are merely seen as an underutilized resource and an instrument in political power struggles or power maintenance.

7

ABD AL-AZIZ AL-BABTAIN: THINKING ABOUT A LIFE OF CONTINUITY AND CHANGE

Abd al-Aziz, Kuwait and the first scholarships

During my visit to Kuwait in October 2016, I travelled by car with Abd al-Aziz al-Babtain to a recording studio. On the way, I asked him about his citizenship status, and he asserted that he is a Kuwaiti citizen. He also regaled me with stories of how his family came to Kuwait. In our brief discussion I also asked Abd al-Aziz about the employment of migrant workers and *bidun* within the al-Babtain Foundation. His answer was vague, and it appeared to me that he was reluctant to engage with the question, or, perhaps, that it was one he rarely reflected upon. It was my error that I did not press the matter. However, I will briefly return to the matter of migrant workers and *bidun* later in the chapter.

To my surprise, the car stopped in front of an older shopping mall that seemed to be in a state of disrepair. At the stairs of the entrance, we were met by a film crew and someone who I later discovered was the host of the programme, Yussuf Abd al-Hamid al-Jassim. The host led Abd al-Aziz and me into the studio. In the studio, Yussuf al-Jassim and Abd al-Aziz drank tea and chatted for a while before the recording of the programme entitled *Mufakkira* started. *Mufakkira* can be translated as "Notebook", but in this instance also carried with it an allusion to the noun *mufakkir,* denoting an intellectual person. The programme produced by al-Majlis TV was a talk show was presented as a friendly conversation with Abu Sa'ud about his life. It focused on his endeavours in the field of culture, the accomplishments of the al-Babtain Foundatio, and the poetry of Abd al-Aziz al-Babtain himself.

In this chapter, my ambition is to reflect on selected parts of Abd al-Aziz Sa'ud al- Babtain's life story and the activities of the al-Babtain Foundation.

I will therefore summarize some of the earlier discussions on the life of Abd al-Aziz and in returning to the initial statements I made with regard to studying a person's life, I will attempt to narrate the individual and the personal as part of a broader history mirroring issues and problems encountered at a particular period in Kuwait's past. In this context, I also regard Abd al-Aziz both as an individual actor involved in the creation of his society and as a representative of interests in Kuwait and the Gulf that developed during the 20th century. Hence, the life of Abu Sa'ud highlights a more personal portrait of the process of development in Kuwait and describes a person shaped by the dynamic conditions in which he lived and prospered. In this way, this chapter explores elements of Abd al-Aziz al-Babtain's life, especially the latter part leading to the creation of the al-Babtain Foundation, and links it to more abstract reflections on developments within Kuwait.[1]

During the visit to the TV studio, Abd al-Aziz was presented as a poet and a "teacher" or "professor" (*al-sha'ir al-ustadh*). The titles given to Abd al-Aziz and the invitation to the TV programme were signifiers of his status and the achievements of someone who never completed a formal education and can therefore be characterized as an autodidact. The modes of address also illustrate the change of the educational system in Kuwait. In Abu Sa'ud's childhood and youth, he learned about poetry from his family, mainly his brother and his father. As a young boy serving tea, he was also permitted to listen to recitation and discussions in the family *diwaniyya*. Abu Sa'ud often describes how the family interest in poetry made him write his first poem at the age of 11. Later, in parallel with his first steps as a businessman, he like many other aspiring entrepreneurs also worked for the government, and he happily tells the story of how he read books on all kinds of topics to increase his general knowledge. The point here is not whether his personal account of his early life is accurate or not, but rather that the quality and availability of all levels of public and private education were strikingly different in the childhood and youth of Abd al-Aziz than in the segregated educational system of modern Kuwait. Free education is provided to citizens, while expatriates, children of the *bidun* and the children of the Kuwaiti women married to labour migrants are disadvantaged by not being eligible for free state education. In higher education, several

---

1 Most of the information in this chapter on the recent developments of the al-Babtain Foundation is available online; see https://www.albabtaincf.org/.

public and private universities and colleges have also been established since the year 2000 and many of them are labelled "American" and are affiliated to institutions of higher learning in the United States.

Abd al-Aziz al-Babtain was born in 1936 and so shares his experience of education with an older generation of entrepreneurs, businesspersons and leaders in the Gulf.[2] They all had limited personal opportunity to attend higher education. They received the schooling of the time and were also educated in the context of their family, learning about local values and principles. In their lives, they have generated personal and family fortunes through various forms of trade and businesses. In later life, they have developed an interest in philanthropy through their support for educational enterprises. Due to the wealth of the state of Kuwait, the limited number of citizens and the privileges in the society attached to a citizenship, they have also actively played a part in the history of the transformation of the Gulf into a collection of independent, highly urbanized and commercial nation-states. In the case of Abu Saʿud, as the very model of an entrepreneur, he has played a dynamic role in Kuwaiti society as a businessman, poet and philanthropist. The terms "businessman" and "poet" are here used as emblematic of his personal and family's success and entrepreneurship in trade and the development of the al-Babtain Foundation, where poetry forms one of the main pillars of the institution. Abd al-Aziz constitutes part of a social layer of entrepreneurs in which their personal experiences of education, success in the business world and social changes in Kuwait and in the Gulf create a link between economic and cultural conditions. In a small state like Kuwait, the intimate relationship between the rulers and successful businesspeople like Abd al-Aziz al-Babtain also creates a bond built on mutual dependency between the state and the elite families concerning local, national and regional power structures. As a general rule, Abu Saʿud usually describes his father as neither rich nor poor.

The advent of oil and the petroleum industry created an opportunity that made it possible for Abd al-Aziz to advance beyond the boundaries set by, for example, tribal affiliation and normative and restrictive systems that customarily hamper a person's opportunities for social mobility – circumstances comparable to the changes that took place in European societies as a result of the Industrial Revolution. The economic, social, political and

---

2 I am using the word businessperson, but almost all of them are male.

religious conditions shaped this group of entrepreneurs, a new financial elite and the rulers and the bonds of mutual loyalty that bind them. Perhaps loyalty is a strong word, but at least persons like Abd al-Aziz are dependent on the framework created for him and his businesses by the state. In Abu Sa'ud's words, his work in the field of culture has generated the respect of the amir and his family for him and his Foundation.

Abd al-Aziz's support of students to study at al-Azhar University in Cairo commenced in 1974 and has since developed considerably. The creation of these scholarships was a response to the need for education in many Muslim majority countries. Nonetheless, it was also connected to the ambition of the small state of Kuwait to actively pursue a foreign policy building on relationships founded on various forms of aid extended to Muslim majority countries. An additional component is Abu Sa'ud's personal appreciation of the importance of education. He and his Foundation provide opportunities for young Muslims and Arabs to obtain a university education – a chance he was never given in his youth. Abd al-Aziz's support of students can also be seen as a recognition of and adaptation to the changed circumstances of everyday life in Muslim majority countries through acknowledging the necessity of university education in order to make societies prosper. In the early stages of the Foundation's scholarship programmes, students were sent only to the prestigious university of al-Azhar in Cairo founded in the 10th century during the Fatimid Caliphate.

In the Sunni Muslim context, the status of al-Azhar for the training of religious scholars is indisputable, and students have come to this university to study Arabic and the classical branches of Islamic learning for centuries. Since the end of the 19th century and early 20th century, changes in the methods of examination and improvement of curricula have been discussed, but it was in the early 1960s that the university transformed and established faculties such as economics, medicine and engineering. Hence, students supported by the al-Babtain Foundation were not necessarily sent primarily to study the classical topics taught at al-Azhar. However, by choosing to send students to al-Azhar and Cairo, the al-Babtain Foundation deliberately chose the most famous Sunni Islamic institution in the world, located in a city that many Arabs consider the cultural capital of the Arab world. The scholarships are granted to students from Muslim majority countries in Central Asia, Africa, Asia and from European countries. Learning Arabic and Arab culture is at the heart of the mission, reconnecting Kuwait and what the Foundation sees as the Arab world with the people and countries that formed extensive networks of trade and cultural exchange in Islamic history. The emphasis on historic connections, the support of training in the Arabic language and the promotion of values seen as being at the heart of *the* Arab culture also reveals that Abd al-Aziz's life is not all about change. In order to create a better society, his life and the idea behind the al-Babtain Foundation are also about continuity.

Expanding the al-Babtain Foundation

The Foundation of the "Abdelaziz Saud al-Babtain's Prize for Poetic Creativity" in Cairo in 1991 was a new departure. In addition to scholarships for students, Abd al-Aziz established a solid framework to promote Arab poets and Arabic poetry. While the annual scholarships were still awarded to students on different levels and from various countries, the new Foundation became a platform for the evolution of a more comprehensive al-Babtain Foundation. The focus on poets and poetry relates to the discussion above on promoting a vision of Arab culture closely connected to the Arabic language and the classical tradition of poetry in Arabic. The focus on classical poetry does not include vernacular poetry.

There are several reasons for Abd al-Aziz's desire to expand and create a new foundation. The first one concerns his personal interest in poetry especially as, after years of engagement in business affairs, he is now at a stage in life when he can cultivate his interest in the Arabic language and the traditions of classical poetry in Arabic. A reflection of the significance of poetry at this point in Abu Sa'ud's life was also the publication of his first book in 1995 and the inception of what he considers one of the Foundation's most important projects, entitled the *al-Babtain Encyclopaedia of Arabic Poets in the Nineteenth and Twentieth Centuries*. This is a multi-volume work, and the hope is that within a few years it will cover the poetry of all major Arab poets from pre-Islamic times to the modern period.

The Foundation has not only focused on a prize and the encyclopaedia. In the early 2000s, courses were developed in prosody, linguistics and the understanding of poetry in Arabic. In comparison to poetry, literature in the form of modern fiction appears relatively late in the contemporary history of Kuwait. The genre of fictional literature is not anchored in the wider population to the same extent as the genre of poetry. The status of poetry is built through the practice of reading and recitation for generations of Kuwaitis. It has the status of an art form and a role as a rhetorical tool in politics. Recitation of poetry and the Arabic language are also connected to understandings of Arabic as God's language and the language of Paradise. For Abd al-Aziz, his support and revival of poetry and poets writing in Arabic is a tool to enhance and anchor his childhood culture in contemporary society, a culture he recognizes as traditional Kuwaiti culture, and also Arab culture in a transnational sense. According to this view, the second point concerns Abu Sa'ud's desire to influence what is broadly understood as culture. In this context, it suffices to define culture as the shared knowledge, norms, beliefs, customs and behaviours that humans acquire through enculturation. He would like to inspire the younger generations to spend less time on the internet, shopping, watching movies or conversing at cafés. Instead, his aim is to foster among young people an awareness of, a pride in and a commitment to Kuwaiti and Arab culture, often through Arabic language and poetry. Abd al-Aziz clearly understands and recognizes the differences between an older generation of an intellectual elite – and their understanding of poetry in Arabic – and the role of the language of Arabic as a foundation for a Kuwaiti and Arab culture and identity on the one hand, and on the other a younger generation's view on the language of Arabic, their aspirations in life and their perception of culture. His objective is to challenge a process of acculturation that is taking place among the young and that is to a large extent global and influenced by popular culture, often presented in English. A third reason for establishing the Foundation and a prize in poetic creativity was to create an alternative to the rise of forms of Islam which Abd al-Aziz considers violent and contrary to the true message of Islam and the Prophet Muhammad.

During our car journey to the TV studio and the recording of the programme *mufakkira,* Abu Sa'ud followed up on a question I had asked earlier, about whether he had ever been involved in conflict resolution. In response, Abd al-Aziz recounted a story of how two Iraqis, a Sunni and Shi'a, visiting his *diwaniyya* the day before had almost got into a fight. He smiled and confirmed that he had been involved in mediation between Algeria and Iran in the 1990s and early 2000s. We never continued the discussion on Algeria and Iran, but Algeria maintains diplomatic relations with all Arab countries as well as with Iran. Kuwait has strong diplomatic relations with Algeria and asked Algeria to mediate in the conflict with

Qatar. Even though Abd al-Aziz repeatedly claims that he is not an active player in Kuwaiti foreign policy, the link between him and Kuwaiti ambitions is paralleled by organizing sessions on poetry and Arabic training in Algeria and Iran, as well as receiving honorary doctorates from universities in both countries. While establishing a foundation dedicated to poetic creativity can be seen as harmless and apolitical, his focus on the promotion of Arab culture and language has a political dimension, since it is also designed to counter certain forms of Islamization of society. It is a deliberate statement on what is important in a society and the enculturation of a collective identity, Arab and Kuwaiti. In taking this stance in support of a particular interpretation of Islam, Abu Saʿud can also been seen as being active in national politics.

The library, changing ambitions and the "dialogue among civilizations"

In the early 2000s, the Foundation grew considerably. A key development was the creation of the al-Babtain Central Library for Arabic Poetry. It is located in the heart of Kuwait City close to the Grand Mosque of Kuwait. The library was inaugurated in the spring of 2006. Today it boasts an extensive collection of classical poetry in Arabic. Abd al-Aziz's interest in modern poetry is limited. Even so, modern texts are included in the library, but the bulk of the collection is classical.

The buildings also contain offices, and the library has become a focal point for the various activities that the Foundation organizes across the world. The formation of this foundation and its award for poetic creativity can be seen as the consolidation of the poet and businessman Abd al-Aziz's engagement in the promotion of Arabic and Arabic literature, but also as a means of strengthening his status as a prominent actor in the field of culture in Kuwait and the broader Gulf. The prominent location of the library in a central area in Kuwait City also adds to the status of Abu Saʿud in Kuwait. As well as being proud of the Foundation at large, he regards the publication of the *al-Babtain Dictionary for Arab Contemporary Poets* and all the subsequent dictionaries as one of his most important accomplishments. The creation of the library and the administrative offices has enabled the foundation to publicly display their work and collections. However, a criticism directed towards the library by one of the employees is that it is

The al-Babtain Foundation and Library in Kuwait City. © the author.

not collaborating with other libraries, and is too focused on poetry. In addition, the library is a publishing house, and there is also concern that its books are not selling. The books that are published are usually given as gifts to visitors or donated to national, regional and international institutions.

Since launching the library in 2006, the Foundation has opened other branches outside of Kuwait. In 2007, the al-Babtain Foundation inaugurated the The al-Babtain Center for the Verification of Poetry Manuscripts. The location of this new branch is in Alexandria, Egypt. This new division of the Foundation is connected with the famous library in Alexandria and with publishers in Egypt upholding Mediterranean traditions of poetry. One of its first publications was a *diwan* of Sicilian poetry. Another example was the establishment of the al-Babtain Center for Dialogue among Civilizations in Córdoba, Spain in 2004. In both cases, these are geographical locations with a strong connection to Arab and Muslim history.

In a conversation with me, Abu Sa'ud stated that the creation of the Centre in Córdoba was a direct result of the tragic events which took place on September 11, 2001, in New York and Washington DC. The label "dialogue among civilizations" was chosen in response to the discussions about a clash of civilizations. The term "civilization" is in the conceptualization of a cultural topography underlying Abd al-Aziz's cultural engagement, where he locates the "Arab world" at the centre, or perhaps at the heart of a broader "Islamic world" as a cultural entity on a par with that of a Christian and secular "West". There is a binary logic to his description.[3] Hence, the choice of Córdoba, he says, was related to the history of al-Andalus and Córdoba during the Umayyad Caliphate (711–1031) as a bridge between cultures. After September 11, 2001, Abd al-Aziz also started to travel more frequently to Europe. The travels extended his network of contacts and the event organized in Córdoba resulted in contacts with UNESCO and a jointly organized seminar in Paris.

The activities of the different branches can be coordinated more effectively. The al-Babtain Foundation is an institution with a physical home in the country of its origin. Through the library, and the offices it is also more visible to external partners, and is the administrative centre for planning activities, as with their support for students abroad. All this is aligned with Kuwaiti foreign policy concerning aid or collaboration with European universities by supporting chairs in Arabic and Arab culture. The library and its offices are the heart of the Foundation and also the centre from which Abd al-Aziz has planned his "dialogue among civilizations".

While at the TV Studio where the programme *Mufakkira* was recorded, Abu Sa'ud recounted the story behind his decision to fund the professorial chair in Arabic at Oxford University. He added how he planned to redirect the objectives of the Foundation and stated that previous initiatives aimed at supporting education in the Arabic language were often time-limited. He said that this applied to subvention for individual students, as well as more far-reaching programmes and courses such as the Arabic language training course at the University of Granada. The idea behind his new initiative, as manifested in his investment in the chair at Oxford, and in many other chairs at European universities such Córdoba University and Leiden University, was to create more permanent forms of support. The chairs are not designed to support research into and teaching in Arabic exclusively, but are

---

3 For discussions on the binary "Islam" and "the West", see the contributions in Stenberg and Wood (eds) 2022.

Abd al-Aziz al-Babtain being interviewed at the TV studio, 2016. © the author.

also meant to extend their activities to the field of Arab culture. This objective is not solely limited to funding chairs at universities in Europe. The intention is to establish similar chairs across five continents, and in his TV interview, Abd al-Aziz mentioned countries such as Togo, China, France, Italy, Kenya and Somalia. The effort is a result of an ongoing restructuring of the Foundation and the goal is to make the practice and study of Arab culture one of its main concerns. Poets and poetry will in the new structure be a part of a Foundation with a broader ambition and scope.

The redirection of the Foundation is perhaps a natural step in the development of the organization and the interests of Abd al-Aziz. In his capacity as the chairperson of the Board of Trustees, Abd al-Aziz is responsible for making all the major decisions at the Foundation. It is his personal choice to develop the scope of the al-Babtain Foundation and follow the broader interest of the Kuwaiti rulers and their foreign policy. The Foundation's new endeavour to create a "dialogue among civilizations" through conferences and the establishment of more enduring chairs in the Arabic language and Arabic culture accords with the interest of the Kuwaiti state in building relations with countries outside the sphere of Arab and Muslim states.

There is a synergy between these ambitions, for the al-Babtain

Foundation's support of students and its augmenting of the quality in education in Muslim majority countries is also a way of reducing the gap between civilizations. Regardless of location, state officials – including royal personages, presidents, prime ministers, ministers and other politicians – have been represented at all the conferences that the Foundation has organized in different countries. Representatives of regional and global organizations like the League of Arab States and the European Union have also attended. Some have been present at multiple events, notably Tokia Saïfi, a member of the European Parliament between 1999 and 2019; Jorge Sampaio, president of Portugal between 1996 and 2006; and Haris Siladjic, prime minister of the Republic of Bosnia and Hercegovina from 1993 to 1996. Examples of participants currently active as politicians are Carmen Calvo, presently the Spanish Vice-prime minister and Rosa Aguilar Rivero, Spanish minister for Environment, Rural and Marine Affairs between 2010 and 2012. A majority of the participating politicians from Europe are from socialist and liberal political backgrounds. These examples show that the aspiration of the Foundation is not only to invite academics and cultural personalities to the conferences, but also influential persons representing states or organizations like the EU. In recent years, the Foundation has also organized conferences in Malta. It has established closed ties with the leadership of Malta and has hosted conferences on the island. Furthermore, the Foundation has addressed questions concerning strengthening of peace initiatives and also organized online talks about responses to the COVID-19 pandemic in collaboration with politicians from Malta such as the former foreign minister Michael Frendo. This connection has also resulted in an agreement with the University of Malta to establish an Abd al-Aziz Sa'ud al-Babtain peace chair to promote and teach a culture of peace.[4]

The recent trajectory of the Foundation can be seen as connected with the objectives of the Kuwaiti state and its rulers' strategy to relate to other countries and contribute to the security and welfare of Kuwait. This strategy is a form of cultural diplomacy (so-called "soft power") that is practised by many states. While Abu Sa'ud would like to influence the development of international relations between what he has defined as civilizations in a positive direction, he also would like to receive further recognition from

---

4 https://www.kuna.net.kw/ArticleDetails.aspx?id=3008547&language=en. Accessed November 23, 2021.

governments and organizations in Europe and North America for his work. Abd al-Aziz is frustrated by being seen as a person on the periphery, both geographically and in his capacity as an Arab and a Muslim. It is my impression that he would like to be recognized for his contributions to poetry, "dialogue among civilizations", and the efforts he and his Foundation make in fostering a culture of peace internationally.

The al-Babtain Foundation and the media

In conjunction with the creation of the library in Kuwait City, the Foundation also started to present its activities to a national and international audience. In conversations with officials working at the library, they revealed that the library has very few Kuwaiti visitors. One official cited just three to four visitors per day and occasional visits of school classes. There are also regular visits by scholars and authors from Kuwait and from the region as well as from other countries. These visits often take place during conferences, workshops and meetings on topics that are within the scope of the Foundation. The Foundation has bought space on the Egyptian Nilesat and the Arab League-founded Arabsat, but in my visit in October 2016 the officials I spoke to were disappointed with the content of the programmes the Foundation produced. The general view was that they were simply too boring, and that both their content and format needed revitalizing. A point was also made that it was unnecessary to purchase space on two satellites, when one would have been enough. Whereas the online presence and social media activity – namely the Facebook page and the Arabic language website – are updated, a corresponding web page in English is lacking and the Facebook page in English is hardly updated. In English one can find more or less random clips on YouTube from Kuwait TV reporting on activities at the library or the Foundation or from Abd al-Aziz's presentations at various different events. The Foundation's YouTube channel in Arabic has a very low number of subscribers – a mere 2,960 as of December 2021. The different clips have been seen by only a few viewers. Bawadi TV, which seems to have a connection to the Foundation, is participating in the production of some of the material shared on the YouTube channel, including a programme entitled "Peace News" reflecting Abd al-Aziz's commitment to dialogue and cooperation between civilizations. One positive aspect is that the YouTube channel interviews give voice to male and female poets and scholars in roughly equal measure. It reflects what has been stated above about the effort expended in the Foundation's poetry events I have attended to give room to as many female poets as possible. Hence, it is no coincidence that Abd al-Aziz has collaborated with the Lebanese female singer Ghada Shbeir in setting his poetry to music. About 10 to 15 of his poems have received this treatment.

In meetings with officials from the Foundation, I have raised the question of why a cohesive media strategy is lacking. I recommended a strategy that would coordinate the message of the Foundation across many social media platforms such as Twitter, Instagram, YouTube, Facebook and blogs, as well as its own dedicated website. I also raised the matter of the poor sales of the Foundation's expensive publications in book form. The answers were defensive, with some of the younger officials, all of them members of the al-Babtain family, maintaining that they were already implementing changes or were about to. Decisions in the Foundation are in the hands of Abd al-Aziz, and he trusts his younger relatives. Their explanations and ideas on how to expand on social media are accepted. My impression is that Abd al-Aziz himself prefers to create and sustain personal relationships with national and international decision makers. He cultivates these relationships through conferences, investments in education and in professorial chairs at different universities as a way of achieving a "dialogue among civilizations". The current tools for augmenting the impact and awareness of the work of the al-Babtain Foundation are not being utilized properly, and his personal desire to receive global recognition globally for his work has not been fully realized.

I cannot comment on Abd al-Aziz's personal knowledge of the social media world and his capacity to navigate in it and evaluate how strategies should be developed to increase the online impact of the work of the Foundation, especially since, in a hierarchical organization like the al-Babtain Foundation, all important decisions have to be approved by Abu Sa'ud. In his role as the chair of the Foundation's Board of Trustees, different administrators and board members vie for influence across the Foundation. Some are family members and others are not. In this structure, social media becomes a problem, or rather a headache, as daily online engagement is needed to create impact and followers, and the work in social media needs a certain degree of trust and a delegation of tasks among employees.

Updates on Facebook and Instagram, postings on YouTube and tweeting in a hierarchical organization are problematic if there is no clear central strategy nor any concerted effort made to carry out such tasks. It is also problematic if the updates and postings always have to be approved by the person at the top of the Foundation. The existing website and Facebook pages become static. This absence of activity, plus the lack of any proper online or social media presence in English, or indeed any language other than Arabic, is an unfortunate position for a Foundation that strives to create dialogue between people, and foster a universal culture of peace. The consequence of this rigidity in the domain of social media, where adaptability and quick response are essential attributes, inevitably means that the good work done by the al-Babtain Foundation is going unrecognized by a wider global audience.

The al-Babtain Foundation has not so far made the best use of the opportunities that exist online and in social media, either to attract visitors to the library in Kuwait City or to maximize the impact of their global and high-profile events. The policy of inviting key decision makers to attend conferences in order to raise the profile of these events also seems to lack a clear strategy. Although it may reflect a belief on the part of Abd al-Aziz and the rest of the Foundation management that such engagements in "high" culture and politics are more effective than the "low" culture of social media, many of the prominent figures invited to the Foundation's events are older – and in many cases former politicians – and only a few maintain a consistent engagement with the Foundation's work by participating regularly in meetings and other occasions. The advantages their involvement brings to the Foundation are questionable.

Interestingly, the library seems something of a throwback to the culture of a *diwaniyya*, or an extension of the actual *diwaniyya* of the al-Babtain family, albeit in a more public context. The Foundation and Abd al-Aziz invite friends and guests for discussions at the library, and sometimes even entertain and dine with them in the *diwaniyya* after the daytime library programme is finished.

Promoting a culture of peace and influencing new generations

Steps in a new and more cohesive direction have been taken by the Foundation in recent years. Many of the changes in the organization and the development of new initiatives and networks can be attributed to Dr Touhami

Abdouli. He began his work at the Foundation in 2016 with the specific task of reorganizing it and focusing on new ideas. The initiative known as the "World Forum for the Culture of Peace" was launched in 2017. In two sessions of the United Nations General Assembly on September 7, 2017 and September 5, 2018, Abd al-Aziz outlined ideas on how to work for sustainable peace under the umbrella of the newly initiated Forum. The project he presented was entitled "Culture of Peace for the Security of the Future Generations". This project is founded on two main precepts. The first is a development of education and a curriculum for teaching a culture of peace and protecting cultural heritage in educational systems from the level of kindergarten to university. This idea was first mooted at an event in The Hague, Netherlands in June 2019 organized by the Foundation under the umbrella of the World Forum and in collaboration with the International Peace Institute, International Committee of the Red Cross, the Carnegie Foundation and Leiden University. The second precept was the organization of the World Forum for Culture of Peace. In 2019 the al-Babtain Foundation also published a book in the name of Abd al-Aziz entitled *Contemplations for Peace*. The book outlines several ways in which people can individually embrace peace as a human value, and is written from the life experience of Abu Saʻud.[5]

In October 2020, the Foundation organized a virtual symposium devoted to the educational programme entitled "Education for a Culture of Peace". The ambition is to arrange yearly events under the aegis of the World Forum for the Culture of Peace. In both the Forum in The Hague and its virtual counterpart, the participants appeared more carefully selected, in that they represented a greater number of countries and were more professionally conversant with the topics discussed. They were all leaders, high-level officials from government and international organizations, NGOs and academics. In the virtual forum, the participants were mainly from countries around the Mediterranean, especially Italy, Malta and Tunisia – states with which Dr Abdouli had an established network as a result of his former role in Tunisian politics. It was fitting that Abd al-Aziz and his Foundation created the World Forum for the Culture of Peace in 2019, a year which marked the 20th anniversary of the United Nations Declaration and Programme of Action on a Culture of Peace.

---

5 al-Babtain 2019.

The new initiative taken by the al-Babtain Foundation to establish a world forum promoting the culture of peace grew from the broader idea of a "dialogue among civilizations" and took on a more cohesive and tangible form. Without passing judgment on the educational programme and the creation of a curriculum on the culture of peace, it certainly represents a much more hands-on approach than previously. The aim of the Foundation is to make discussions more pragmatic and to provide practical and tangible solutions on how to make the culture of peace a reality. The idea is that the discussions should generate concrete projects such as the curriculum and identify solutions to current social challenges. The prominence of the partners and collaborators in these activities constitutes a notable shift in this respect. Partnering with the International Committee of the Red Cross and the Carnegie Foundation as well as academic institutions such as Leiden University or Oxford University strengthens the brand name of the Foundation. Integrated in this shift is an expansion of the strategy to emphasize the collaboration with organizations and strong brand names rather than with well-known individuals. Earlier publications published by the Foundation in honour of Abu Sa'ud largely consisted of brief accounts of his achievements and served very little purpose other than personally praising Abd al-Aziz. These recent developments may also be presumed to make the relationship of the Foundation and Abd al-Aziz with the government and the rulers of Kuwait resilient.

On a personal level, Abu Sa'ud also strives to find ways to raise his international profile as someone contributing to the creation of a better world through concrete actions. The World Forum in the Hague focused on Iraq and Yemen and was designed explicitly to discuss the role of international organizations in protecting the world heritage in those countries. Abu Sa'ud's underlying ambition is to be seriously considered for the Nobel Peace Prize. The hiring of Dr Abdouli with his personal network of contacts is one part of this objective. The work of the Foundation in collaborating with distinguished partners to produce tangible results may also help promote this ambition. At the same time, the collaboration strengthens the position of the al-Babtain Foundation nationally and internationally.

The desire to influence younger generations of Arabs and Muslims has thus far not been realized. At least not if we gauge its success from the internet and social media strategies and presence of the al-Babtain Foundation. Many initiatives aimed at young people, such as the educational initiative to teach a culture of peace, have been developed in top-down fashions. The objective of reaching out to younger generations is seen as vital and before creating the chair at the University of Malta, the al-Babtain Foundation established a professorship for culture and peace at the Altiero Spinelli Centre at the University of Rome in late 2017. This chair has been entrusted to lead the development of the programmes in the culture of peace from kindergarten to university level. The al-Babtain Foundation also established an international committee that discussed the proposals of the teaching models in a conference in Lisbon in spring 2018. Later, the teaching manuals were presented by Abd al-Aziz at the meeting in the UN in the same year. Since the presentation at the UN, teams of educational specialists have drafted various versions of the manuals and adapted them to different school systems. Supervision and teaching of the programmes was assigned to the European Centre for Democracy and Human Rights, an organization which has connections with numerous universities.

Another new initiative to reach the younger population of Kuwait was launched in 2017 under the name of Akadimiyya al-Babtain (the al-Babtain Academy). The Academy implemented training courses for young people in poetic creativity. Students of several nationalities were enrolled on the courses – hailing from Egypt, Indonesia, Iran, Iraq, Jordan, Kuwait, Lebanon, Palestine, Saudi Arabia, Senegal and Syria. Later that same year, the Foundation established a joint Diploma in poetic creativity in collaboration with the International Academy of Poetic Creativity in Verona, Italy. The al-Babtain Foundation also awards two prizes annually to young poets writing in Arabic, one for the best poem and another for the best poetry collection. In October 2017, the Foundation's Academy also started lessons in Arabic to non-native speakers of the foreign diplomatic missions. A total of 130 diplomats representing about 30 foreign embassies in Kuwait enrolled on the first course. Another way of reaching the younger generations is also the investment in and ongoing financial support for several professorial chairs in the Arabic language and Arab culture at universities around the world.

These professorial chairs are concentrated in countries around the Mediterranean, especially Spain but also in Italy, France and one chair in Tunisia. The chairs are mostly in Arab culture, and the most extensive programme is the master's programme in contemporary Arab studies at the Autonomous University of Barcelona. In this programme, agreed upon in 2016, Arabic is used as a language of teaching. Beyond chairs and educational programmes as models for fostering new thinking among young and university-educated students at European universities, the al-Babtain Foundation has forged links with areas that have had a strong historical connection with Arab and Muslim culture. This initiative also builds on the idea of a common Mediterranean connection between people in the form of shared cultures and identities. The centre for translation, created in 2004, is not devoted to the translation of books directed only at the younger population, but a more general effort to contribute to an increase in the translation of books into Arabic. The Foundation recognizes the translation of books as a real spur for an intellectual renaissance in Arab countries and a need to acquire knowledge that can contribute to cultural, human and economic development. The aim is not to translate fiction or books on politics. The purpose is to translate books on the conditions of life in Europe and North America and books on history. An additional goal is to translate books on science and technology. The point the Foundation makes concerning translations is that the translated books should inform the reader about the knowledge acquired and the experiences made in the process leading to, for example, invention in science. The books should inspire the reader and encourage him or her to be creative and engage with science and new technology.

For Abd al-Aziz al-Babtain, an overarching task is to strengthen an Arab identity and the awareness of an Arab culture among young people in Kuwait, and among Arabs in general. The ambition is general and in the context of an authoritarian state such as Kuwait, ideas on identity are politically sensitive. Citizens, men and women, are not equal according to the constitution or in actuality, and citizens are not equal to the majority of the population in the country. A paternalistic attitude is taken by the ruling family primarily towards Kuwaiti part of the population. The rulers and the state also promote the image of the country as an Arab nation built on an Arab history linked to seafaring, maritime trading, pearl-diving and tribal heritage. Kuwait has always been slightly unusual compared to its neighbours due to the longer history of its national identity. This identity has not always been easy to maintain and has been forged in discussions and conflicts between different groups in society, but also in conflicts such as the Gulf War.

Poetry, Arab culture, Islam, identity politics and nationalism

The Kuwaiti form of Arabism, the Arabic language, Arab culture, and "Arab identity" as articulated through the concept of Kuwait as an Arab nation amounts to a complex idiom of simultaneous inclusion and exclusion. The idea of an Arab and Kuwaiti national community corresponding to the borders of the state includes most Kuwaiti citizens, albeit not on equal terms, but excludes other people such as labour migrants, those who identify or are identified as Iranians, and the *bidun*. In the dominant Kuwaiti understanding of being an Arab, just as in Abd al-Aziz's, genealogy, being of a Najdi and tribal origin, is important not only as a factor determining the right to citizenship, but also the hierarchy of tribes linked to Arabness. Tribes and large families are not equal. They play a part in nation-building and as the case of the ruling al-Sabah family indicates, hierarchy among them has not been static over time, but has proved adaptable, allowing for social mobility of a tribe or an individual within the system. Abu Sa'ud's assertion that the amir respects his work and that he lives close to the quarters of the amir in Kuwait City illustrates the trajectory of his social movement and his place in the system. The citizens of Kuwait share a feeling that they are at the core of the nation. Even if there are cracks in the system and many do not feel a particularly strong attachment, especially not in their daily life, to an invented Arab culture, citizens are proudly connected to Kuwait and to the benefits they see themselves entitled to in their capacity as nationals.

Aside from the Arab culture and identity sponsored by the state and deemed to be embodied by the nation of Kuwait, the question of how the state differentiates between different types of religious affiliation and incorporates religion into national identity remains largely ambiguous. Kuwait's constitution and legal system are rooted in the Sunni tradition. The Public Authority for Civil Information, the agency providing information on the population of Kuwait, classifies the population of the country by religion and gender, yet there are no accurate statistics with regard to a sensitive topic like the numbers of Sunni compared to the Shi'a population of Kuwait. Likewise, the category of *bidun* as well as their religious affiliation is not discernible in the statistics. Defining all Muslims as "Muslims" with no breakdown reflecting the composition of the population in terms of ethnic and religious majority and minorities is part of an official strategy with reference to the promotion of a national Kuwaiti identity, whereby the rulers and the state shape a common understanding of the meaning of Kuwait and Kuwaiti identity that is built on a constructed understanding of Arabness and Arab culture as well as a certain interpretation of Islam and the implication of being Muslim. It comes out in a form of an ethno-nationalism and religio-nationalism that is celebrated in the commemoration of shared historical memories such as the pearl-diving culture or the liberation from Iraqi occupation. It is a nationalism in which the cherished memories of traditions are cultivated in parallel with a culture that embraces a modernity that is still changing the country's infrastructure and values at a rapid pace. Recognizing social change in the current society, new lifestyles and the awareness of the world beyond Kuwait have also made the state address the changes and promote their understanding of the Kuwaiti national identity through the educational system. One of the problems in the construction of Kuwaiti identity founded on the construction of a shared collective history and a certain Arabness and Muslimness is that the citizens are a minority population in the country, with stateless minorities and expatriates/immigrants making up more than 50 per cent of the population. Another problem is that identities such as Shi'a, *bidun* or being a young person or a woman are mobilized in the pursuit of status and identity recognition and even become vehicles for protest against broader conditions of injustice. Their evocation challenges the state-promoted and constructed image of a homogeneous citizenry and of a united Kuwait.

In the context of Kuwaiti nation-building, the terms "Arab" and "Islam" are vaguely defined and often conceptualized in general and positive terms and become objects that have to be both institutionalized and controlled as anchors of identity and as part of a general process establishing institutions and endowing them with legitimacy.

The appropriation of culture, history and heritage to nurture the understandings of a Kuwaiti individual and collective identity also aims to legitimize the inequalities that exist in the country and within the citizenry. This is especially the case concerning gender, but also in the way these inequalities exist between the different classes of citizenship, and between citizens and non-citizens. The discourse on culture including religion and heritage also endorses a claim among the citizens of Kuwait to ownership of the country. In this context, nation-building and appropriation of histories are manifested in education and celebrations, and also institutionalized in museums in which the objects and histories on display represent and support the official narrative of the national heritage.[6]

The al-Babtain Foundation is an institution that supports the ruler of Kuwait and the Kuwaiti state's nation-building project. As can be expected of most successful and wealthy Kuwaiti nationals, Abd al-Aziz's *diwaniyya* manifests his relationship to the ruling family. In January 2016, the *diwaniyya* had a large image of the former amir Sheikh Sabah al-Ahmad al-Jabir al-Sabah and the current amir Nawaf al-Ahmad al-Jabir al-Sabah above the entrance. The text under the two rulers of the al-Sabah family plays with the greeting in Arabic *sabah al-khayr* ("Good morning") and states *sabahak khayr ya Kuwait* ("Your Sabah is prosperous Kuwait"). Hence, Abu Sa'ud is not explicitly critical of the politics of the state and the ruling family, and his activities are aligned with the foreign policy of the state. As already discussed, the Foundation's projects in the Comoros and in Central Asian states are examples in which the Foundation is working in conjunction with the foreign policy of Kuwait. In more recent years, the Foundation's initiative to create dialogues between civilizations and to work for a culture of peace seems aligned with the Kuwaiti state's objective to become a voice representing smaller countries in international discussions – an ambition that also became a reality, however briefly, when the state of Kuwait was elected as a non-permanent member of the United Nations Security Council between 2018 and 2019.

Broadly speaking, there are three positions in the discussion on political reform in Gulf countries: those of the ruling families, Islamist individuals and movements that work within the political framework, and liberal individuals and organizations.[7] Abd al-Aziz al-Babtain represents a generation of successful businesspersons that throughout their life have been in a symbiotic relationship with the rulers and the state. Alongside their entrepreneurial skills and ambitions, this interdependence has been the foundation of their wealth. They have been an important source of support in a state where the nationals are few and organized in a hierarchical, tribal system.

Abd al-Aziz rarely makes strong political statements and has clearly stated that he is not interested in mixing Islam or any other religion with politics. In his opening statements at various inaugurations of the poetry events I have attended, he has shared his understanding of Islam as a non-violent

---

6 al-Ragam 2014
7 Hamzawy 2008: 158

Entrance of the al-Babtain *diwaniyya*. © the author.

religion, premised on tolerance. Perhaps these are not particularly compromising statements coming from a devout man at first sight, but his view of Islam could be seen as different from the understanding held among some of the individuals and movements that are branded as Salafi. Indeed, several of his statements appear to indicate that for him Islam is also a religion to be practised by the individual and not to be mixed with statecraft. His views on religion can also be linked to his understanding of Arabness and Arab culture as inextricably linked to religion. Some programmes on the al-Babtain YouTube channel connected to Islam are titled *adab al-Islam,* broadly translated in this context as the "moral culture of Islam". These programmes concern the literature on social behaviour, good practices and morals that should be upheld by the individual Muslim. Again, the theme connects to the view that focuses on the individual behaviour of Muslims and not on Islam as the foundation for a state ruled by one or the other interpretation of Islamic law. On a few occasions, the Foundation has combined the Arab and the Islamic, such as in the organization of the Malaga Islamic Fair in 2009 organized jointly with Malaga University and in which the term "Arab-Islamic civilization" was prominent in the presentations of the fair.

Aside from the moral dimension of Islam, Abu Saʿud sees it as having the potential to reinforce the Kuwaiti nation-building project. Islam in this context is not so very different from the official state interpretation and presentation in which it becomes an instrument that can be utilized to underline commonality among Kuwaitis. Accordingly, the al-Babtain Foundation does not present a unique understanding of Islam and the meaning of being Muslim and seeks to intertwine Islam and Arabness along the lines suggested above.

Since the start of the Foundation's efforts to promote poetry, the underlying discussion on poetry in Islamic interpretative traditions does not appear as an issue. If poetry is the cousin of music and Arabic is a language closely connected to God, language and poetry becomes a companion to piety. I am here referring to Arabic as the language of the revelation and the Quran, and the major language of interpreting Islam across the various schools that have developed in history. The question of how poetry can be discussed is a question of eloquence, grammar and content. The question of content is the most important one in relation to Islam, and also a reason for the programmes on the social behaviour of the Muslim referred to above. Content that can border on sensitive questions focusing on, say, sexuality or moral behaviour that would be understood as going against the Arab or Muslim norms and values is not featured and performed at the poetry festivals. The only exceptions to this involve European and North American writers or poets.

According to Abd al-Aziz, Arab culture and the Arabic language need to be reinvigorated to become the glue that binds Kuwaitis (and Arabs) together. The state and the Foundation appear to stress Arab culture more than an Islamic culture as a common bond between Kuwaiti nationals, or to see Islam as inextricably linked with Arabness, and the cultural project of reinvigorating it. If this is a choice, it is understandable since the segments of the Kuwaiti population that identify either as Sunni or Shiʿa make Islam a volatile point of reference in a nation-building process and in the creation of common national histories. The implicit assumption in the work of the Foundation is that the social and cultural transformation of Kuwait over recent decades has weakened the link among younger generations to an Arab culture and to the Arabic language. At the time of its inception and establishment, the Foundation had the ambition not only to reinvigorate Arab culture, but also to rejuvenate the perception of an Arab identity that is broader, integrative, forward looking and founded on shared aspirations and values that bind Kuwaiti society together.

Abd al-Aziz has justified the Foundation's efforts in supporting poetry and Arab culture by pointing to the fact that poets are people with essential and special qualities. Poets are in some regard cultural heroes who carry the values of a culture from one generation to another. Abu Sa'ud's claim on this point is a reminder of the role ascribed to poets as carriers of tribal memory in the pre-Islamic era, and in the times of early Islam, in which oral tradition was prominent on the Arabian peninsula. Abd al-Aziz's characterization of poets is perhaps a peculiar instantiation in which poets become like prophets – important for the creation of culture and the collective memory of a nation.

The way Abd al-Aziz understands the needs of Kuwait and his effort to reinstitute the status of poetry and Arab culture relate to the experiences he has collected throughout his life. The stories he tells about his childhood in interviews and in the media mostly describe his personal relationship to literature, reading and composing poetry and the family *diwaniyya*. His shared recollections may be responses to questions focusing on his childhood and Abu Sa'ud's expectation concerning what the interlocutor would like to hear, but in the stories he shares about his childhood and his long and extraordinary life, he also reflects his self-image. Abd al-Aziz connects his early life being brought up in a family with a passion for language and poetry with his recent work as the chairperson at the al-Babtain Foundation. The years he spent in commercial activities and the businesses that have since 2006 been led by his sons and other members of the family are not often mentioned, but are always present in the background through the wealth they generate. He portrays himself as an Arab and sees himself as part of the long history of the Arab tribes that he has learned by heart and in which he can locate his personal tribal and family affiliation and history. Abd al-Aziz has his place in the tribal system, but to describe him on the basis of his tribal belonging is too simple a way of characterizing him. In his life story, he has been an example of social mobility: building his fortune and position in society instead of merely inheriting it. He states that he favours the simple life of the Arab and the Bedouin, but he is difficult to characterize as being on a certain side socially. He moves between the notions of being the Bedouin that belongs in the desert and the urban entrepreneur belonging to the centre of power in Kuwait City or in any capital of the world. He also belongs to a variety of Kuwaiti and global networks. Abd al-Aziz stresses the need for a culture he regards as fairly static and describes as the Arab culture in a definite form. However, his personal life is fluid, and he is not afraid of new challenges and to take on new initiatives that cultivate his accomplishments, such as starting the Forum for the Culture of Peace late in life, or to move from his childhood life in the small Kuwait City to meetings with world leaders, royalty, scholars of high standing and several influential businesspeople.

8

FINAL REFLECTIONS

It is true that before the Uqair Convention in 1922, when borders were delineated between Saudi Arabia and Kuwait, no clear borders had existed defining Kuwait. Passports, immigration controls and citizen documentation too – all instruments for the symbolic demarcation of a Kuwaiti territory, suggesting the act of "crossing" and its monitoring – were relative latecomers in the 20th century. Before the demarcation of borders, people had moved and mixed with each other independently of different affiliations, but often linked to each other by notions of a common and shared Arab, tribal and Islamic origin.[1] The drive to establish borders and demarcate a geographical area termed "Kuwait" was the first step in an endeavour to conceptualize the meaning of Kuwait and what defines it.[2]

Today 100 years have passed since the settlement in Uqair, and the history of the contemporary State of Kuwait demonstrates that, over time, the country, like any other, can be comprehended in different ways. On an abstract level, it is probably true that many Kuwaiti nationals, if asked about what binds them together as Kuwaitis, share ideas and point to common identity markers such as religion, history, language, culture and Arabness. On the individual level, and on the level of certain modalities of belonging such as the tribal, or to a specific religious group, these perceptions of common bonds between Kuwaitis are contested. The definition of Arab culture, and the emphasis on the need for Kuwait to rejuvenate a sense of Arabness among the population, advocated by Abd al-Aziz al-Babtain and the al-Babtain Foundation, is not shared by all in the diverse population. Important in the discussion of belonging and Kuwait as a nation is the role

---

1 AlShehabi 2015: 5
2 This discussion is inspired by Brubaker 2015.

of religion in Kuwaiti society. In the cases in which religion is intertwined with the nation-building efforts of the rulers and the government, it is in the form of an all-embracing "Islam", and rarely, if ever, divided into the branches of Islam that exist in Kuwait. Abd al-Aziz is an example. For him, Islam is defined broadly as the Sunni version. He also shows a considerable and genuine respect for other Islamic traditions such as the Shi'a. This is underlined by his relationships with universities and leaders in the Islamic Republic of Iran, and his inclusion of Shi'a voices in the conferences and events the Foundation has organized in Europe and elsewhere. The general position taken by the al-Babtain Foundation on Islam fits within the ambition of the state to create a controlled space assigned to religion. Abu Sa'ud's more personal views of Islam as a matter of the individual and not the state also appear to be in line with the Kuwaiti rulers' aspiration to be publicly seen as devout, but not aiming for an Islamization of the state. In the end, Islam in an all-encompassing and undefined version becomes an instrument interwoven with nationalism in certain contexts. The aim of celebrations of the ruling family and the nation during Ramadan or at other religious holidays is to make religious traditions and practices a vehicle binding people together, regardless of whether they are citizens or not. On special occasions, the rulers and state officials also refer to the language of the Quran and the traditions of the Prophet Muhammad common to most Muslims.

However, these references to a general and all-embracing Islam also become an identity marker of difference and exclusion when Shi'a Islam is not visible on particular occasions and their ritual celebrations are not permitted. Identity markers like religion and Arabness are fluid and borderless. Abd al-Aziz may refer to a stable "Arab culture", but his life story and the way the remit and operation of the al-Babtain Foundation have shifted over time underline the fluidity of the meaning of being Arab. The shift of the work of the Foundation towards promoting the culture of peace is not only pragmatic and an end in itself, it is a move away from an emphasis on poetry and literary expression to the quest for peace in the understanding of what is important for contemporary Arabs and in Arab culture. In Abd al-Aziz's perspective, it is important to understand who you are before defining a culture of peace. Even if borders can be porous in an abstract meaning between contemporary Kuwait and other countries, many boundaries exist inside the society: social, economic, religious and political. The idea of a common Arab and Islamic origin is currently not enough to constitute the foundation for the creation of a nationalism sufficient to connect people thoroughly to the nation of Kuwait.

On February 26 every year, Kuwait celebrates the liberation and the end of the Iraqi occupation in 1991. Liberation Day is an official holiday commemorating the US-led military operation that ousted the Iraqis and reinstalled the al-Sabah family as the rulers of the state. In contemporary Kuwait, most of the people living in the country, citizens or non-citizens, have no personal experience of the occupation and the liberation. A majority of the citizens were not born before 1991, and most of the labour migrants have arrived after the war. It has become a celebration similar to D-Day in Europe and is filled with aspirations to become a collective memory for Kuwaitis that tie them together. It is a collective memory for a small part of the population as the diversity among the people in Kuwait is manifested in everyday life politically, socially and religiously, not to mention in the discussions on labour migration, gender and women's rights. The obvious aspect in the comparison between the different lives of the labour migrants, the *biduns* and the privileged citizens is the rulers' aspirations concerning the identity of Kuwait. For Abu Saʿud, the Iraqi occupation, liberation and its aftermath are experiences that convinced him of the necessity of an Arab solidarity that transcends the borders of individual Arab states.

The meaning of citizen, citizenship and non-citizen are central to developments in Kuwait. Migration has in many ways transformed the state, and inequality founded on different belongings among the current population is built into the legal system as well as social and public life. For the citizens of the country, the fairly long existence of the idea of a Kuwait, the long reign of the al-Sabah family and the experience of periods of democratic governance make the state of Kuwait distinct within the Arab Gulf and may provide some degree of legitimacy allowing the rulers and the government to address the various current and future challenges that the state of Kuwait faces.

On September 29, 2020, the amir Sabah al-Ahmad al-Jabir al-Sabah passed away. He was succeeded a day later by Crown Prince Nawaf al-Ahmad al-Jabir al-Sabah (r. 2020–present). The peaceful transition in the second half of 2020, the slow process concerning the "Kuwaitization" of the labour force and the carefully introduced changes to the taxation system and citizenship legislation are all examples that indicate that the rulers of Kuwait are very cautious when it comes to decisions that affect the people

View of the *suq* in Kuwait City hung with posters of
the ruling family, 2016. © the author.

living in Kuwait, especially changes that may upset the everyday life of the
privileged citizens. One reason beyond the obvious concerns about security
and maintenance of power for the cautious politics of the ruling family and
the government is the role that the rulers have ascribed to themselves.

The ruling al-Sabah family has succeeded in establishing themselves as
Kuwait's ruling dynasty since the mid-18th century. Land in Kuwait belongs
to the state, and it is in the hands of the ruler. Law-making, nation building
and the relationship of the ruling family to Kuwaitis are inextricably linked
to the ruling family's link to the land. It becomes a paternalistic relationship
in which the ruler/landowner provides for his or her clients. The development of Kuwait's welfare system is a telling instance of this bond in which
the rulers provide for the citizens.

When viewing contemporary Kuwait, it is possible to describe the state
as an exemplar of tribal modernity, in which the instrumental aspects of
modernity exist, but where its values and norms are informed by traditions
that at best can be understood as expressions of a multiple modernity. One
example is the debate concerning women's rights and gender relations. The

al-Sabah family has built the relationship between state and ruler over many years and their status in Kuwait is underlined by the writing of the constitution and inscribed in the legal system.

In the history of Kuwait, scholars have portrayed the links between the amir and the nationals in terms of a family bond.[3] In conjunction with a perception of Arab and tribal culture, the amir is often represented as the father who provides for the family members. This relationship surpasses the public and private spheres and builds on relationships between people, such as the symbiotic relationship between Abd al-Aziz and the Kuwaiti ruling family or the land laws of Kuwait which stipulate that the land of Kuwait belongs to the ruler. This is not only a relationship between male Kuwaitis – the ruler as the father and the male Kuwaiti citizens as the sons of the nation. Women are also placed into this constructed family relationship mainly as the mothers of the nation responsible for catering to the family. In this interpretation, women's emancipation and female participation in politics and in education are either a threat or an incentive for a reconstruction of the composition of the relationship between the amir and the people of Kuwait through the lens of a family. Connecting the nation and nation-building to a family conceptualization is by no means unique, as the idiom of the family and family bonds (nation as brotherhood or fraternity) is frequently used in such processes to render abstract connections between members of the nation or between the nation and its members more concrete and durable.

Being older than the state of Kuwait itself, Abd al-Aziz al-Babtain, has an intimate historic relationship with the notion of "Kuwait" as it has developed over the years. Abu Sa'ud supports the idea of the Kuwaiti nation and contributes in a loyal manner to its development. He is also grateful for the benefits and opportunities that the independent state of Kuwait has given him. This interdependence – the fruitful relationship between family and its members (variations of which have developed between the state and the majority of Kuwaiti citizens) – has underpinned the development of Abu Sa'ud's Foundation that works closely with the state to promote the nation.

Abu Sa'ud's charitable work and engagement in education, culture and dialogue reflects not only his but also Kuwait's experience of statehood and the ambiguities of Kuwaiti identity. A reflection of domestic Kuwaiti politics

---

3 For example, Dresch 2013, Krause 2009 and al-Mughni 1997.

and identity can be discerned in his understanding of Arabness, steeped in the coexistence of a traditional, hierarchical culture with a common sense of belonging to a broad Arab community. Islam, and its inextricable links to Arab culture and history, is also present in this visualization of Arabness (and Kuwaitiness) in a way similar to the instrumentalization of Islam by the Kuwaiti state and the ruling family as a cultural force bringing cohesion and informing societal values and not as a political project under which statecraft is subsumed. Yet, this topography underlying the work of Abd al-Aziz al-Babtain is a fluid one, marked by permeable borders reflecting the emphasis on dialogue and crossing civilizational boundaries that has become central in his more recent work. The notion of Islam deployed within it is illustrative of this; although Sunni Islam is undoubtedly at the centre of this cultural topography, the boundaries between Sunni and Shia Islam are considered to be sufficiently porous, as they have often been in Kuwait's dynastic and parliamentary politics, in order not to challenge the overarching notion of Arab culture and identity that occupies a central position both in the official Kuwaiti identity narrative (and foreign policy) and Abd Al Aziz's, and his Foundation's work. This depoliticized and tacitly repoliticized (in the sense of tying it to the political project of building Kuwaitiness) version of Islam, central in the work of the al-Babtain Foundation, but also in the foreign and aid policy of the Kuwaiti state, extends the topography delineated by Abd al-Aziz's work to a broader notion of an Islamic world that had once shared, or still shares, an appreciation for Arab culture and its achievements, and an affinity with the Arab world, of which both Kuwait and al-Babtain seek to be ambassadors and custodians. In this way, the shifting character of the al-Babtain Foundation reflects, and at the same time contributes to, the ongoing nation-building project in Kuwait and the forging of the emirate's international personality and quest for a place in a rapidly changing world.

Finally, I should like to return to the story with which I began book. The point of the story about the meeting between Abd al-Aziz al-Babtain and a high-level Iraqi official was that it was a meeting between two successful and eminent persons. They discussed important political matters and relations between states. The story, which was recounted to me at my first private meeting with Abd al-Aziz, in retrospect set the tone for all my subsequent interactions with him. In other words, for Abu Sa'ud all stories told about him reflect his ambitions and his views on how to achieve a continuity of

I Love Kuwait mural, Kuwait City, 2016. © the author.

what needs to be preserved and change what needs to be changed.

Abd al-Aziz al-Babtain and al-Babtain Foundation uphold the idea that effective impact in the world is achieved through elite action. This view permeates not only his personal understanding of the world, but also the daily work of the Foundation. The hierarchical standpoint is the same if it concerns the preservation and promotion of poetry, Arabic language and culture, in the "dialogue among civilizations", and in the creation of a culture for peace. The idea that an elite has a form of primary agency is also visible in establishing chairs in academia and in the organization of the conferences on peace, inviting people considered to be influential and who can support the initiatives of the Foundation from a top-down perspective. Abd al-Aziz's hierarchical view on society is also mirrored in his views on Arab culture and Islam, and is visible in his and his Foundation's efforts in strengthening Arab culture in the Comoros, Central Asia and in Mali. Also, the support for individual students is carried out in a top-down manner in which the Foundation has identified what a student should study or what kind of education that is needed in a country. In more recent years, such as in the book titled *Contemplations for Peace*, Abd al-Aziz's personal experience founded on a successful life becomes a role model and the underpinning for how peace can become a value within humanity.

The prism of a high and low philosophy in the agency of Abd al-Aziz and the al-Babtain Foundation also elucidates why things like social media, or indeed the library, have yet to become fully functioning parts of the Foundation's strategy. Hierarchy is also a foundation for how he tells the story about his life, and how he reiterates his Arab and tribal background as well as the relationship to the ruling family. The individual can change his or her personal life, but the transformation of a society is built on a hierarchy that also gives those at the top authority over cultural and societal change.

KUWAIT TIMELINE

1500s ► Region known as modern Kuwait comes under
Portuguese control

1613 ► Kuwait City founded

1700s ► al-Sabah family settles in Kuwait early in the 18th century

1752 ► Sheikhdom of Kuwait established and Sabah bin Jabir
elected as ruler, and the position of sheikh becomes
hereditary within the al-Sabah family

1750s ► Kuwait becomes a major stop on the trading route between
the Gulf, Indian subcontinent and Europe

1850 ► The al-Babtain family moves from al-Kharj (south of Riyadh)
to al-Rawda (northwest of Riyadh); later in the 19th century
they move to the city of al-Zubayr (south of Basra)

1855 ► The grandfather of Abd al-Aziz al-Babtain arrives in Kuwait

1875 ► Kuwait is incorporated into the Ottoman administrative
region of Basra

1896 ► Mubarak al-Sabah becomes ruler of Kuwait

1899 ► Kuwait becomes a British Protectorate

1900s ► Economic decline in the first years of the new century

1912 ▶ al-Mubarakiyya school established

1915 ▶ Death of Mubarak al-Sabah

1922 ▶ The Uqair agreement establishes the borders of Kuwait

1930s ▶ Great Depression

1932 ▶ Ibn Saud becomes the king of Saudi Arabia

1934 ▶ First oil concession is signed between the al-Sabah ruler and the Kuwait Oil Company

1936 ▶ Birth of Abd al-Aziz al-Babtain

1937 ▶ First school for girls is built

1938 ▶ Discovery of oil in Burgan

1945 ▶ Start of the Golden Era

1946 ▶ The exporting of oil begins
▶ First public hospital constructed

1948 ▶ Nationality law signed

1950 ▶ Abd Allah al-Salim al-Sabah is declared the new ruler (after independence in 1961, he becomes the first amir of Kuwait)

1951 ▶ Kuwait's first broadcasting station launched

1952 ▶ The National Bank of Kuwait and the Kuwait Commercial Bank are established
▶ First secondary school for girls built

1953 ▶ Creation of Kuwait Investment Authority to manage Kuwaiti government funds

1954 ► Abd al-Aziz al-Babtain's first paid employment as a
secretary in the al-Shuwaykh secondary school library

1955 ► Abd al-Aziz al-Babtain starts working at the Ministry
of Education

1956 ► Abd al-Aziz al-Babtain starts his business career trading
in a small village shop

1958 ► *al-Arabi*, the first printed magazine in Kuwait published

1959 ► The Central Bank of Kuwait is established
► Abd al-Aziz al-Babtain makes his first agreement with
a tobacco company and becomes their agent in Kuwait

1960 ► Kuwait becomes a founding member of the Organization
of Petroleum Exporting Countries (OPEC)

1961 ► Independence from Britain; state of Kuwait is fully
established with the end of the Anglo-Kuwaiti treaty
► The Kuwaiti Dinar is issued as the national currency
► Launch of the first English language daily newspaper,
Kuwait Times
► Kuwait's first television broadcast

1962 ► First constitution of the state of Kuwait is written
and ratified
► Abd al-Aziz al-Babtain becomes the representative of
Marlboro in Kuwait, Saudi Arabia and Afghanistan

1963 ► First election to the National Assembly
► Kuwait joins the United Nations

1964- ► Abd al-Aziz al-Babtain opens offices and stores in Iran,
1965 Pakistan, Iraq, Turkey, Cyprus, Egypt and Italy

1966 ► Creation of Kuwait University

1968 ▸ Abd al-Aziz al-Babtain establishes new companies in Saudi Arabia

1970 ▸ al-Babtain's commercial enterprises expand into property. Later in the decade, consumer goods and food products become important parts of the business
▸ al-Babtain becomes involved with the developing electronics industry, with links to European, Chinese and North American companies

1973 ▸ The Arab-Israeli War and ensuing OPEC oil embargo rages on

1974 ▸ al-Babtain grants the first scholarships for students to study abroad

1975 ▸ The nationalization process of the Kuwait Oil Company is completed

1976 ▸ Kuwait Future Generations Fund is established
▸ The first satellite TV channels arrive in Kuwait

1977 ▸ Jabir al-Ahmad al-Jabir al-Sabah is appointed the new amir

1979 ▸ The revolution in Iran begins

1980 ▸ The war between Iran and Iraq starts

1981 ▸ Creation of the Gulf Cooperation Council (GCC)

1982 ▸ Suq al-Manakh stock-market crash
▸ End of the Golden Era

1986 ▸ Suspension of the 1962 constitution

1988 ▸ The war between Iran and Iraq ends

1989 ▶ al-Babtain Foundation begins activities in Cairo and creates the Abdulaziz Saud al-Babtain Prize for Poetic Creativity

1990 ▶ Iraqi invasion of Kuwait on August 2

1991 ▶ Liberation from Iraqi occupation and end of the First Gulf War in February

1992 ▶ al-Babtain Foundation establishes regional offices in Jordan, Kuwait, Tunisia and, later on, Spain

1993 ▶ Internet is introduced in Kuwait

1994 ▶ Abd al-Aziz al-Babtain's company granted the franchise to sell Marlboro products in Saudi Arabia

1995 ▶ Publication of Abd al-Aziz al-Babtain's first poetry book *Bawh al-Bawadi* and the Foundation publishes the first of the al-Babtain encyclopaedias of Arab poetry

1999 ▶ National Assembly annuls decree granting women the right to vote and run for office

2003 ▶ The Second Gulf War or Iraq War; US-led coalition overthrows the Iraqi regime of Saddam Hussein between March and May, but the conflict doesn't end until 2011

2004 ▶ al-Babtain Foundation supports the first chair in Arabic language and culture at the University of Córdoba, Spain

2005 ▶ Kuwaiti women granted the right to vote and stand for office

2006 ▶ Death of amir Jabir al-Ahmad al-Jabir al-Sabah
▶ al-Babtain Central Library for Arabic Poetry opens in Kuwait City
▶ Abd al-Aziz al-Babtain retires from business life to focus on his Foundation

2010 ▶ Jasmine Revolution in Tunisia begins, followed by protests and conflicts in several other Arab countries

2011 ▶ Civil unrest begins in Kuwait, with protests forcing the resignation of the prime minister, Sheikh Nasir al-Muhammad al-Sabah; unrest continues into 2012

2012 ▶ al-Babtain Foundation establishes the Euro-Arab Institute for Dialogue between Cultures in Rome in collaboration with partners in Italy, Belgium and Tunisia

2012 ▶ All Kuwaiti female MPs lose their seats in the general election and the Assembly convenes without any female representatives

2014 ▶ Civil war in Yemen starts

2015 ▶ The official name of the al-Babtain Foundation changes to the Abdulaziz Saud al-Babtain Cultural Foundation
▶ Foundation begins to focus more on the "dialogue among civilizations" and the promotion of Arabic language and culture

2017 ▶ Relations between Qatar and other Gulf states, including Kuwait, begin to deteriorate

2018 ▶ Launch of the al-Babtain Leiden University Centre for Arabic Culture

2020 ▶ Death of amir Sabah al-Ahmad al-Jabir al-Sabah
▶ Nawaf al-Sabah al-Ahmad al-Jabir al-Sabah becomes the amir

BIBLIOGRAPHY

Abdulaziz Saud al-Babtain: Biography & Cultural Achievements 2017. The General Secretariat of the Foundation. Kuwait Second edition.

Abdulaziz Saud al-Babtain: Impressions and Testimonials by Statesmen and Intellectuals 2015. Elain Publishing house, Cairo.

Abdulrahim, Masoud A., Ali A. J. al-Kandari and Mohammed Hasanen 2009. "The Influence of American Television Programs on University Students in Kuwait: A Synthesis", in *European Journal of American Culture*. Vol. 28, No. 1.

Alahmad, Barrak et al. 2020. "Extreme Temperatures and Mortality in Kuwait: Who is Vulnerable?", in *Science of the Total Environment*. Vol. 732. https://doi.org/10.1016/j.scitotenv.2020.139289

Alebrahim, Abdulrahman 2019. *Kuwait's Politics Before Independence: The Role of the Balancing Powers*. Exeter Critical Gulf Series. Gerlach Press, Berlin.

Alkhamis, Abdulwahab, Amir Hassan and Peter Cosgrove 2013. "Financial Healthcare in Gulf Cooperation Council Countries: A Focus on Saudi Arabia", in *The International Journal of Health Planning and Management*. Vol. 29, Issue 1.

Alnajdi, Abdullah Ahmad 2014. *Shaikh Abdullah Al-Salim Al-Sabah, 1895–1965*. Thesis for the Degree of Doctor of Philosophy in Arab and Islamic Studies. Submitted to the University of Exeter, Institute of Arab and Islamic Studies.

Alzuabi, Ali Z. 2016. "Socio-political Participation of Kuwaiti Women in the Development Process: Current State and Challenges Ahead", in *Journal of Social Service Research*. Vol. 42, No. 5.

AlShehabi, Omar 2015. "Histories of Migration to the Gulf", in Abdulhadi Khalaf, Omar AlShehabi and Adam Hanieh (eds). *Transit States: Labour, Migration & Citizenship in the Gulf.* Pluto Press, London.

An Overview of Abdul Aziz Saud Al-Babtain 2015. Compiled by the General Secretariat of the Foundation. Kuwait.

Atzori, Daniel 2014. "Poetry, a message for humanity. Interview with Abdul Aziz Saud al-Babtain", *Papers of Dialogue*. No 2.

al-Awadi, Abdul-Rahman 1957. "Education in Kuwait", in *The Vocational Aspect of Secondary and Further Education*. Vol. 9, No. 19.

al-Awadi, Hesham 2014. "Kuwait", in Ellen Lust (ed.) *The Middle East*. CQ Press, Thousand Oaks. 13th edition.

Ayoob, Mohammed 1981. *The Middle East in World Politics*. Croom Helm, London.

Azoulay, Rivka 2020. *Kuwait and Al-Sabah: Tribal Politics and Power in an Oil State*. I. B. Tauris, London.

Azoulay, Rivka and Madeleine Wells 2014. "Contesting Welfare State Politics in Kuwait", in *Middle East Report*. No. 272, Fall.

Babar, Zahra R. 2011. *Free Mobility within the Gulf Cooperation Council*. Center for International and Regional Studies, Georgetown University School of Foreign Service in Qatar, Occasional Paper No. 8.

al-Babtain, Abdulaziz Saud 2019. *Contemplations for Peace*. Abdulaziz Saud al-Babtain Cultural Foundation, Kuwait City.

Bagchi, Amiya Kumar 2000. *Private Investment in India 1900–1939. The Evolution of International Business 1800–1945, Volume V*. Routledge, London. First published by Cambridge University Press in 1972.

Bagnied, Mohsen and Hanas Cader 2016. "Shopping Malls and Commercial Strips: An Examination of Factors Affecting Shoppers' Behaviour in Kuwait", in *International Journal of Leisure and Tourism Marketing*. Vol. 5, No. 1.

al-Baharna, Husain M. 1968. *The Legal Status of the Arabian Gulf States: A Study of their Treaty Relations and their International Problems*. Manchester University Press, Manchester.

Bano, Masooda and Keiko Saurai 2015. *Shaping Global Islamic Discourses: The role of al-Azhar, al-Medina and al-Mustafa*. Edinburgh University Press and The Aga Khan University Institute for the Study of Muslim Civilisations, Edinburgh.

Barakat, Sultan and John Skelton 2014. *The Reconstruction of Post-war Kuwait: A Missed Opportunity?* Kuwait Programme on Development, Governance and Globalisation in the Gulf States, No. 37. London School of Economics and Political Science, London.

Beaugrand, Claire 2016. "Deconstructing Minorities/Majorities in Parliamentary Gulf States (Kuwait and Bahrain)", in *British Journal of Middle Eastern Studies*. Vol. 43, No. 2, April.

Beaugrand, Claire 2018. *Stateless in the Gulf: Migration, Nationality and Society in Kuwait*. Library of Modern Middle East Studies. I. B. Tauris, London.

Beaugrand, Claire 2020. "The *Bidun* Protest Movement as an Act of Citizenship", in Roel Meijer and Nils Butenschøn (eds). *The Crisis of Citizenship in the Arab World*. Brill, Leiden.

Beblawi, Hazem and Giacomo Luciani 1990: "The Rentier State in the Arab World", in Giacomo Luciani (ed.). *The Arab State*. Routledge, London.

Behar, Ruth 1990. "Rage and Redemption: Reading the Life Story of a Mexican Marketing Woman", in *Feminist Studies*. Vol. 16, No. 2, Summer.

Benthall, Jonathan and Jerome Bellion-Jourdan 2009. *The Charitable Crescent: Politics of Aid in the Muslim World*. I. B. Tauris, London.

Bilboe, Wendy 2011. "Vocational Education and Training in Kuwait: Vocational Education Versus Values and Viewpoints", in *International Journal of Training Research*. Vol. 9, Issue 3.

Bowen Jr., Richard LeBaron 1951. "The Pearl Fisheries of the Persian Gulf", *Middle East Journal*. Vol. 5, No. 2.

Bratton, Michael and Nicolas van de Walle 1997. *Democratic Experiences in Africa: Regime Transitions in Comparative Perspective*. Cambridge University Press, Cambridge.

Brennan, P. 1990. "Greater Burgan Field", in E. A. Beaumont and N. H. Foster (eds). *AAPG Treatise of Petroleum Geology: Atlas of Oil and Gas Fields, Structural Traps I*, AAPG, Tulsa.

Brown, Nathan J. and Mara Revkin 2018. "Islamic Law and Constitutions", in Anver M. Emon and Rumee Ahmed (eds). *The Oxford Handbook of Islamic Law*. Oxford University Press, Oxford.

Brubaker, Rogers 2015. *Grounds for Difference*. Harvard University Press, Cambridge, MA.

Bulloch, John and Harvey Morris 1991. *Saddam's War: The Origins of the Kuwait Conflict and the International Response*. Faber and Faber, London.

Buscemi, Emanuela 2016. "Abaya and Yoga Pants: Women's Activism in Kuwait", in *AG About Gender International Journal of Gender Studies*. Vol. 5, No. 10.

Buscemi, Emanuela 2017. "Resistant Identities: Culture and Politics among Kuwaiti Youth", in *Contemporary Social Science*. Vol. 12, Issue 3–4.

Cammett, Melani, Ishac Diwan, Alan Richards and John Waterbury 2015. *A Political Economy of the Middle East*. Westview Press, Boulder. Fourth edition.

Casey, Michael S. 2007. *The History of Kuwait*. Greenwood Press, Westport.

Celine, K. 1985. "Kuwait Living on it Nerves", in *Middle East Report*. No. 130, February.

Chay, Clemence 2016. "The *Dīwāniyya* Tradition in Modern Kuwait: An Interlinked Space and Practice", in *Journal of Arabian Studies – Arabia, the Gulf, and the Red Sea*. Volume 6, Issue 1.

Chejne, Anwar 1965. "Arabic: Its Significance and Place in Arab-Muslim Society", in *Middle East Journal*. Vol. 19, No. 4.

Chisholm, Archibald H. T. 1975. *The First Kuwait Oil Concession Agreement: A Record of the Negotiations 1911–1934*. Frank Cass, London.

Coates Ulrichsen, Kristian 2012. "Kuwait's Uncertain Path", in *Foreign Policy*, September 26.

Coates Ulrichsen, Kristian 2013. "Domestic Implications of the Arab Uprisings in the Gulf", in Ana Echague (ed.). *The Gulf States and the Arab Uprisings*. FRIDE and the Gulf Research Center, Madrid.

Coates Ulrichsen, Kristian 2014. "Politics and Opposition in Kuwait: Continuity and Change", in *Journal of Arabian Studies – Arabia, the Gulf, and the Red Sea*. Vol. 4, Issue 2.

Coates Ulrichsen, Kristian 2017. *Economic Diversification in Gulf Cooperation Council (GCC) States*. Center for Energy Studies. Rice University's Baker Institute for Public Policy, Houston.

Cole, Donald P. 1975. *Nomads of the Nomads: the Al Murrah Bedouin of the Empty Quarter*. Harlan Davidson, Chicago.

Commins, David 2014. *The Gulf States: A Modern History*. I. B. Tauris, London.

Crystal, Jill 1989. "Coalitions in Oil Monarchies: Kuwait and Qatar", in *Comparative Politics*. Vol. 21, No. 4.

Crystal, Jill 1990. *Oil and Politics in the Gulf: Rulers and Merchants in Kuwait and Qatar*. Cambridge University Press, Cambridge.

Crystal, Jill 1992. *Kuwait: The Transformation of an Oil State. Routledge Library Editions: Society of the Middle East*, Routledge, London. First published by Westview Press in 1992.

Darwiche, Fida 1986. *The Gulf Stock Exchange Crash: The Rise and Fall of the Souq Al-Manakh*. Croom Helm, London.

Daun, Holger, Reza Arjomand & Geoffrey Walford 2004. "Muslims and Education in a Global Context", in Holger Daun and Geoffrey Walford. *Educational Strategies among Muslims in the Context of Globalization: Some National Case Studies*. Muslim Minorities Vol. 3. Brill, Leiden.

Daun, Holger and Geoffrey Walford 2004. *Educational Strategies among Muslims in the Context of Globalization: Some National Case Studies*. Muslim Minorities, Vol. 3. Brill, Leiden.

Devlin, John F. 1991. "The Baath Party: Rise and Metamorphosis", in *The American Historical Review*. Vol. 96, No. 5, December.

Dickson, Harold 1949. *The Arab of the Desert: A Glimpse of Badawin Life in Kuwait and Saudi Arabia*. George Allen & Unwin, London.

Donner, Fred 2010. *Muhammad and the Believers: At the Origins of Islam*. Harvard University Press, Cambridge, MA.

Dresch, Paul 2013. "Debates on Marriage and Nationality in the United Arab Emirates", in Paul Dresch and James Piscatori (eds). *Monarchies and Nations: Globalisation and Identity in the Arab States of the Gulf*. I. B. Tauris, London.

Dresch, Paul 2013b. "Societies, Identities and Global Issues", in Paul Dresch and James Piscatori (eds). *Monarchies and Nations: Globalisation and Identity in the Arab States of the Gulf*. I. B. Tauris, London.

Duffy, Matt J. 2014. "Arab Media Regulations: Identifying Restraints on Freedom of the Press in the Laws of Six Arabian Peninsula Countries", in *Berkeley Journal of Middle Eastern and Islamic Law*. Vol. 6, No. 1.

Dustur: A Survey of the Constitutions of the Arab and Muslims States 1966.

E. J. Brill, Leiden.

Eickelman, Dale F. 1985. *Knowledge amnd Power in Morocco. The Education of a Twentieth-Century Notable*. Princeton University Press, Princeton. Paperback edition 1992.

Eickelman, Dale F. and James Piscatori 2004. *Muslim Politics*. Princeton University Press, Princeton. Paperback edition 1996.

Elman, Miriam Fendius 1995. "The Foreign Policy of Small States: Challenging Neorealism in Its Own Backyard", in *British Journal of Political Science*. Vol. 25, Issue 2.

Finnie, David H. 1992. *Shifting Lines in the Sand: Kuwait's Elusive Frontier with Iraq*. Harvard University Press, Cambridge.

Forslund, Magnus 2002. *Det omöjliggjorda entreprenörskapet: Om förnyelsekraft och företagsamhet på golvet*. Växjö University Press, Växjö.

Freedman, Lawrence and Efraim Karsh 1993. *The Gulf Conflict, 1990–1991: Diplomacy and War in the New World Order*. Faber and Faber, London.

Freer, Courtney 2015. *The Rise of Pragmatic Islamism in Kuwait's Post-Arab Spring Opposition Movement*. Working paper, Rethinking Political Islam Series. Brookings Institution, Washington D. C.

Freer, Courtney 2018. *Kuwait's Post-Arab Spring Islamist Landscape: The End of Ideology?* Rice University's Baker Institute for Public Policy. Issue Brief 08.08.18.

Freeth, Zahra 1972. *A New Look at Kuwait*. Allen & Unwin, London.

Fukuyama, Francis 2019. *Identity. Contemporary Identity Politics and the Struggle for Recognition*. Profile Books, London.

Ghabra, Shafeeq 1991a. "The Iraqi Occupation of Kuwait: An Eyewitness Account", *Journal of Palestine Studies*. Vol. 20, No. 2, Winter.

Ghabra, Shafeeq 1991b. "Voluntary Associations in Kuwait: The foundation of a New System?", in *Middle East Journal*. Vol. 45, No. 2.

Ghabra, Shafeeq 1993. "Kuwait: Elections and Issues of Democratization in a Middle Eastern State", in *DOMES-Digest of Middle Eastern Studies*, Vol. 2, Issue 2, Spring.

Giddens, Anthony 1990. *The Consequences of Modernity*. Stanford University Press, Stanford.

Gause III, F. Gregory 1994. *Oil Monarchies: Domestic and Security Challenges in the Arab Gulf States*. Council on Foreign Relations Press, New York.

Gulf News Kuwait, October 17, 2016.

Gunter, Barrie and Roger Dickinson (eds) 2013. *News Media in the Arab World: A Study of 10 Arab and Muslim Countries*. Bloomsbury Academic, London.

Hafidh, Hasan 2017. *From Diwaniyyat to Youth Societies: Informal Political Spaces and Contentious Politics in Bahrain and Kuwait*. PhD-thesis in Comparative Politics of the Middle East, School of Languages, Cultures and Societies, University of Leeds: http://etheses.whiterose.ac.uk/19820/1/Hasan percent20Hafidh percent20- percent20Thesis percent20 percent28Complete percent29.pdf

Halevi, Leor 2019. *Modern Things on Trial. Islam's Global and Material Reformation in the Age of rida, 1865–1935*. Columbia University Press, New York.

Halliday, Fred 1984. "The Yemens: Conflict and Coexistence", in *The World Today*. Vol. 40, No. 8/9, Aug/Sep.

Halliday, Fred 1991. "The Gulf War and Its Aftermath: First Reflections", in *International Affairs*, Vol. 67, No. 2.

Hammond, Andrew 2007. *Popular Culture in the Arab World: Arts, Politics and the Media*. The American University in Cairo Press, Cairo.

Hamzawy, Amr 2008. "Debates on Political Reform in the Gulf: The Dynamics of Liberalising Public Spaces", in Alanoud Alsharek and Robert Springborg (eds). *Popular Culture and Political Identity in the Arab Gulf States*. SOAS Middle East Issues, Saqi Books, London.

Henry, Clement M. & Robert Springborg 2001. *Globalization and the Politics of Development in the Middle East*. Cambridge University Press, Cambridge.

Herb, Michael 1999. *All in the Family: Absolutism, Revolution, and Democracy in the Middle Eastern Monarchies*. State University of New York Press (SUNY Series in Middle Eastern Studies), New York.

Herb, Michael 2009. "A Nation of Bureaucrats: Political Participation and Economic Diversification in Kuwait and the United Arab Emirates", in *International Journal of Middle Eastern Studies*. Vol. 41, No. 3.

Herb, Michael 2016. *The Origins of Kuwait's National Assembly*. LSE Kuwait Programme Paper Series 39.

Herrera, Linda 2007. "Higher Education in the Arab World", in J. J. F. Forest and P. G. Altbach (eds). *International Handbook of Higher Education*. Springer International Handbooks of Education, Vol. 18. Springer, Dordrecht.

Hertog, Steffen 2020. *Reforming Wealth Distribution in Kuwait: Estimating Costs and Impacts*. LSE Middle East Centre Kuwait Programme Paper Series 5, July 2020.

Hijazi, Ahmad 1964. "Kuwait: Development from a Semitribal, Semicolonial Society to Democracy and Sovereignty", in *The American Journal of Comparative Law*. Vol. 13, No. 3, Summer.

Hijji, Yaqub Yusuf 2010. *Kuwait and the Sea: A Brief Social and Economic History*. Arabian Publishing, London.

Hill, Peter 1969. "The Changing World: The Population of Kuwait", in *Geography*. Vol. 54, No. 1.

Hjorth, Daniel and Chris Steyaert (eds) 2004. *Narrative and Discursive Approaches in Entrepreneurship. A Second Movements in Entrepreneurship Book.* Edward Elgar, Cheltenham.

Hofheinz, Albrecht 2007. "Arab Internet Use: Popular Trends and Public Impact", in Naomi Sakr (ed.). *Arab Media and Political Renewal: Community, Legitimacy and Public Life.* I. B. Tauris, London.

Ingham, Bruce 1997. "Men's Dress in the Arabian Peninsula: Historical and Present Perspectives", in Nancy Lindisfarne-Tapper and Bruce Ingham (eds). *Languages of Dress in the Middle East.* Routledge. London and New York.

Kaboudan, Mahmoud A. 1988. "Oil Revenue and Kuwait's Economy: An Econometric Approach", in *International Journal of Middle Eastern Studies.* Vol. 20, No. 1.

Kamrava, Mehran 2013. *Qatar: Small State, Big Politics.* Cornell University Press, Ithaca.

Kapiszewski, Andrzej 2006. "Elections and Parliamentary Activity in the GCC States: Broadening Political Participation in the Gulf Monarchies", in Abdulhadi Khalaf and Giacomo Luciani (eds). *Constitutional Reform and Political Participation in the Gulf.* Gulf Research Center, Dubai.

Karam, Jasem M. 1993. "Kuwaiti National Assembly – 1992 A Study in Electoral Geography", in *GeoJournal.* Vol. 31, Issue 4

Khadduri, Majid & Edmund Ghareeb 1997. *War in the Gulf, 1990–91: The Iraq- Kuwait Conflict and Its Implications.* Oxford University Press, Oxford.

Khalaf, Abdulhadi, Omar AlShehabi & Adam Hanieh (eds) 2015. *Transit States: Labour, Migration & Citizenship in the Gulf.* Pluto Press, London.

Khalaf, Sulayman 2008. "The Nationalisation of Culture: Kuwait's Invention of a Pearl-Diving Heritage", in Alanoud Asharekh and Robert Springborg (eds). *Popular Culture and Political Identity in the Arab Gulf*

States. SOAS Middle East Issues. Saqi Books, London.

Khalaf, Sulayman and Hassan Hammoud 1987. "The Emergence of the Oil Welfare State: The Case of Kuwait", in *Dialectical Anthropology*. Vol. 12, No. 4.

Khallaf, Mahi 2008. "The State of Kuwait", in Barbara Lethem Ibrahim and Dina H. Sherif. *From Charity to Social Change: Trends in Arab Philanthropy*. Cairo University Press, Cairo.

Khouja, M. W. and P. G. Sadler 1979. *The Economy of Kuwait: Development and Role in International Finance*. Macmillan Press, London.

al-Khouri, Riad 2008. *Kuwait Rentierism Revisited*. Carnegie Endowment for International Peace, Washington DC.

Kinninmont, Jane 2013. *Citizenship in the Gulf*. Chatham House, London.

Kostiner, Joseph 2009. *Conflict and Cooperation in the Gulf Region*. VS Verlag für Sozialwissenschaften, Wiesbaden.

Krause, Wanda 2009. *Gender and Participation in the Arab Gulf*. Kuwait Programme on Development, Governance and Globalisation in the Gulf States and the Centre for the Study of Global Governance. London School of Economics and Political Science, London.

Kuwait: Land Ownership and Agricultural Laws Handbook. Volume 1, Strategic Information and Basic Laws 2011. International Business Publications, Washington DC.

Kuwait Today: A Welfare State 1963. Ministry of Guidance and Information (*Wizarat al-irshad wa al-anba'*), Quality Publications, Kuwait.

Lauterpacht, E., Greenwood, C. J., Weller M. and Daniel Bethlehem (eds) 1991. *The Kuwait Crisis: Basic Documents*. Cambridge International Documents Series, Vol. 1. Cambridge University Press, Cambridge.

Lawson, Fred 1985. "Class and State in Kuwait", in *Middle East Report. No. 132*.

Lawson, Fred 1996. *Why Syria Goes to War: Thirty Years of Confrontation.* Cornell University Press, Ithaca and London.

Legrenzi, Matteo 2015. *The GCC and the International Relations of the Gulf: Diplomacy, Security and Economic Coordination in a Changing Middle East.* I. B. Tauris, London and New York.

Leichtman, Mara A. 2017. *Kuwaiti Humanitarianism: The History and Expansion of Kuwait's Foreign Assistance Policies.* Policy brief series edited by Agnieszka Paczynska. School for Conflict Analysis and Resolution, George Mason University, Stimson Center.

Levins, John M., 1995. "The Kuwaiti Resistance", in *The Middle East Quarterly.* March 1995, Vol. 2, No. 1.

Lindisfarne-Tapper, Nancy & Bruce Ingham (eds) 1997. *Languages of Dress in the Middle East.* Routledge, London and New York.

Loewenstein, Andrew B., 2000. "'The Veiled Protectorate of Kowait': Liberalized Imperialism and British Efforts to Influence Kuwaiti Domestic Policy during the Reign of Sheikh Ahmad Al-Jaber, 1938–50", in *Middle Eastern Studies.* Vol. 36, No. 2.

Longva, Anh Nga 2009. "Nationalism in Premodern Guise: The Discourse on Hadhar and Badu in Kuwait", in *International Journal of Middle East Studies.* Vol. 38, No. 2.

Longva, Anh Nga 2013. "Neither Autocracy nor Democracy but Ethnocracy", in Paul Dresch and James Piscatori (eds). *Monarchies and Nations: Globalisation and Identity in the Arab States of the Gulf.* I. B. Tauris, London.

Looney, Robert E. 1990. "Structural and Economic Change in the Arab Gulf after 1973", in *Middle Eastern Studies.* Vol. 26, No. 4.

Lorimer, John Gordon 1915. *Gazetter of the Persian Gulf.* Vol. 1, Historical part 1A & 1B. British Library: India Office Records and Private Papers, IOR/L/PS/20/C91/1, in *Qatar Digital Library,* https://www.qdl.qa/archive/81055/vdc_100023575946.0x0000aa.

Accessed November 14, 2017.

Louër, Laurence 2008. *Transnational Shia Politics: Religious and Political Networks in the Gulf.* Hurst, London.

Luomi, Mari 2012. *The Gulf Monarchies and Climate Change: Abu Dhabi and Qatar in an Era of Natural Unsustainability.* Hurst, London.

Lust, Ellen (ed.) 2017. *The Middle East.* Sage, Singapore.

Maktabi, Rania 2017. "Ti år etter kvinners stemmerett I Kuwait: Quo vadis?", in *Babylon: Nordisk Tidskrift for Midtøstenstudier.* Nummer 1, 15 Årgang.

al-Marashi, Ibrahim 2003. "Saddam's Security Apparatus During the Invasion of Kuwait and the Kuwaiti Resistance", in *Journal of Intelligence History.* Vol. 3, Winter.

Meleis, Ibrahim Afaf, Nagat El-Sanabary and Diane Beeson 1979. "Women, Modernization and Education in Kuwait", in *Comparative Education Review.* Vol. 23, No. 1.

Mitchell, Charles et al 2014. "A Body of Dissatisfaction: A Study of the Effects of Media Imperialism in Kuwait", in *American Journal of Humanities and Social Sciences.* Vol. 2, No. 1.

Mohamed, Enaam Abdullah 2019. "The Impact of Political Reform on the Stability of the State of Kuwait since 2010", in *Journal of Humanities and Applied Social Sciences.*

Molyneux, Philip and Munawar Iqbal 2005. *Banking and Financial Systems in the Arab World.* Palgrave Macmillan, Basingstoke.

al-Moosa, Abdulrasool A. 1984. "Kuwait: Changing Environment in a Geographical Perspective", in *British Journal of Middle Eastern Studies.* Bulletin British Society for Middle Eastern Studies, Vol. 11, 1984, Issue 1.

Moss, Robert 2009. *The Secret History of Dreaming.* New World Library, Novato, California.

Morony, Michael G. 1984. *Iraq after the Muslim Conquest*. Princeton University Press, Princeton.

Mottahedeh, Roy 1985. *The Mantle of the Prophet: Religion and Politics in Iran*. Simon and Schuster, New York.

Mottahedeh, Roy 2001. *Loyalty and Leadership in an Early Islamic Society*. I. B. Tauris, London. First published in 1980 by Princeton University Press.

Moore, Pete W. 2001. "What Makes Successful Business Lobbies? Business Associations and the Rentier State in Jordan and Kuwait", in *Comparative Politics*. Vol. 33, No. 2.

al-Mughni, Haya 1996. "Women's Organizations in Kuwait", in *Middle East Report*. No. 198.

al-Mughni, Haya 1997. "From Gender Equality to Female Subjugation: The Changing Agendas of Women's Groups in Kuwait", in Dawn Chatty and Annika Rabo (eds). *Organizing Women: Formal and Informal Women's Groups in the Middle East*. Berg, Oxford.

al-Mugni, Haya 2001. *Women in Kuwait: The Politics of Gender*. Saqi Books, London.

Nader, Kathi & Robert S. Pynoos 2014. "The Children of Kuwait after the Gulf Crisis", in Lewis A. Leavitt and Nathan A. Fox (eds). *The Psychological Effects of War and Violence on Children*. Psychology Press, Taylor & Francis Group, New York. First published in 1993 by Lawrence Erlbaum Associates.

al-Nakib, Farah 2014. "Revisiting Hadar and Badu in Kuwait: Citizenship, Housing and the Construction of a Dichotomy", in *International Journal of Middle East Studies*. Vol. 46, No. 1.

al-Nakib, Farah 2016. *Kuwait Transformed: A History of Oil and Urban Life*. Stanford University Press, Stanford.

al-Nakib, Rania 2015. *Education and Democratic Development in Kuwait:*

Citizens in Waiting. Research paper, Middle East and North Africa Programme, Chatham House, The Royal Institute of International Affairs, London.

Naser, Mohamed 2017. "Kuwait's Foreign Policy towards Regional Issues in the Middle East from 2003 to 2014", in *Asian Social Science*. Vol. 13, No. 11.

Nonneman, Gerd 2011. "Political Reform in the Gulf Monarchies: From Liberalization to Democratization? A Comparative Perspective", in Anoushiravan Ehteshami and Steven Wright (eds). *Reform in the Middle East Oil Monarchies*. Ithaca Press, Reading.

Nosova, Anastasia 2018. "Private Sector and Diversification in Kuwait", in Ashraf Mishrif and Yousuf Al Balushi (eds). *Economic Diversification in the Gulf Region. The Private Sector as an Engine of Growth, Volume 1*. The Political Economy of the Middle East. Palgrave Macmillan, London.

Nyrop, Richard F. et al 1977. *Area Handbook for the Persian Gulf States*. Wildside Press, Rockville.

Okasha, Ahmed, Elie Karam and Tarek Okasha 2012. "Mental Health Services in the Arab World", in *World Psychiatry: Official Journal of the World Psychiatric Association (WPA)*. Vol. 11, Issue 1.

Olimat, Muhamad S. 2009. "Women and Politics in Kuwait", in *Journal of International Women's Studies*. Vol. 11, Issue 2.

Olimat, Muhamad S. 2012. "Arab Spring and Women in Kuwait", in *Journal of International Women's Studies*. Vol. 13, Issue 5.

Olver-Ellis, Sophie 2020. *Building the New Kuwait. Vision 2035 and the Challenge of Diversification*. LSE Middle East Centre Paper Series 30, London.

Ostovar, Afshon 2017. "The Visual Culture of Jihad", in Thomas Hegghammer (ed.). *Jihadi Culture: The Art and Social Practices of Militant Islamists*. Cambridge University Press, Cambridge.

Owen, Roger and Sevket Pamuk 1999. *A History of Middle East Economics in the Twentieth Century*. Harvard University Press, Cambridge, MA.

Ozkirimli, Umut 2017. *Theories of Nationalism. A Critical Introduction*. Palgrave, London, Third edition.

Parolin, Gianluca 2009. *Citizenship in the Arab World. Kin, Religion and Nation-State*. IMISCOE Research, Amsterdam University Press, Amsterdam.

Parolin, Gianluca 2016. "Winter is Coming. Authoritarian Constitutionalism Under Strain in the Gulf", in Rainer Grote and Tilmann J. Röder (eds). *Constitutionalism, Human Rights, and Islam after the Arab Spring*. Oxford University Press, New York.

Pfeifer, Karen 2002. "Kuwait's Economic Quandary", in *Middle East Report*. No. 223, Summer.

Phillips, Christopher 2016. *Everyday Arab Identity: The Daily Reproduction of the Arab World*. Routledge, London.

Pillai, R. V. and Mahendra Kumar 1962. "The Political and Legal Status of Kuwait", in *The International and Comparative Law Quarterly*. Vol. 11, No. 1.

The Politics of Rentier States in the Gulf, 2019. Project on Middle East Political Science, POMEPS Studies 33, Institute for Middle East Studies, George Washington University.

Qattan, Lidia 2013. "Dr Al-Babtain a Self-Made Tycoon. Poet of Special Merit", in *Arab Times*, February 25.

Qattan, Lidia 2018. "Abdul Aziz Emerges into a Remarkable Business Tycoon", in *Arab Times*, April 2.

al-Ragam, Asseel 2014. "The Politics of Representation: The Kuwait National Museum and processes of Cultural Production", in *International Journal of Heritage Studies*. Vol. 20, Issue 6.

Rajab, Jehan S. 1993. *Invasion Kuwait: An English Woman's Tale*. The Radcliffe Press, London.

Randeree, Kasim 2012. *Workforce Nationalisation in the Gulf Cooperation Council States*. Center for International and Regional Studies, Georgetown University School of foreign Service in Qatar, Occasional Paper No. 9.

Regan Wills, Emily 2013. "Democratic Paradoxes: Women's Rights and Democratization in Kuwait", in *The Middle East Journal*. Vol. 67, No. 2.

Renner, Michael and Paul Aarts 1991. "Oil and the Gulf War", in *Middle East Report. No. 171*, July/August.

Rogan, Eugene L. 2009. *The Arabs: A History*. Basic Books, New York.

al-Sabah, Souad M. 2014. *Mubarak Al-Sabah. The Foundation of Kuwait*. I. B. Tauris, London.

al-Sabah, Souad M. 2015. *Abdullah Mubarak Al-Sabah. The Transformation of Kuwait*. I. B. Tauris, London.

al-Sabah, Y. S. F. 2018. *The Oil Economy of Kuwait*. Routledge Library Editions: Kuwait. Vol. 6. Routledge, New York. First edition 1980.

Sadowski, Yahya 1991. "Arab Economies after the Gulf War: Power, Poverty, and Petrodollars", in *Middle East Report*. No. 170, May/June.

Sadowski, Yahya 1997: "The End of the Counterrevolution? The Politics of Economic Adjustment in Kuwait", in *Middle East Report*. No. 204, July/September.

Safwat, Ismail 1993. *The System of Education in Kuwait*. A PIER World Education Series Working Paper. American Association of Collegiate Registrars and Admissions Officers and NAFSA: Association of International Educators, Washington DC.

Sailer, Matthias and Stephan Roll 2017. *Three Scenarios for the Qatar Crisis: Regime Change, Resolution or Cold War in the Gulf*. Stiftung

Wissenschaft und Politik -SWP- Deutsches Institut fur Internationale Politik und Sicherheit, Berlin.

Sakr, Naomi 2001. *Satellite Realms: Transnational Television, Globalization & the Middle East.* I. B. Tauris, London.

Salih, Kamal Osman 1991. "Kuwait: Political Consequences of Modernization, 1750– 1986", in *Middle Eastern Studies.* Vol. 27, No. 1.

Salih, Kamal Osman 1992. "The 1938 Kuwait Legislative Council", in *Middle Eastern Studies.* Vol. 28, No. 1.

al-Sallabi, Ali Muhammad not dated. *'Umar ibn al-Khattab: His Life and Times.* Volume One, Islamic History Series Part II, The Rightly Guided Caliphs 2, International Islamic Publishing House. Kalamullah.Com. Translated by Nasiruddin al-Khattab.

Satti, Mohamed 2013. "International Media and Local Programming: The Case of Kuwait", in *Arab Media and Society.* Issue 18, Summer.

Schlumberger, Oliver (ed.) 2007. *Debating Arab Authoritarianism. Dynamics and Durabiltiy in Nondemocratic Regimes.* Stanford University Press, Stanford.

Schumpeter, Joseph A. 2017. *Essays on Entrepreneurs, Innovations, Business Cycles and the Evolution of Capitalism.* Routledge, New York. First published in 1951.

Selvik, Kjetil 2011. "Elite Rivalry in a Semi-Democracy: The Kuwaiti Press Scene", in *Middle Eastern Studies.* Vol. 47, No. 3.

Senturk, Recep 2005. *Narrative Social Structure: Anatomy of the Hadith Transmission Network 610–1505.* Stanford University Press, Stanford.

Shah, Nasra M. 1986. "Foreign Workers in Kuwait: Implications for the Kuwaiti Labor force", in *The International Migration Review.* Vol. 20, No. 4. Special Issue: Temporary Worker Programs: Mechanisms, Conditions, Consequences, Winter.

Shah, Nasra, M. 2012. "Socio-demographic Transitions among Nationals of GCC Countries: Implications for Migration and Labour Force Trends", in *Migration and Development*. Vol. 1, Issue 1.

Shalaby, Marwa. 2015. *Women's Political Representation in Kuwait: An Untold Story*. James A. Baker III Institute for Public Policy, Rice University, Houston.

Shakoor, Farzana 1989, "Pakistan-Bangladesh Relations-A Survey", in *Pakistan Horizon*. Vol. 42, No. 2. Pakistan Institute of International Affairs.

al-Shamlan, Saif Marzooq 2001. *Pearling in the Arabian Gulf: A Kuwaiti Memoir*. Translated by Peter Clarke. London Center of Arab Studies (LCAS), London.

Shepherd, Benjamin 2013. *GCC States' Land Investments Abroad. The Case of Ethiopia*. Center for International and Regional Studies, Georgetown University School of Foreign Service in Qatar, Summary Report No. 8.

Shryock, Andrew 1997. *Nationalism and the Genealogical Imagination: Oral History and Textual Authority in Tribal Jordan*. University of California Press, Berkeley.

Shultziner, Doron and Mary Ann Tétreault 2011. "Paradoxes of Democratic Progress in Kuwait: The Case of the Kuwaiti Women's Rights Movement", in *Muslim World Journal of Human Rights*. Vol. 7, Issue 2.

Shultziner, Doron and Mary Ann Tétreault 2012. Representation and Democratic Progress in Kuwait, in *Representation*. Vol. 48, Issue 3.

Skovgaard-Petersen, Jakob 2010. "al-Azhar, Modern Period", in Gudrun Kramer, Denis Matringe, John Nawas and Everett Rowson (eds). *Encyclopedia of Islam*. Brill, Leiden.

Smith, Pamela Ann 2009. "Gulf Telecoms' Billion Dollar Shopping Spree", in *The Middle East*. June.

Smith, Simon C., 1999. *Kuwait, 1950–1965: Britain, the Al-Sabah, and Oil*. Bap Series, British Academy, Oxford University Press, Oxford.

Smith Diwan, Kristin 2018. *Kuwait: Finding Balance in a Maximalist Gulf.* The Arab Gulf States Institute in Washington DC. Issue paper No. 4.

Smoor, Pieter 2006. "Abu 'L-'Ala' Ahmad Ibn Abd Allah, Al-Ma'arri", in Josef W. Meri (ed.), *Medieval Islamic Civilization: An Encyclopedia.* Vol. 1, A-K, Index. Routledge, New York.

Sorkabi, Rasoul 2012. "The Great Burgan Field, Kuwait", in *GEOExPro.* Vol. 9, No. 1.

Starret, Gregory 1998. *Putting Islam to Work. Education, Politics, and Religious Transformation in Egypt.* University of California Press, Berkeley.

Stenberg, Leif 1996. "The Revealed Word and the Struggle for Authority: Interpretation and Use of Islamic Terminology among Algerian Islamists", in David Westerlund (ed.). *Questioning the Secular State. The Worldwide Resurgence of Religion in Politics.* Hurst, London.

Stenberg, Leif and Philip Wood (eds) 2022. *What is Islamic Studies? European and North American Approaches to a Contested Field.* Exploring Muslim Context Series. Edinburgh University Press, Edinburgh.

Stephenson, L. (2011). "Women and the Malleability of the Kuwaiti Dīwāniyya", in *Journal of Arabian Studies.* Vol. 2, Issue 1.

Teitelbaum, Joshua (ed.) 2009. *Political Liberalisation in the Persian Gulf.* Hurst, London.

Tétreault, Mary Ann 1991. "Autonomy, Necessity, and the Small State: Ruling Kuwait in the Twentieth Century", in *International Organization.* Vol. 45, No. 4.

Tétreault, Mary Ann 1993. "Civil Society in Kuwait: Protected Spaces and Women's Rights", in *Middle East Journal.* Vol. 47, No. 2.

Tétreault, Mary Ann 2001. "A State of Two Minds: State Cultures, Women, and Politics in Kuwait", in *International Journal of Middle Eastern Studies.* Vol. 33, No. 2.

Tétreault, Mary Ann 2009. "Kuwait: Slouching toward Democracy?", Joshua Teitelbaum (ed.). *Political Liberalisation in the Persian Gulf.* Hurst, London.

Tétreault, Mary Ann 2011. "Bottom-Up Democratization in Kuwait", in Mary Ann Tétreault, Gwenn Okruhlik and Andrzej Kapiszewski (eds). *Political Change in the Arab Gulf States: Stuck in Transition.* Lynne Reiner, Boulder.

Tétreault, Mary Ann, Andrzej Kapiszewski and Gwenn Okruhlik 2011. "Twenty- First-Century Politics in the Arab Gulf States", in Mary Ann Tétreault, Gwenn Okruhlik and Andrzej Kapiszewski (eds). *Political Change in the Arab Gulf States: Stuck in Transition.* Lynne Reiner, Boulder.

al-Thakeb, Fahed 1985. "The Arab Family and Modernity: Evidence from Kuwait", in *Current Anthropology.* Vol. 26, No. 5, December.

Toll, Chistopher and Jakob Skovgaard-Petersen (eds) 1995. *Law and the Islamic World: Past and Present.* Historisk-filosofiske Meddelelser 68, The Royal Danish Academy of Sciences and Letters, Copenhagen.

Ulaby, Laith 2010. "Mass Media and Music in the Arab Persian Gulf", in Michael Frishkopf (ed.) *Music and Media in the Arab World.* The American University in Cairo Press, Cairo.

Voll, John O. 2011. "The Middle East in World History", in Jerry H. Bentley (ed.), *The Oxford Handbook of World History.* Oxford University Press, Oxford.

Wakeley, James Moreton 2018. *The Two Falls of Rome in Late Antiquity: The Arabian Conquests in Comparative Perspective.* Palgrave Pivot, London.

Webb, Peter 2017. *Imagining the Arabs. Arab Identity and the Rise of Islam.* Edinburgh University Press, Edinburgh.

Weber, Alan 2010. *Web-based Learning in Qatar and the GCC States.* Center for International and Regional Studies, Georgetown University School of Foreign Service in Qatar, Occasional Paper No. 5.

Wheeler, Deborah 2000. "New Media, Globalization and Kuwaiti National Identity", in *The Middle East Journal*. Vol. 54, No. 3.

Wiseman, John A. 1995. "The Movement Towards Democracy: Global, Continental and State Perspectives", in John A. Wiseman (ed.). *Democracy and Political Change in Sub-Saharan Africa*. Routledge, London.

Yamada, Makio and Steffen Hertog 2020. "Revisiting Rentierism: The Changing Political Economy of Resource-Dependent States in the Gulf and Arabian Peninsula", in *British Journal of Middle Eastern Studies*. Special issue, Vol. 47, No. 1.

Years of Cultural Output 1989–2015 2015. The Foundation of Abdulaziz Saud al- Babtain's Prize for Poetic Creativity. Kuwait. Ninth Edition.

Yetiv, Steve 2002. "Kuwait's Democratic Experiment in Its Broader International Context", in *Middle East Journal*. Vol. 56, No. 2.

Yom, Sean 2019. "Roles, Identity, and Security: Foreign Policy Contestation in Monarchical Kuwait", in *European Journal of International Relations*. Vol. 26, issue 2.

Zeghal, Malika 1999. *Religion and Politics in Egypt: The Ulema of Al-Azhar, Radical Islam, and the State (1952–54)*. Cambridge University Press, Cambridge.

INDEX

*Page numbers in italics refer
to illustrations; a page number
followed by 'n' refers to a footnote.*

A

Abd al-Aziz al-Babtain Cultural
    Waqf 156
Abd al-Aziz Sa'ud al-Babtain
    Laudian Professor in Arabic,
    Oxford University (*see also*
    academic chair [al-Babtain
    sponsored]) 13, 100, 231
Abd al-Aziz Sa'ud al-Babtain
    peace chair, University of
    Malta (*see also* academic chair
    [al-Babtain sponsored]) 233,
    239
Abd al-Karim Qasim, General
    94n, 144
Abdouli, Touhami 3, 116, 197,
    237
Abdulaziz Saud al-Babtain
    Center for Intercultural
    Dialogue 181, 198
Abdulaziz Saud al-Babtain
    Cultural Foundation *see*
    al-Babtain Foundation
Abdulaziz Saud al-Babtain Prize
    for Poetic Creativity 156, 179,

227
Abila, Albert 87
academic chairs (al-Babtain
    sponsored) 13, 100, 122, 127,
    181, 188, 231–4, 235, 239, 290,
    255
Afghanistan 79, 141, 184
Africa 128, 183, 186–7 (*see also*
    Algeria; Chad; Comoros;
    Egypt; Libya; Mali)
al-Ahmad branch, al-Sabah
    family 196
Akadimiyya al-Babtain, *see* the
    al-Babtain Academy
Algeria 12n, 57, 228–9
Altiero Spinelli Centre 13
American University of Kuwait
    125
Anglo-Persian Oil Company
    (later the Anglo-Iranian Oil
    Company, eventually British
    Petroleum) 54
Arab Cooperation Council 147
Arab-Israeli War 134, 136
Arab League (formally the
    League of Arab States) 73,
    95, 147
Arab Satellite Agreement
    Organization (Arabsat) 111

Arab Thought Foundation 186
Arab Women Development
    Society (AWDS) 214
Arafat, Yasser 158
al-Ariba (branch of Qahtani
    tribe) 38
Asia 41, 186–7 (*see also*
    Bangladesh; India; Pakistan)
Asians 9, 10, 98, 158, 209, 212
Australian College of Kuwait 125
al-Azhar University, Cairo 33n,
    156, 179, 188, 226
Aziz, Tariq 152

B
al-Babtain, Abd al-Aziz
    (grandfather of Abu Saʻud')
    45, 46, 47
al-Babtain, Abd al-Karim
    (brother of Abu Saʻud) 131,
    142
al-Babtain, Abd al-Latif (brother
    of Abu Saʻud) 77
al-Babtain, Abd al-Muhsin (uncle
    of Abu Saʻud) 84
al-Babtain, Abd al-Rahman
    (nephew of Abu Saʻud) 143
al-Babtain, Abd al-Rashid
    (brother of Abu Saʻud) 131
al-Babtain, Abd al-Wahab
    (brother of Abu Saʻud) 131,
    142
al-Babtain, Saʻud (father of Abu
    Saʻud') 47, 48–9, 103
al-Babtain Academy 239
al-Babtain family 68, 90, 143, 156
al-Babtain Center for Dialogue

among Civilizations,
    Córdoba, Spain 230
al-Babtain Center for the
    Verification of Poetry
    Manuscripts 230
al-Babtain Central Library for
    Arabic Poetry 123, 126, 156,
    180, 220, 229–34, *230*, 236, 256
al-Babtain Cultural Foundation
    for Poetic Creativity *see*
    al-Babtain Foundation
al-Babtain *diwaniyya* 16–17, 17,
    17, *18*, 103–5, 243, *244*
al-Babtain Electronic Company
    90
al-Babtain Foundation 7, 12–13,
    16, 33–4, 37, 78, 105, 116–17,
    122–3, 126–8, 143, 156, 179–89,
    197–8, 220, 226–47, *230*, 250,
    254, 255
al-Babtain Leiden University
    Centre for Arabic Culture
    13n
Bahbahani, Murad 111
Bahrain 14, 62, 170, 173, 177, 189
Baker, James 152
Bangladesh 15
Bangladeshis 212
Bani Khalid 40–1
Basra 36, 41, 42, 95, 108
Bawadi TV 234
Bedouins 22, 37, 38–8, 40, 44,
    53, 98, 247
bidun 22, 121–22, 176, 183, 196,
    200, 209, 210n, 223, 224, 241,
    242, 251
Bishara, Abd Allah 13, 134

Blair, Tony 174
Bourguiba, Habib 104
British Bank of the Middle East
88–9
British Petroleum Oil (BP) 54,
55
Bubiyan 144, 148, 168
al-Bukhari, Muhammad 198
Burgan 54, 55
Bush, George H.W. 146, 152

C
Cairo 33
Calvo, Carmen 233
Carnegie Foundation 238
Central Bank of Kuwait 89
Centre for Mediterranean
Europe Studies, Belgium 13
Centre for Middle Eastern
Studies, Oxford University 13
Centro di Eccellenza Altiero
Spinelli *see* Altiero Spinelli
Centre
Chad 184
Chakra, Dr Faruk Abu 26
Cinescape 112
Cole, Donald P. 39
Comoros 127, 180, 183–4, 198
Cooperation Council for the
Arab States of the Gulf *see*
Gulf Cooperation Council
(GCC)
Córdoba, Spain 230–1
Córdoba University 180, 181,
230, 231
Credit and Savings Bank 89
Cultural and Social Society 204

D
Dammam 111
Demafelis, Joanna 211
Dhoinine, Ilkiliou 184
Dickson, Harold 54–5
Dole, Robert 146
Al Driss, Sara 194

E
Egypt 14, 72, 112, 134, 142, 189,
230
Egyptian Muslim Brotherhood
205
Egyptians 212, 213
Eickelman, Dale 29
Essebsi, Mohamed Beji Caid 104
Euro-Arab Institute for the
Dialogue between Cultures
13
Europe 188
European Centre for Democracy
and Human Rights 239
European Union 233
Europeans 209, 210

F
Facebook 116, 234, 236
Fahd, King of Saudi Arabia
149–50
al-Fatat, Nadi 214
Faylaka 168
FGF (Kuwait Future
Generations Fund) 107
Filipinos 212
Forslund, Magnus 30
Foundation of Mediterranean
Studies, Tunisia 13

Freedom House 25, 103n, 113
Frendo, Michael 233
Future Generations Fund (FGF) 107

G
Gaz de France Suez 173
General Reserve Fund (GRF) 107
Glaspie, April 146
Gulf Cooperation Council (GCC) 13–14, 91, 109, 134, 147, 170, 171, 173, 174, 189, 192, 195, 208
Gulf Oil 54, 55
Gulf Research Center (GRC) 208
Gulf University for Science and Technology (GUST) 125
Gulf War, First (*see also* Iraqi occupation) 16, 17, 24, 31, 73, 144–67, 216, 240, 251
Gulf War, Second 24

H
Herb, Michael 16
Hizb al-Ba'ath (the Ba'ath Party) 3
Hussein, King of Jordan 149
Hussein, Saddam 2, 15, 24, 144, 145–6, 152–3

I
Ibn Khaldun 36
Ibn Qutaybah 36, 38
Ibn Sa'ud 52, 53
Ibn Taymiyya 36

ICM (Islamic Constitutional Movement) 205–6, 207
Ikhwan 52
IMF (International Monetary Fund) 170, 172, 174, 178
India 184 (*see also* Asians)
Industrial Bank of Kuwait 89
International Academy of Poetic Creativity 239
International Committee of the Red Cross 238
International Islamic Charitable Organization (IICO) 128
International Monetary Fund (IMF) 170, 172, 174, 178
Iran 132–3, 134, 142, 145, 171, 178, 184, 187, 195, 229
Iran-Iraq War 15, 96, 134, 144, 178
Iraq 2, 15–19, 24, 90, 94n, 95, 96, 142, 144–54, 160, 167, 178, 187, 238
Iraqi occupation 15, 16, 17, 19, 31, 73, 105, 108, 111, 112, 147–67, 170, 179n, 180n, 210n, 215, 221n, 242, 251
Islamic Constitutional Movement (ICM) 205–6, 207
Israel 134, 146
Italy 142, 182, 237, 239

J
al-Jahiz 36
al-Jalahima 41
al-Jam'iyya al-Khayriyya Charitable Society 187n

Jariah 48
al-Jassim, Yussuf Abd al-Hamid
223
Jordan 39, 156, 180

K
Kazakhstan 184
Kent (tobacco company) 87
KFAED (Kuwait Fund for Arab
Economic Development) 128,
178, 185
KFAS (Kuwait Foundation for
the Advancement of Sciences)
176
al-Khalifa family 41
al-Kharj 23
al-Khattab, Umar ibn 34
Khuja Group 185
KOC (Kuwait Oil Company)
54, 55, 57, 62
KUNA (Kuwait News Agency)
73
Kurdish Autonomous Republic
154
Kuwait Center for Islamic and
Arabic Studies, Comoros 184
Kuwait City 6, 19, 52, 76–7, 148,
154, 156, 157, 159, 252, 255
Kuwait Commercial Bank 89
Kuwait Foundation for the
Advancement of Sciences
(KFAS) 176
Kuwait Fund for Arab Economic
Development (KFAED) 128,
178, 185
Kuwait Future Generations Fund
(FGF) 107

Kuwait International Airport
159
Kuwait Investment Authority
107
Kuwait Liberation Day 158
Kuwait Library and Information
Society 123
Kuwait National Cinema
Company 112
Kuwait News Agency (KUNA)
73
Kuwait Oil Company (KOC)
54, 55, 57, 62
Kuwait Television 111, 234
Kuwaiti Central Bank 9
Kuwaiti Cultural Hall, Palestine
182
Kuwaiti Fund for Arab
Economic Development
(KFAED) 128
Kuwaiti Investment Office 137
Kuwaiti Muslim Brotherhood
204–5, 206–7
Kuwaiti Oil Company 55, 136
Kuwaiti Women's Union 214
Kyrgyzstan 184

L
League of Arab States see Arab
League
Lebanon 141, 178
Lebanese civil war 178
Leiden University 231, 238
Libya 15
Lubnani, Samir 84–5

M

al-Ma'arri, Abu al-Ala 3
Maastricht Business School 125
al-Majid, Ali Hasan 151
al-Majlis TV 223, 224, 231, *232*
Maktabi, Rania 21–2
Malaga Islamic Fair 244–5
Mali 182
Malta 233, 237, 239
al-Manakh, Zakia Abd al-Aziz
    (wife of Abu Sa'ud) 141
al-Maqsud Khuja, Abd 185–6
Marlboro (tobacco company)
    87, 141
Meseuro Foundation *see* Centre
    for Mediterranean Europe
    Studies, Belgium
al-Mirqab 84
Mobile Telecommunications
    Company (MTC) 116
Mossadegh, Muhammad 132–3
Mottahedeh, Roy 29
Mubarak (Egypt's president)
    149–50
al-Mubarak, Massouma 217, 218
al-Mubarakiyya 118–19
Muhammad Reza Pahlavi 3
Musallam al-Barak 194
Muslim Brotherhood 204–5,
    206–7

N

al-Na'im, Muhammad bin Salih
    185
Najd 23, 40, 44–7, 52
National Assembly of Kuwait 8,
    19–22, 60, 154, 161, 173, 174,
176, 190–3, 196n, 199–200,
    206, 216–17, 218
National Bank of Kuwait 9, 89,
    140
National Committee for
    Educational Support 123
North Americans 98, 209, 210
North Yemen 14

O

Oman 15, 173, 178, 189
Organization of the Petroleum
    Exporting Countries (OPEC)
    15, 95, 133, 134, 145, 168, 178
Ottomans 40, 41–3, 52
Oxford University, Centre for
    Middle Eastern Studies 13,
    231, 238

P

Pakistan 15, 142, 178
Palestine 182
Palestine Liberation
    Organization (PLO) 96, 178
Palestinians 97, 119, 126, 157, 178
Pearl-Diving Festival 102
Peninsula Shield Force 14
Philippines 211 (*see also*
    Filipinos)
Public Authority for Civil
    Information 209, 241

Q

al-Qadi, Abd al-Muhsin 47
Qahtani(or Qahtan) tribe 23, 38
Qatar 14, 208, 220

R

Radio Kuwait 110–11

al-Rahman, Abd al-Muhsin 45, 47

al-Rashid, Harun 128

al-Rawda 45

Real Estate Bank of Kuwait 89

Rivero, Rosa Aguilar 233

Rome 182

al-Rumayah, Abd al-Aziz 85–6

S

al-Sabah, Abd Allah III al-Salim (r. 1950–65, amir 1961–65) 7, 64–6, 75–6, 80–1, 94, 109, 198

al-Sabah, Ahmad al-Jabir (r. 1921–50) 52n, 54, 56, 62, 63, 64–5, 67–8, 71–2, 75

al-Sabah, Jabir al-Ahmad al-Jabir (amir 1977–2006) 16, 17, 18, 19, 105, 144, 146, 148–9, 151, 160–1, 177

al-Sabah, Jabir al-Mubarak al-Hamad, prime minister 109, 172

al-Sabah, Jabir II al-Mubarak (r. 1915–17) 74

al-Sabah, Mubarak (r. 1896–1915) 42–4, 54, 74, 94, 95, 118, 160n, 196

al-Sabah, Nasir al-Muhammad, prime minister 174, 190, 191

al-Sabah, Nawaf al-Ahmad al-Jabir (amir 2020–present) 207, 243 251

al-Sabah, Sabah al-Ahmad al-Jabir (amir 2006–2020)

14, 108, 171, 207, 243, 251

al-Sabah, Sabah al-Khalid al-Hamad, foreign minister 195

al-Sabah, Sa'd Abd Allah al-Salim, crown prince 144, 148

al-Sabah, Salim al-Mubarak (r. 1917–21) 52, 74

al-Sabah family 20, 41, 42, 47, 49, 51, 59, 62, 63, 64, 65, 69, 71, 74, 83, 84, 108, 162–3, 166, 168n, 190, 196, 199, 201, 202, 207, 241, 243, 251, 252–3

al-Sabah hospital 109

al-Sabani, Nouria 214

Saïfi, Tokia 233

Salafis 204, 205, 206, 244

Saleh, Abdallah 115

Saleh, Mulla 61–2

Salih, Kamal Osman 49

al-Salim branch, al-Sabah family 196

Saudi Arabia 4, 14, 15, 39–40, 53, 79, 90, 111, 134, 141, 142, 145, 148, 150, 152, 173, 185, 189, 202–3, 220 (see also Najd)

Savant, Dr Sarah Bowen 36

Schumpeter, Joseph A. 29–30

Schwarzkop, General, Norman 17, 18, 153

Second World War 7, 55, 56, 57, 60, 64, 72, 88, 108, 110n, 160n

Shatt al-Arab 38, 40

Shbeir, Ghada 235

Shi'a community 11–12, 61–2, 74, 98, 121, 195, 196, 204, 215,

216, 242, 250, 254
Shryock, Andrew 39
Shuwaykh 171
Siladjic, Haris 233
Social Reform Society 204
South Yemen 15
Soviet Union 153
Spain 156, 181, 230, 231
al-Subaih, Nuriya 217
Sunni community 11–12, 47, 61,
    74, 121, 196, 215, 216, 226, 254
Suq al-Manakh 9, 138, 139, 164
al-Suyuti 36
Syria 72, 134, 178, 189, 196n

T
al-Talfah, Adnan Khayr Allah 2–3,
    144
al-Talfah, Sajida 2
Ta'if, Saudi Arabia 148, 160
Tehran University 187
Trump, Donald 195
Tunisia 104, 156, 180, 189, 237
Turkey 53, 142

U
UNESCO 231
United Arab Emirates 14, 141, 147,
    208, 220
United Arab Republic (UAR)
    72–3
United Nations 95, 109, 151–2, 177,
    178, 214, 237, 243
United States 56, 133, 138, 146,
    152, 170–1, 188, 195, 225 (see also
    North Americans)
University of Cairo 156

University of Córdoba 181n, 231
University of Granada 231
University of Kuwait 123, 124–5
University of Malta 233, 239
University of Rome, Altiero
    Spinelli Centre 239
University of the Comoros 184
University of Yazd, Iran 187

W
Wahhabi 42
Warba 144
al-Watan TV 115
Webb, Peter 36
Women's Cultural and Social
    Society (WCSS) 214
World Bank 170
World Forum for the Culture of
    Peace 237
World War I 43, 48n, 52, 54

Y
Yemen 23, 38, 178, 189, 195, 238
YouTube 116, 234, 244

Z
Zain 116
al-Zubayr 45–6, 49, 83